Slavery and the Politics of Liberation 1787-1861

Slavery and the Politics of Liberation 1787-1861

A Study of Liberated African Emigration and British Anti-slavery Policy

Johnson U. J. Asiegbu

Africana Publishing Corporation

Published
in the United States of America 1969
by Africana Publishing Corporation
101 Fifth Avenue
New York, N.Y. 10003

Library of Congress catalog card no. 70-94834

S.B.N. 8419-0027-2

Printed in Great Britain

Contents

Acknowledgements

Growing out of my Doctoral thesis in history for the University of Cambridge, this book, except for Chapter 1 which makes extensive use of secondary sources,[1] is based on the use made of the series of original documents at the Public Record Office in London, and at the archives at Fourah Bay College in Sierra Leone, all dealing with liberated African emigration. As a rule, the sources are cited in the footnotes.

I am deeply grateful to those who showed so much confidence and keen interest in my projected study and gave me every encouragement in my work. I must record my thanks to Professor J. E. Flint, formerly of King's College, London, but now of Dalhousie University, Halifax, Canada. He unofficially supervised a greater part of my work at Cambridge and was always very helpful with constructive criticisms and suggestions. Professor G. Shepperson of Edinburgh University and Dr R. E. Robinson, Fellow of St John's College, Cambridge, both showed very keen interest in my work and kindly gave me the benefit of their advice and encouragement in adapting the thesis for publication.

I am very grateful to Mr D. A. Barrass, Fellow of Churchill College, Cambridge, for the great pains he took in reading through the final drafts and pointing out some errors for correction.

I am deeply indebted to Captain S. W. Roskill, R.N. also a Fellow

---

1. Mainly the following works:
Fyfe, C. H., *A History of Sierra Leone* (Oxford, 1962).
Butt-Thompson, F. W., *Sierra Leone in History and Tradition* (London, 1926).
Ingham, E. G., *Sierra Leone after a Hundred Years* (London, 1894).
Kuczynski, R. R., *Demographic Survey of the British Colonial Empire*, Vol. 1 (London, 1948).
Hoare, P., *Memoirs of Granville Sharp* (London, 1820).

of Churchill College, from whom I received much fatherly kindness, advice and assistance in various ways. I must thank the staffs of the various archives and libraries in London, Oxford and Cambridge, on whose unfailing courtesy and readiness to assist the research worker can always count.

Finally, I must thank my wife for the great secretarial skill she displayed both in taking shorthand notes at odd hours and in typing the manuscript accurately from my heavily smudged notes.

FOURAH BAY COLLEGE   J.U.J.A.
UNIVERSITY OF SIERRA LEONE
FREETOWN

List of Abbreviations

C.O.	Colonial Office
C.O.L.	Colonial Office Library
F.O.	Foreign Office
W.I.C.	West India Committee
PP.	Parliamentary Papers
SP.	State Papers

Foreword

I first met Johnson Asiegbu in 1963, when I joined the staff of the ill-fated University of Nigeria at Nsukka, which was one of the first casualties of the Nigeria-Biafra war. For all those in the graduating year of 1963 it had been an uphill struggle in a new institution bedevilled by confusion in its administration, its goals and its standards. But in every university the outstanding man will make his mark, and Asiegbu was one of these. It is thus with a particular pleasure that I respond to the request to contribute a foreword to this book.

The British campaign against the West African slave trade appears at first glance to be a well-worn theme, and, since Eric Williams published his *Capitalism and Slavery*, a controversial one. The emphasis in previous studies, however, has been on motivation and policy, seen in the context of British imperial history. What this book does is to take the theme of liberation out of the realms of political theory and legal status, and consider the liberated Africans themselves, what experiences they were subjected to as a result of liberation, and the fluctuating attitudes of British policy towards them. The result provides historians with a large body of additional information from sources which have received little attention, and a number of interpretations of the nature of the anti-slavery movement which must surely provoke further controversy on a major topic of British and African history.

Dalhousie University   JOHN E. FLINT
Halifax, Canada
July 1969

Preface

Sensational themes, such as the Atlantic slave trade and the nine-teenth-century humanitarian movement, have engaged the attention of historians for many years. Christopher Fyfe's recent paper, *A Historiographical Survey of The Atlantic Slave Trade From West Africa*[1] has revealed the existence of a mine of literature on the subject. Yet 'Slave Trade Studies' still remain as topical for historians as they have been productive of continuing academic controversy, mainly between two opposing schools of thought.

The first, the 'Coupland school', comprising a galaxy of British historians, upholds a humanitarian interpretation of the abolition movement and the suppression of the Atlantic slave trade and slavery:

> The unweary, unostentatious, and inglorious crusade of England against slavery may probably be regarded as among the three or four perfectly virtuous pages comprised in the history of nations.[2]

Professor Lecky's dictum was an only slightly extreme form of the view commonly held by notable British historians—Coupland, Mathieson, H. A. Wyndham (later Lord Leconsfield), C. M. Mac-Innes, G. R. Mellor, and a host of others. When Professor A. J. P. Taylor styled the members of this school the 'chaplains of the pirate ship' and made Professor Coupland their 'Chaplain-General',[3] he

---

1. This paper by C. H. Fyfe is to be found in *The Transatlantic Slave Trade from West Africa*—a compilation of papers read by various scholars during a History Seminar at the Centre of African Studies, Edinburgh University, in June 1965. All references to this compilation will hereafter be denoted by *Seminar*, Edinburgh 1965. I am very grateful to Professor G. Shepperson for drawing my attention to this Seminar.
2. Lecky, W. E. H., *A History of European Morals*, 6th ed. (London, 1884) Vol. 2, p. 153.
3. Cited in *Seminar*.

was probably brooding over what must have appeared to him to be a narrow and over-simplified humanitarian interpretation of an important and complicated subject.

The appearance in 1944 of Dr Eric Williams' *Capitalism and Slavery*, upholding a socio-economic interpretation and so establishing the second school of thought on the subject, constituted a major challenge to the Coupland school and hence to the old accepted views on the abolition of slavery and the suppression of the slave trade.

In 1951 was published G. R. Mellor's *British Imperial Trusteeship 1783–1850*, which appeared as the most determined attempt made by the Coupland school to meet some of the arguments posed by Eric Williams. How successful have they been? Their efforts, some scholars feel, fell far short of the target. Rather than counter Williams' charges, the 'chaplains of the pirate ship', only 'pulled out more stops on the chaplain's organ and played a bit louder'.[1] Yet, even with the assistance of some younger and perhaps more sophisticated voices, the humanitarian crescendo still remains faint and weak against the background of Williams' economic baritone.

In his *Critique* of *Capitalism and Slavery* Dr Anstey, clearly with more sophistication than the traditionalists possessed, had tried to come to grips with Williams' arguments, but suddenly calls the contest off. Neither Williams nor himself, he pleads, has as yet acquired sufficient strength of evidence:

> On the vitally important day to day events in the prohibition of the slave trade to British subjects in 1807, in the abolition of British colonial slavery in 1833, in the question of the Sugar Duties, in the action against the foreign transatlantic slave trade, much of the detailed work on primary sources remains to be done. Only when this has been done will any sort of clear picture emerge.[2]

It does little credit to historians that, more than a century after these important events have happened, the big problem of historical determinism lingers on[3] as to the factors which may be judged to have *dominated*, at each particular period, the calculations or actions of the 'political nation' at Whitehall, in the course of the abolition movement against slavery and the Atlantic slave trade. The contest between the Coupland school and the Eric Williams school seems to be as yet unresolved.

---

1. Fyfe in *Seminar* (Edinburgh, 1965).   2. Anstey, R., *op. cit.*
3. Fyfe, *Seminar*. Anstey, *op. cit.*

The charge has been made against *Capitalism and Slavery*, that it ignored or under-rated the humanitarian factor in the abolition movement. By no means did Williams ignore or under-rate the abolitionists, but indeed, as Professor Fage has pointed out, he showed himself more aware of the importance of the humanitarian movement for abolition than the Coupland school did of the economic trends which affected the circumstances of the movement.[1] The point, however, was that his bloodhound methods, sniffing at everybody and their property, their utterances, and their interests both inside and outside Parliament, did not spare even the 'Saints'. It was after a searching scrutiny that Williams tried, perhaps unconsciously, to grade or classify the abolitionists. Thus what he says of Thomas Clarkson, James Stephen and Granville Sharp, for instance, is different from what he has to say about other members of the Clapham sect.[2]

Since *British Imperial Trusteeship* missed its target, further opposition to *Capitalism and Slavery* has indeed come, but mainly by the hit and run method of taking issues with only specific points in Williams' arguments, while still dodging the major question raised by the thesis, namely, the determinism as to the *dominant* factor in the official minds at Whitehall who, after all, exercised the final executive control over the national policy. Even Dr Anstey's *Critique* is aware of these hit and run tactics, and the negative result they have so far produced for the opponents of *Capitalism and Slavery*. 'Whatever the reasons for the absence of a sustained criticism, the Williams thesis itself continues to ride high.'[3]

It is important to note that practically every critic of the thesis has been obliged to concede new points here and there: Dr Anstey agrees for example that the decline of mercantilism made action against slavery and the slave trade *more possible*.[4] Professor Hargreaves concedes that between 1783 and 1807 commercial expansion and American independence had changed the British economy to such an extent as to *permit* action against the slave trade and slavery.[5] But beyond these points these scholars are not prepared to enter fully into Williams' argument of abolitionism as an economic necessity or

---

1. See Fage, J. D., in his introduction to Coupland, *The British Anti-Slavery Movement* (London, 1964).
2. *Capitalism and Slavery* (Carolina, 1944) pp. 179–86.
3. Anstey, R., *op. cit.*   4. *Ibid.*
5. Hargreaves, J. D., 'Synopsis of A Critique of Eric Williams' Capitalism and Slavery' in *Seminar*.

as a movement whose main course was very largely determined by
the economic factor.

At this point, perhaps one or two questions might be asked: Since
the advantages of mature industrialism and capitalism must have
been seen as a permanent phenomenon and therefore *necessitating*
the permanent abolition of slave or forced labour in 1834, why was
forced labour again resorted to after 1838, in order to save West
Indian plantation industry and capital?

It seems that *Capitalism and Slavery* needs to make some reconciliation between the *necessity* of abolition in 1834, because of
mature industrialism, and the *necessity* of forced or indentured labour
after 1834, in the face of mature industrialism. Likewise, for the
Coupland school to maintain their stand on the dominance of humanitarianism in the abolition of slavery and the slave trade, there
has to be a reconciliation between British humanitarianism in the
abolition of 1834, and the lack of that humanitarianism in the recruitment of forced labour with its encouragement of the slave trade
on the West Coast after 1840.

The present work, although touching on those issues at various
points, deals, in the main, neither with the abolition of 1807 nor with
the history of the abolition of British Colonial slavery in 1834. Its
theme concerns the liberated Africans, the immediate and direct
beneficiaries of the acts of abolition.

The liberated Africans, settled at the Colony of Sierra Leone from
1787, not only owed their freedom to British policy; indeed, on its
vagaries depended whether they eventually found themselves in the
West Indies as labourers, or in West Africa as agents of Christianity,
commerce and European culture. But more than that, it is of vital
importance to know how much the British anti-slavery policy itself,
the diplomatic negotiations on international abolition, was affected
after 1840 by the British official policy towards liberated Africans;
and of how and why and with what consequences the liberated
Africans were despatched to the West Indies as voluntary emigrants.
Indeed, by studying the official policy pursued towards them some
useful light might be shed on the real weight and achievements of
British humanitarianism as well as on the point of contest between
Capitalism and Slavery and its critics. If the present work is able to
throw out any information which may be found useful in itself, or
which may help to elucidate or resolve the controversy between the
'chaplains' and the 'economists' of the abolition movement, then the
author's efforts will not have been in vain.

Chapter 1
Introductory: The Sierra Leone Settlement and the Birth of a British African Policy 1787–1840

Before 1783 only a few Englishmen had any thought about the morality of the trade in human beings. The abolition of the Atlantic slave trade and the consolidation of the British humanitarian tradition were great historic events which must for all time be associated with the names of a small minority of Englishmen, whose selfless devotion to high causes, scrupulous honesty and frank appeal to Christian conscience epitomised all that was best and virtuous in the nineteenth-century humanitarian enlightenment. Indeed the 'Saints', as the leading abolitionists were nicknamed, raised anti-slavery sentiment to the status of a religion in England. But perhaps even more important than their public campaigns and organisations at home was the idea which they hatched of a colony for freed slaves in West Africa. It can be rightly claimed that, through the establishment of the Sierra Leone Colony for freed slaves, the 'Saints' bequeathed to Whitehall a positive African policy, which was to be pursued for upwards of half a century, and the consequences of which were far-reaching not only for the liberated Africans at Sierra Leone, but indeed for the subsequent history of the whole of West Africa.

The years between 1787–1840, representing a period when abolitionist opinion had enjoyed the greatest influence and respect in official as well as public circles, may be called the era of the abolitionists. For after 1840 the abolitionists increasingly lost voice[1] in the dispensation of British humanitarianism to liberated Africans and in the execution of the African Policy—the suppression of the Atlantic slave trade and the civilisation of Africa.

---

1. Pilgrim, E. I., 'Anti Slavery Sentiment in England, Its Decline and Fall, 1841–1854' (Cambridge Ph.D., 1953).

Many Africans lived in England in the eighteenth-century as domestic servants or slaves imported from West Africa or the trans-atlantic colonies. After the famous Somerset case in 1772 all were free. But the freedom of other slaves after Somerset was soon to pose an awkward social problem: some of the freed slaves had remained as paid servants with their masters; some had found employment elsewhere, while several hundred of them had drifted into idleness and destitution. After 1783 the problem was intensified by the demobilisation of the American Negroes who had served with the British forces in the American War and of whom some had been despatched to Nova Scotia and some to London. Friendless, often destitute, most of these freed slaves wandered about the streets, distressing the kind-hearted and alarming the timorous and the men of property. Anti-slavery sentiment in England occurred in the fulness of time. For some time relief of some sort was afforded by private charity, Granville Sharp, hero and victor of the Somerset case, maintaining a growing number of these destitute blacks out of his own pocket. It was soon evident that the problem was more than private charity could cope with.

A sign of the new trends of thought on slavery was that in the University of Cambridge.

In 1784 Dr Peckard, Master of Magdalene College, preached a rousing humanitarian sermon that set the minds of his young students thinking on the slave trade:

> There is a great part of the human race, most unfortunate men, whose external complexion indeed is different from our own, but who are formed of the same blood with ourselves; who partake in common with us of all the faculties, and of all the distinguishing excellencies of our nature. These persons we, being of greater power, and deeper proficiency in iniquity, deprive of their natural liberty: we steal them we buy them we sell them, we consign them to perpetual slavery.[1]

In the following year, 1785, Peckard proposed a Latin essay composition for his undergraduates: *Anne liceat inviteos in servitutem dare?* Through this event an important new member was to be added to that brilliant band of Saints who were soon to found the Liberated African Settlement at Sierra Leone.

Young Thomas Clarkson, then a student of St John's College,

---

1. Dr Peckard's Sermon from 1 Peter 11, verse 17: 'Honour all men, love the Brotherhood, Fear God, Honour the King' (Church sermon delivered January 30th, 1784).

Cambridge, won first prize in that competition with his famous composition: *An Essay on the Slavery and Commerce of the Human Species, particularly to Africans*. Thereafter Clarkson was to devote the rest of his life to the cause of abolition. The efforts of the Saints helped the public to understand the true nature of the slave trade. In 1786, fourteen years after Granville Sharp had won a single handed victory against the West Indian slave holders in the Mansfield judgement, a few gentlemen met to hear Thomas Clarkson discuss the point of his famous College essay: 'Is it right to make slaves of others against their will?'

They met in the Battersea home of Henry Thornton, a rich London city banker, and amongst them were Granville Sharp, the Rev. James Ramsay, who had lived for nineteen years at St Christopher and who had published his opinion of the slave plantations there. These gentlemen in 1786 formed a committee which, in the next year, merged into the Society for Effecting the Abolition of the Slave Trade, whose best-known member was William Wilberforce, and whose main support came from such influential abolitionists as Josiah Wedgwood, Bennet Longton, William Warburton (Bishop of London), Jonas Hanway, and later, Zachary Macaulay, Henry Brougham and James Stephen.

In that same year, 1786, these abolitionists also got up another Committee, headed by Jonas Hanway. The Committee for the Relief of the Black Poor, as this body was called, raised about £800 in a few months. The Committee distributed food daily at public houses in Paddington and Mile End Green, opened a hospital and found berths for those who wanted to go back to sea.[1] But meanwhile the thoughts of Granville Sharp, a leading member of the Committee, had turned to the possibilities of a safe settlement, somewhere in Africa, for the increasing number of destitute and friendless blacks in London; for since the Mansfield judgement there had been cases of re-enslavement in which Sharp had had to intervene with a writ of Habeas Corpus before he could refree the slaves again. *The Committee for the Black Poor* printed, over the name of its Chairman, Jonas Hanway, a Manifesto[2] written by Dr Henry Smeathman, an amateur botanist who had visited the Banana Islands near Sierra Leone in 1771 to gather specimens for collectors in London. Inviting the 'London Blacks' to avail themselves of a free passage and

---

1. Fyfe, C. H., *A History of Sierra Leone* (Oxford, 1962) p. 14.
2. Smeathman, Henry: *Plan of a Settlement*. . . . See Appendix I.

return to a free colony to be formed in West Africa, the Manifesto breathed nothing but the enthusiasm of its writer. It painted a land of immense fertility perfectly healthy for those who lived temperately, where the soil need only be scratched with a hoe to yield grain in abundance, where livestock propagated themselves with a rapidity unknown in cold climates, where a hut provided adequate shelter at all seasons. Smeathman stressed the commercial advantages of a settlement which would repay initial outlay by opening new channels of trade.[1] The Committee were impressed and promptly recommended his plan to the Treasury.

Long anxious for an opportunity to rid London of the nuisance of black beggars, the Government readily consented to the Committee's plan and accepted financial responsibility for the 'Black Poor', leaving the Committee to make arrangements for their departure.

Such being the Government's attitude on the issue, it was left to the philanthropists responsible for the scheme to bring a new breath of vision and purpose to the experiment. The settlement of 1787 owed much of its success to the personal exertions of Granville Sharp, a man who should forever be honoured in Sierra Leone. From the outset Sharp intended the Sierra Leone settlement to be more than a receptacle for unwanted vagrants. In Somerset's case in 1772 he had provided them with a charter of freedom; in Sierra Leone he designed to provide a country and a constitution. With his characteristic thoroughness Sharp found out all there was to be known of the land: he invited Smeathman home to gather more information about Sierra Leone and had interviews with John Newton, then Curate of Olney but once a Slaver resident in the Banana and Plantain islands off the coast, near Sierra Leone.

Meanwhile the freed slaves in London, their minds agitated by the Smeathman Manifesto, went in groups to see Sharp who was in friendlier touch with them than any other member of the Committee for the Black Poor, to get his opinion. The fifteen corporals, or headmen, chosen to represent them told Sharp that one of their number, a native of Sierra Leone, had assured them the people would receive them joyfully. Sharp continued in his efforts to ensure the success of the scheme and the safety and happiness of his protégés. He addressed himself to the task of working out the details and making the final arrangements for the transportation of the Africans to their proposed new settlement in Sierra Leone.

---

1 Fyfe, *op. cit.*, p. 14.

Headmen were chosen to be instructed and prepared for the responsibilities of self government. Every prospective settler had to sign a contract which included a clause where each 'binds and obliges himself or herself to the other settler for the Protection and Preservation of their common Freedom'. Sharp's *Short Sketch of Temporary Regulations (until better shall be proposed)* was a constitution bound by a social contract rooted in history, in the institution of the Anglo Saxon monarchy, and of Israel under the judges. Its bond was the old English system of frank-pledge. Every ten householders would form a tithing, every ten tithings a hundred collectively responsible for preserving order and keeping watch against outside enemies, each householder with a voice in a Common Council.[1]

As they insisted on documentary proof of their being free, to protect them against slave traders, they were given parchment certificates bearing the Royal Arms, granting them the status of free citizens of 'the Colony of Sierra Leone or the Land of Freedom'. Not being passports, the certificates of freedom were only signed by the Clerk of the Acts of the Navy. Once established they became free settlers of the land, the Province of Freedom, as Sharp called it, their own country, ruling themselves without reference to higher authority, though they had sworn allegiance to the King.

Desiring the settlers to avoid the evils of a monetary economy, Sharp proposed instead a medium of exchange based on individual labour, with a special tax on those too proud or idle to work.

He was ready to take in any industrious Europeans (if Protestant), particularly those who could teach a craft. The sailing list of settlers included about twenty artisans, some with families, a town-major to build fortifications, five doctors and a sexton. Sharp persuaded the Archbishop of Canterbury to let Patrick Fraser, a Scottish Presbyterian who wanted to go as chaplain, be ordained into the Church of England; the Society for the Propagation of the Gospel allowed him £50 a year and books. Dr Smeathman having died, the Committee asked his friend, Joseph Irwin, to succeed him as Agent Conductor. He was to have charge of the settlers while they were on board, and on arrival was to have the town laid out in lots and built.

The expedition was now being fitted out on a scale far exceeding the Committee's earlier estimate. The Navy Board was given a free

1. Fyfe, *A History*, pp. 15–16; G. Sharp, *Short Sketch of Temporary Regulations* (London, 1787).

hand by the Treasury: Over £10,000 worth of stores and provisions were supplied; the final bill stood at over £15,000.

Towards the end of October 1786, the Navy Board sent three transports, *Atlantic*, *Belisarius*, and *Vernon*, to Deptford to take the settlers. Meanwhile the whole scheme was seriously threatened with failure by the effects of the false stories and reports being spread by the hostile press about the expedition: the settlers were being sent to a penal colony; they were being taken away to be abandoned to slave traders on the West Coast! Such false reports and other stories discrediting the expedition killed the original enthusiasm of many of the prospective settlers. In the end, out of about 700 who had signed the agreement to go, only 259 were found on board the vessels.

In the middle of January 1787 the *Atlantic* and *Belisarius* left the Thames for Portsmouth where Captain T. Boulden Thompson was waiting for them with a Navy ship, the *Nautilus* sloop. The Committee was now obliged to get the City authorities to round up any blacks still found begging in the streets. This proved unavailing for by January 1787 only two ships were filled. In the meantime, while the ships waited at the London harbour, some seventy white prostitutes and persons of low character were embarked. After all sorts of delays and difficulties on board, the ships finally left London on April 8th with a total of 411 passengers .

The convoy put in at Teneriffe, stayed nearly a week and, on May 10th, entered the Sierra Leone river, finally anchoring in Frenchman's Bay at the historic watering place.

Captain Thompson's instructions were to take the settlers to Sierra Leone, acquire a settlement from the chiefs, land the stores, and stay in the river to help them as long as provisions and crew's health allowed. On May 11th Thompson, after saluting Chief (King) Tom, native ruler at the watering place, went ashore to negotiate. Tom was only a sub-chief under Naimbana who lived up the river at Robana and Robaga and was overlord of the Bulom shore. Although Naimbana came down after a fortnight, spent a night on board, he left without making any agreement, leaving Tom and his sub-chiefs to conclude the arrangements.

In return for some £59 worth of trade goods—muskets, gunpowder, swords, laced hats, cotton goods, beads, iron-bars, tobacco and rum—Tom and his men gave up the shore from the watering place to Gambia Island, a stretch of nine or ten miles, a depth of twenty miles. On May 15th, the settlers disembarked and cut their way through the bush to the top of the hill overlooking the watering place (the present Government House site), where they planted the British flag.

At Thompson's suggestion the people started their settlement at that spot. The hill was named St George's Hill, Frenchman's Bay became St George's Bay, and the settlement Granville Town, after Granville Sharp. The settlers then elected their officers, following Sharp's instructions, and chose one of them as Chief in Command, or Governor, of the Province of Freedom. They started erecting tents for temporary shelter, and town lots were laid out and allotted.

The 'Saints' responsible for the scheme had done their limited best, the officers and seamen of the convoying party had provided what comforts they could, but the fact remained that the voyage had been a disastrous one. Eighty-four of the party had died since leaving England while nearly two hundred were lying in their bunks prostrate and helpless when the ships anchored at Sierra Leone. The long delays in sailing brought them to land at the worst time of year. The rainy season had commenced when they arrived, and now fever and dysentery broke out while rain, heavier that year than for many years, beat down on their tents. Within three months about a third were dead. Without legal powers over them, Captain Thompson did what he could to maintain discipline among the disheartened remainder, and encouraged them to build a store-house, and plant rice. By the end of August the stores were unloaded and the transports sent home. On September 16th, after landing the settlers' arms and ammunition, and sending Chief Tom a present, he himself sailed away.

The high mortality rate among the settlers continued, Sharp blaming it on the intemperance of settlers who over-ate salt food and over-drank their daily rum rations; while Captain Thompson blamed the choice of settlers, declaring them vicious, drunken and lawless, unfit to colonise.

When the rains lessened, the surviving settlers began cultivating. It was assumed that the soil Smeathman had declared so fertile would support an agricultural community. Sharp himself imagined he was planting a breed of sturdy farmers and dreamed of the primitive simplicity of pastoral life. But the first attempts at agriculture proved a big failure. Nothing would grow on the rocky hill where the people had first settled. Unable to gain a livelihood from the soil, the settlers, faced with starvation, had to barter their stores, even their muskets and clothes, with the Temne for rice. Very soon they began drifting away to work on passing ships or for neighbouring slave traders. James Reid, a literate settler who had just been

elected to succeed another as headman or Governor, wrote asking
Sharp whether some business agent could not come out to supply
them with goods and credit, till their crops were established. This
request, perhaps, was to be the origin of Sharp's plan to form a
Sierra Leone Company.

Early in 1788, he determined to send out another ship, the *Myro*,
with more settlers, well supplied with livestock and supplies. He had
already paid out nearly £500 in gifts to the community or in loans
he was unlikely to recover to individuals. He now persuaded the
Treasury, which had already spent over £15,000 on the first expedition, to give another £200 towards livestock. A friend, probably
Samuel Whitbread, the brewer, donated 100 guineas. Sharpe bore a
greater part of the cost of the new venture. By the end of 1788 he
reckoned he had spent altogether £1,735 18s. 8d. on the Province of
Freedom. In June Captain John Taylor, owner and master of the
Myro brig, was engaged to take out the new emigrants, 39 of them
and mostly whites, to Sierra Leone. In August the second expedition
arrived to see the settlement seriously reduced by death and desertion
to about 130 settlers. With the *Myro*'s arrival, however, many who
had left the settlement returned with new hopes.

King or Chief Tom died about this time. King Naimbana who
had never agreed to the first treaty, now insisted on a new treaty
of land purchase before he would allow the settlers to stay. It fell to
Taylor to make this new treaty and repurchase the land from the
Temne chief, to whom he paid £85 1s. 7d. in goods. Taylor's treaty
with Naimbana, signed August 22nd, 1788 and superseding Thompson's treaty with King Tom in 1787, is deemed the legal beginning
of the Colony.

Even with those who returned when the *Myro* arrived, the total
population was not more than 200. The settlers still lived in temporary huts; the planned church, court house and prison were un-
built. And now many of the Europeans whom Sharp had sent in the
Myro to help the young settlement, went off to the slave trade. What
distressed Sharp most was hearing that some of the settlers did the
same, particularly that Henry Demane, whom he had rescued from
slavery in 1786 by sending a writ of Habeas Corpus on board a ship
already under sail from Portsmouth, had crossed to the Bullom
Shore to trade in slaves. Disappointed by the behaviour of his
protégés and by the news of the hostility shown to the young settlement by the slave traders on the coast, Sharp remained undaunted.

By 1790 he was already working on the idea of forming a Company and making contacts among his friends on the Black Poor Committee and Thomas Clarkson's Abolition Society. Sharp's proposed St George's Bay Company was no bait to self-interested capitalism: though he pointed out in the prospectus he published anonymously, 'Free English Territory in Africa', that the West African barter trade provided a profitable market for cheap English manufactures, Sharp made it clear that the Company was formed at the settlers' request, and for their benefit, not to make profits for the subscribers.

From Thomas Clarkson's letter to Josiah Wedgwood in 1793, concerning the sale of shares in the Sierra Leone Company, we also find some of the finest sentiments that motivated Sharp, Clarkson and their class of humanitarians in the philanthropic experiment at Sierra Leone:

> But, I should not chuse [sic] to permit anyone to become a purchaser, who would not be better pleased with the good resulting to Africa than from great commercial profits to himself; not that the latter may not be expected, but in case of a disappointment, I should wish his mind to be made easy by the assurance that he has been instrumental in introducing light and happiness into a country, where the mind was kept in darkness and the body nourished only for European chains.[1]

In February 1790 twenty-two people, including Wilberforce and Henry Thornton, attended the first meeting to subscribe as an act of kindness rather than as an investment. Through Wilberforce they bought a thirty-four ton cutter, the *Lapwing*, seized by the customs for smuggling, to send to the settlers.

In April came the news that the settlement had been attacked and destroyed by King Tom's successor, King Jimmy. Sharp and his associates were hard put to it to find a means to resucitate the Colony. He begged Pitt for help, for a naval ship to go out with marines to restore the settlers, and for a further grant of £300. He pointed out how valuable Sierra Leone was to England and the unwisdom of abandoning it to other European powers. He wrote four letters between April and August, but Pitt made no reply. A letter to the Treasury elicited no more than formal acknowledgement.

Denied Government help, Sharp had to turn to private sources. Thirty-eight shareholders petitioned for incorporation by Act of Parliament as a Company with possession of the land granted the settlers, exclusive trading rights for thirty-one years, a grant towards

---

1. Farrer, K. (ed.), *The Correspondence of Josiah Wedgwood* (London, 1906) Vol. I, 215–16, June 17th, 1793, cited in Williams, Eric, *op. cit.*, p. 179.

a fort and soldiers, and powers to make laws until the settlers were capable of making their own. The humanitarian colonisation promised education of the natives and opposition to the slave trade.

The directors met with the great hostility in Parliament of all connected with the African trade. Slave traders, in any case hostile to a body sponsored by Sharp, Wilberforce and Clarkson, were enabled to oppose the petition on grounds of public as well as private interest. 'Reasons against giving a territorial grant to a Company of merchants to colonise and cultivate the peninsula of Sierra Leone'[1] were given and widely distributed in many pamphlets. The Company met the attack with some strategy, withdrawing their application, changing their name from St George's Bay to the Sierra Leone Company, and putting out a new and changed Manifesto. They sought wider support. In February 1791, with their number increased to about 100, they petitioned Parliament for incorporation. Realising that philanthropy may be made more attractive by the inducement of earthly as well as heavenly rewards, the directors now stressed their commercial rather than their philanthropic intentions. Their project offered those who supported abolition on humanitarian principles a practical way of encouraging alternative forms of African trade. Thus the 'Saints' through their new Company, attracted the attention and sympathy of other abolitionists all over England: when shares were eventually offered to the public almost as many were taken up in the provinces as in London.

In April a Bill to incorporate the Company was introduced into the House of Commons. After much opposition the bill passed by eighty-seven votes to nine and became law on June 6th, 1791 (31 Geo III Cap. 55). The Act vested management in thirteen directors, elected annually by the shareholders, and allowed the Company to make its own laws for those concerned in its affairs. Thus a colony governed by absentees in England replaced the self governing Province of Freedom. Sharp had to submit, realising the alternative was abandoning the settlers altogether. His fellow directors, putting business before philanthropy, elected Thornton, not him, Chairman; henceforth Sharp's influence in the direction of the affairs of the young settlement counted for little. The Company took full charge.

As a joint-stock Company their capital was limited to £50,000,

---

1. Campbell, F., 'Reasons Against Giving a Territorial Grant to a Company of merchants to colonise and cultivate the peninsula of Sierra Leone' (London, 1791).

but before half that sum was raised they commenced operations from Sierra Leone House, Brichin Lane, London, establishing at a trifling expense a few small factories chiefly on Sierra Leone rivers, and purchasing the French factory on Gambia Island. They reimbursed Sharp the sum of £1,850. The capital, afterwards raised to £230,000, was gained from fifty pounds subscriptions, the first thirteen directors holding most of the shares.

At last the *Lapwing* was sent out in December and arrived in Sierra Leone in January 1791. Driven from Granville Town in 1790 by King Jimmy and his henchmen, the settlers found temporary shelter at Bobs Island, near Bance Island. Some found employment on ships, or at the slave factories. Some were taken in by Namina Modu, the Sanko chief of Port-Loko, and about fifty by Pa Boson, a nearby chief, who let them have a church and hold regular services.

A few weeks after despatching the *Lapwing*, the directors sent an agent, Alexander Falconbridge, to relieve and if possible resettle them. Formerly a ship's surgeon employed in the slave trade, Falconbridge had turned against it with the uncompromising violence of a religious conversion and had helped Clarkson collect evidence. The directors judged him chiefly by his opinions, overlooking his lack of self-control and addiction to drink. Falconbridge came out with his wife, Anna Maria, a young lady from Bristol. Not the first English woman to visit Sierra Leone, she was the first to record her experiences in print in her *Letters* and *Narrative of Two Voyages* from which sources much useful information can be had about some of the events which occurred in the settlement during this early period.

On arriving in the Colony, Falconbridge went to persuade Naimbana to let the surviving settlers return, stressing that the land had been twice paid for. Seven times he went to meet the chief at Robana, twice with his wife, for protracted palavers, until the assembled chiefs consented, in return for about £30 worth of tobacco, rum, iron bars and gold-laced hats.

About fifty men and women gathered under Falconbridge's care. Granville Town was overgrown with bush, so having agreed to keep away King Jimmy, the hostile Temne chief, Falconbridge took his party eastwards to the east side of what is now Cline Bay (then Fora Bay). They settled by the shore, north of where Kissy Village was later built, in a village abandoned for being haunted by evil spirits. To this new site, they gave the old name, Granville Town.

In a few weeks they built huts and a store and planted cassava and

other crops for the coming year. They had arms to defend themselves; a militia was organised to keep guard. By mid-June 1791
Falconbridge could safely leave them to report to the directors.

Having heard the Governor's report, the directors called a shareholders' meeting to decide on future policy. They decided on generous capital outlay as the only way to secure an adequate return.
Originally it was proposed to raise £42,000; the meeting resolved to
raise £100,000. Eventually some £235,000 was subscribed. £30,000
was estimated for initial expenditure in the first year; recurrent annual expenditure £7,000, out of which £2,000 was to pay for salaries
of the Company's employees. Prospective settlers were to have free
passages, rations for three months, half rations for another three, and
grants of sixpence, to be made according to size of family. Land was
to be subject to two shillings an acre quit-rent for two years, then to
an annual tax. The Company was to establish factories or stores for
marketing goods and produce at reasonable charges. The Company
was not intended to make huge profits but its business, it was hoped,
would prosper commercially and yield the shareholders a return for
their investment. Finally, the directors drew up a declaration to be
explained to the neighbouring tribes—that the Company renounced
the slave trade, and would keep a large stock of goods to exchange
for other commodities. Those who came to live within their jurisdiction would be governed by English law without prejudice as to
colour; and the Company further promised to establish schools to
give free education to all children brought to them by the natives.

By the February of 1792, some 119 Company officials were sent to
the Colony, including a superintendent (afterwards called a Governor), eight councillors, a chaplain, three physicians, a botanist, a
mineralogist, a commercial agent, land and building surveyors, a
secretary, an accountant, a chief storekeeper, clerks, gardeners,
bakers, artificers, store keepers, thirty women and ten children;
and a military bodyguard. It was now a humanitarian Colonisation
on a grand scale, far exceeding the humble estimates of 1787.

The successive Superintendents or Governors of the Sierra Leone
Company's administration were John Clarkson, 1792; William
Dawes, 1792–3, 1795–6, 1801–3; Zachary Macaulay, 1794–5, 1796–9;
John Gray, 1799–1800; William Day, 1803, 1805; Thomas Ludlam,
1799, 1803–5, 1806–8.

John Clarkson, a younger brother of the more famous Thomas
Clarkson, was born at Wisbech. At the time of his appointment he
was an assistant to the Abolition Committee. A man of frail health,

he was devotedly religious and of a mild disposition. His last action in the Colony was the preaching of a sermon in the church to the settlers. His short period of service shows him to have been without the power of discipline owned by others, but possessing a great personal magnetism that was a control in itself, endearing him to the liberated African settlers.

William Dawes was once in the Royal Marines and had also seen some service at Botany Bay established at Port Jackson. He was first employed by the Sierra Leone Company as a Surveyor, and then as one of Clarkson's two assistants. A man of capacity, cool, sensible and business-like, he attempted in Freetown the methods he had been familiar with at the convict establishment and thus ran into trouble with the settlers.

Clarkson, when handing over to Dawes, had endeavoured to impress upon the minds of the colonists favourable ideas respecting his successor, for some of the settlers had been prejudiced against him, not being acquainted with his real disposition. 'These poor people', stated Clarkson, 'suspicious in the highest degree, mistake the serious and sedate conduct of this gentleman for pride and want of feeling towards them, and from their ignorance cannot be prevailed upon to believe that he has their interest at heart. Most sincerely do I hope that the colonists will be induced to show Mr. Dawes more attention, and place more confidence, and also that he will endeavour to unbend a little, and try to show his good intention by a little more conciliation.'[1]

Mortality amongst the settlers was very severe during the administration of Clarkson and the first year of Dawes; so much so that the hastily-made graveyard at the foot of Thornton Hill was continuously being enlarged. By the end of 1792 only about forty white men were left in the Colony, which soon acquired the unsavoury title of the 'White Man's Grave'.

Zachary Macaulay succeeded Mr Dawes as Governor of the Colony. Born in 1768, Macaulay had been sent at the age of sixteen by a Scottish business house as book-keeper to an estate in Jamaica, and soon became sole manager of the estate. His position brought him into close contact with slavery, a social system he had been educated to respect as scriptural. Young Macaulay's heart was soon wounded by cruelties practised on the slaves at the will and pleasure

---

1. John Clarkson, cited in Butt-Thompson, F. W., *Sierra Leone In History and Tradition* (London, 1926) p. 82.

of a thousand petty despots on the West India plantations. Unable to alleviate the hardships of the plantation slaves, Macaulay finally resigned his position in Jamaica and returned home. It was then he came in contact with Henry Thornton, chairman of the Sierra Leone Company's board of Directors, and was soon afterwards appointed Governor in 1794.

Macaulay was by his past Jamaican experiences admirably adapted for the arduous task of planting a Negro colony. Incapable of being frightened or fatigued, he stood as a centre for order, authority and discipline amidst the seething chaos of inexperience and insurbordination at the Sierra Leone settlement. He was Governor during the most eventful period of the colony's early history.

The staff was so miserably insufficient that the Governor had to be in the counting-house, the law court, the school, and even the chapel. He was his own secretary, his own postmaster, his own envoy. He posted ledgers, he conducted correspondence with the directors at home and visited neighbouring tribal chiefs on diplomatic missions which made up in danger what they lacked in dignity.

The Governor preached sermons and performed marriages, and yet had time to establish something resembling order, knowing that a reasonable measure of prosperity had commenced.

He experienced the French attack on the town in 1794 and some of the insurrections and hostilities of the settlers and the natives; he settled the currency question, extended the Colony westward to the sea, and stayed until the settlers were thriving and his Company was seeing some return on its expenditure.

John Gray, who succeeded Macaulay, was a member of the Colony's 'Council of Eight' before being appointed Governor. His total unfitness for any part in a settlement of this kind is seen in his subsequent action of setting up as a slaver at Bassam where he died in 1807. To Thomas Ludlam, who succeeded Gray, fell the honour of proclaiming the transfer of the Colony to the Crown, in 1808 and of remaining in charge until the arrival of the first Crown Governor. Captain William Day, from whom Ludlam took over after 1805, had first arrived in the Colony in 1803. After a few months as Governor he was recalled to appear before a Committee of the House of Commons, appointed in 1803 to investigate the merit of a petition from the Court of Directors for the continuance of the Parliamentary grant. Day returned in January 1805, with the full confidence of all at home. He is remembered for his vigorous work fortifying the Colony; for restoring confidence amongst the settlers and the neigh-

bouring chiefs; and for compelling respect from the Colony's enemies. During this time, the spirit of the settlers revived, the native
labourers, *grumettas*, returned to their work on the farms, and cultivation was successfully resumed.

One of the early administrative bodies set up in the Colony by the
Company directors was the so-called 'Council of Eight'. Comprising
eight men with equal authority to each other and to the Governor,
the Council of Eight constituted one of the greatest obstacles to some
of the early Governors. Mrs Falconbridge contrasted the 'amiable
and unostentatious' Governor Clarkson with 'those opinionated up-
starts' who so tied the Governor up and 'so thwarted him' that
Clarkson could neither do anything without them nor do the good
things he wished for the settlers. Clarkson's own diary contains
other evidence of the difficulty created by the council. 'The officers',
he lamented, 'have been ruined by being placed in situations they
were never calculated to fill; and their brains have been turned from
being allowed to wear a flaming sword and epaulette, when a jacket
and trousers would have been more consistent for those employed
in forming a colony.' The wives also troubled him; 'their mutual
jealousies and absurd notions of their rank and consequence gave
rise to many private piques, which often cause open dissensions
amongst the gentlemen; the mischief they have occasioned me from
the day the ships left the Downs to the present day cannot be estimated'.[1] With the subsequent arrival of settlers from the New
World, other Superintendents of the humanitarian experiment at
Sierra Leone soon faced more administrative problems than Clarkson had experienced with the Company's officials and their wives.

The American War of Independence had an impact on the history
of the Sierra Leone Colony.

After the surrender of Lord Cornwallis to Washington, on October
19th, 1781, the British began to disband their army; many of the
slaves who had fought on the British side had now to quit America,
for most of them the land of their birth, for good. A few found their
way to England, thence to Sierra Leone; others later found themselves planted in the cold forests of Nova Scotia and New Brunswick.
Having served under the Crown they were entitled, as disbanded
soldiers, to grants of land.

In fact when they landed at Halifax, Nova Scotia, their first as-
signment was the building of a town, Shelburne, for the white

---

1. *Op. cit.*, p. 86.

ex-soldiers whom the British authorities sought to help. When land
was eventually distributed most of these humbler loyalist immigrants
were overlooked. Some were told to wait; others were granted tracts
of remote, impenetrable bush.

Before long many of these loyalists became servants or labourers
to new white masters in Nova Scotia under a system of apprenticeship. In Thomas Peters, their comrade and able leader, the Nova
Scotian negroes found a mouth-piece, and their grievances soon
reached the ears of the humanitarians in England. Having arrived
in London to present the case of his fellow loyalists before the
authorities, Peters criticised the non-grant of the farm lands which
had been promised them and denounced the Nova Scotia apprenticeship system as a new form of slavery no different from that from
which they had fled. So like slavery was this system that 'masters
sold or disposed of their apprentices as they thought proper'.[1]

Granville Sharp quickly took up the case of the Nova Scotians;
in Parliament Wilberforce repeated Peters' words; Thomas Clarkson
wrote of him to his friends; Thornton had him out to Battersea; and
the Sierra Leone Company adopted him and his cause. Backed by
these friends, Peters spoke in a committee room of the House of
Commons. Parliament went into 'ways and means', and John Clarkson, younger brother of the more famous Thomas Clarkson, was
dowered with ships and money and provisions to bring the
'Nova Scotians', as they were now called, from Canada to Sierra
Leone.

On arrival at Halifax, Clarkson found the situation even worse
than Peters had painted it. Twelve months later, in a letter to
William Dawes recommending the Nova Scotians to his care, Clarkson, after speaking of the war services of the blacks, stated that these
men when brought to Nova Scotia

> were promised a certain quantity of land, with provisions for three
> years, with every other encouragement, such as implements of
> husbandry, a musket each, and various other things. When I tell you
> that upwards of 3,000 people embarked for Nova Scotia, you will be
> surprised to hear that not 300 got their promises performed; and that,
> although I brought with me 1,200 people, yet the majority of those
> who remained in America are at this moment upon the lands of white
> men in a species of slavery; for they are obliged to cultivate the ground
> of another man, while he pays them part of the produce—say, a few

---

1. Butt-Thompson, *op. cit.*, p. 92.

bushels of potatoes half-yearly, when they have more right to the land than the men who claim it.[1]

The fifteen vessels carrying the Nova Scotians started from Halifax on January 15th, 1792, and arrived at Freetown on March 28th with some 1,030 settlers, about one hundred of the original number having died during the voyage. The elements were against the expedition and during the passage the ships saw little of each other. Sickness and deaths on board had made the voyage tedious and unpleasant but all this was quickly forgotten when the survivors at last entered what they looked upon as their 'Promised Land'. The fleet anchored in and about Kru Bay, and there the Nova Scotians were landed in boats along the eastern bank of King Tom's Brook, where one of their number, the venerable William Ash, led them in 'prayer and thanksgiving'. They then 'ordered themselves into bands' and went up from the shore in a singing, joyful procession.

On the ground where the colonial hospital now stands they put up tents for the women and children, for the hope of the directors that they would find houses erected for them had been a vain one. The advance party of officials had only provided dwellings for themselves. The first building the Nova Scotians erected was a Meeting House, under the shade of King Jimmy's gris-gris tree, a vast silk-cotton tree that still stands at the City Centre by the present Law Courts. Here, the three denominations they represented met in a daily 'Praise-giving Service'.

In Sierra Leone the Nova Scotians soon again experienced difficulty over grants of land. The Manifesto read to them in Nova Scotia had stated that 'every free black accepted by the Company shall have a grant of not less than twenty acres of land for himself, ten for his wife, and five for every child, upon such terms, and subject to such charges and obligations, with a view to the general prosperity, as shall hereinafter be settled by the Company'. The settlers arrived only to be first employed on Company land and in the gardens of the officials. At last, when the grants were made, they got only one fifth of the promise, no family having more than five acres and some considerably less.

Labour was another source of trouble. Much of the time which settlers needed to cultivate their land and build their houses was taken up in public labour such as erecting a church, a hospital, warehouses and other buildings, fencing and cultivating 'a garden

---

1. Cited in Butt-Thompson, *op. cit.*, pp. 94–5.

of experiment', and executing 'some measures for the defence of the colony'. Wages were paid in kind and the storekeeper had his own ideas concerning values; sometimes the stores were irrelevant to the settlers' needs.

The first Governor, for instance, was obliged to observe regretfully:

> The *Felicity*'s cargo does not appear to be well selected, considering our wants; she has brought out an immense number of garden watering pots, which seem to occasion a smile from everyone.[1]

The conduct of the seamen of the Company's vessels was a constant irritation to the settlers; Clarkson found the action of some of the seamen 'an open insult' and tried without much success to check them. The Nova Scotians especially resented the 'degrading expressions' flung at them. 'These people', remarked Clarkson, 'have delicate feelings, and just ideas of right and wrong, and as they have been ill-treated and deceived through life, they are very suspicious of the conduct of white people.'[2]

The Nova Scotians soon took to various occupations: some became shopkeepers, some farmers, some merchants in rice or camwood or livestock, some fishermen, whilst many proved to be good mechanics. Within the first twenty-four months, about fifty of them owned canoes and a few had bought small coasting schooners. Some migrated up river where they cultivated large plantations of rice, land having been given them freely by the natives. Their gardens contained rice, yams, plantains, cabbages, indian corn and cotton, while their yards became alive with pigs and poultry. Most of the Nova Scotian farmers eagerly entered into a competition for the money prices offered by the company.

Community work and social organisations were a common feature of life in the settlement. The first Thrift Society took the form of a Burial club. The three denominations put up their own places of worship; the Baptists, about the end of 1792, in Rawdon Street; the followers of the Countess of Huntingdon Church, about the same time, in Wilberforce Street where the 'Zion' church now stands, and the Wesleyan Methodists after 1792, also built in Rawdon Street, where College Chapel now stands. The preachers came from among their own particular denominations and often achieved considerable influence among their own sect. It was widely felt even among the

---

1. Butt-Thompson, *op. cit.*, p. 99.   2. *Ibid.*

authorities that the discipline which these preachers preserved in their little congregations contributed considerably to the maintenance of the general morals.

Town planning was also undertaken during this time, the first streets bearing to this day the names of Oxford, Westmoreland, Bathurst, Liverpool, Percival, Pultney and Walpole. Substantial houses appeared, that of Thomas Peters being the first to be built of stone.

Trial by Jury was established, the settlers acting as Jurymen, one of the company's servants as Judge. A defence force was formed, the veterans of the American War once again shouldering arms. For the purposes of local government the town was divided into Tithings (districts of ten families) after the old-English custom of frank-pledge.

Each district elected a Tithingman to represent it, and every ten of these officials chose one of their members to be their Hundreder; these, in their turn, elected from amongst themselves a Headman for the town. Thomas Peters was the first Headman of Freetown, and continued in that position until in 1799, when the Company published a new Regulation and from that date began appointing an official of their own as Mayor, when he was appointed Town Marshal. During the reign of the Sierra Leone Company many of the Nova Scotians took active part in the government of the colony: Thomas Cox, George Ross, Alexander Smith, Peregrine Francis Thorne, A. Vanneck, D. Molloy Hamilton, Walter Robinson, Francis Leedham had all acted as the Mayor and the alderman of the town. A Legislative Council was created of which Thomas Peters and another Nova Scotian, David George, were among the first members.

After the French attack on the Colony in 1794 the directors, having lost so much, decided to supplement their meagre trading returns by tapping a source of income which they had never yet exploited: the quit-rents on the Nova Scotians' land. The quit-rent was to be imposed as a land tax to yield the Company revenue. Between 1796 and 1800, the issue of quit-rent remained a constant source of trouble between the Nova Scotians and the Company's Administration. In June 1796 a notice was issued fixing them at a shilling an acre per annum, chargeable from January 1st, 1797, the half-yearly payment of 6d. an acre to be made in July 1797.

Nothing the directors or their employees could say would efface their memory of Clarkson's firm promise to them before they left

Nova Scotia, that they would never have to pay rent for their land. Now all their suspicions revived. Vehemently opposed to the quit-rent law, they charged the Company of breach of faith over the promised allotments and over the idea of payments for their plots. Macaulay, admitting their grievance, thought it offset by the Company's extra, unpromised, services, free schools and medical care, and by their having received rations so long, credit at the store, and employment. Both parties felt aggrieved, the Nova Scotians at the breach of faith, the Company at their want of gratitude. Later the Company's published report, while carefully giving them credit for their good qualities, deplored their ingratitude for the benefits the Company was conferring on them.[1] The constant trouble between the Nova Scotians and the Administration in Sierra Leone ended in Thomas Peters and David George being summoned to England to appear before the directors, who received the delegates and their people's case with great disfavour.

The difficult experiences with the Nova Scotian Settlers did not prevent the Company from countenancing an appeal by the Jamaican Maroons to be sent over from Halifax to Sierra Leone. The negotiations in London between the Halifax representatives and the Sierra Leone Company were not protracted and in the correspondence there appears a general conspiracy to say all the nice things possible of the Maroons.

The Sierra Leone Company, when accepting the charge, after being assured that the Government would bear the expense of removal, issued a Manifesto, in which all the Maroons who subscribed to it were promised the rights and privileges of citizenship in Freetown, or other parts of their land. Each male of the age of twenty-one was to have three acres for himself, two for his wife and one for each child. One-third of the land was to be given in the first year and the remainder within three years. Each holder was to have his ground cleared and his house built within one year of arrival.

Hastily embarked at Halifax, because of the increasing hostility of the tribesmen and the Nova Scotians towards the Settlement, some 550 sturdy Maroons arrived at Freetown in September 1800, in time enough to defend the Colony against attack by the surrounding tribes and the turbulent Nova Scotian settlers.

Except for some antagonism between them during the first years, the Maroons and the Nova Scotians lived on together in the Colony

---

1. Fyfe, *A History*, p. 57.

without any serious conflicts. Eleven years after their arrival the Maroons were found to have increased by more than fifty per cent, but later their number decreased, many of them returning to Jamaica. After the Maroons in 1800, the only other settlers arriving in the Colony from the New World were the 1,222 Negro pensioners and their families from the West Indian Royalist Regiments in 1818, and in 1819 eighty-five Negroes involved in an insurrection in Barbados.[1]

Up to 1796 the Sierra Leone Company bore the expense of the settlement, keeping up a more or less regular communication by its own ships, and being responsible for the wages of the Governor, chief judge, secretary and a host of other officials. From 1796, however, the British Government began making grants to assist the Company. Starting with a grant of £4,000 in 1796 the Government raised the sum to £10,000 per annum by 1798.

In the December of 1803 a Special Committee was appointed by the House of Commons to investigate the condition of the Colony. Following the report the grant was raised by £4,000 for purposes of defence. Three years later the Company, then heavily in debt, asked the Government to relieve it of its charge, and the following year a Bill was carried through Parliament to this effect, receiving the Royal Assent in the August, and being put into operation in 1808.

History seems to have dealt unkindly in its assessment of the Company's role in the effort of resettling freed slaves in Sierra Leone. Its humanitarian intentions, no less than its real achievements, were obliterated by clouds of criticisms that studiously advertised its financial embarrassments and over-emphasised its administrativs weaknesses. Many years after the Company had relinquished ita authority over the Settlement, the West India interests, in persuading the Government to reverse the old policies adopted by the Company in preference for a policy of voluntary emigration, painted the Company's work in the blackest terms.[2]

Governor Ludlam, who had been asked to continue in office until a successor was appointed by the Crown, explained the general want of success as follows:

---

1. C.O. 300/4, MacGregor Laird, 'Memorandum on Sierra Leone' (London, 1842).
2. McQueen, J., *The Colonial Controversy* (Glasgow, 1825)—in which the author, an agent of West India interests, delivered a classic invective against the Company; Macgregor Laird, 'Memorandum on Sierra Leone', C.O. 300/4.

Few places have met with greater discouragement; frequently the colony has been threatened, and twice was actually attacked by the natives. Once it was ruined by the French; twice its own people have broken out into insurrection. When extensive commerce was carried on the French destroyed it. When cultivation flourished, the natives first drove away the labourers, and then drove the settlers from their farms.

'The wonder', concluded Ludlam, 'is that the colony exists rather than that it has not flourished.'[1]

The Company's achievement was modest enough: it had to point with pride to the twenty-six African children brought to England from Sierra Leone between 1791 and 1800, to be trained at the Company's expense.[2] Yet in the history of the British anti-slavery movement before 1807, no achievement was as impressive, venturesome and selfless as the founding of a liberated African colony at Sierra Leone. The humanitarian directors of the Company, though disappointed over the numerous embarrassments they had to face in running the settlement, justly prided themselves in having laid a good foundation, a liberated African Settlement, which could serve as a base for the deployment of more ambitious policies in the subsequent decades. When in 1807 the British Parliament announced the legal abolition of the slave traffic and from 1808 started on its long career of recapturing and protecting African slaves intercepted from foreign slavers on the high seas, the question of where to resettle or rehabilitate those it rescued did not arise. Still more, in the agricultural and educational policies pursued by the short-lived Sierra Leone Company, the Government was provided with a store of precedent and experience to guide its course. The Company could rightly claim on the eve of its demise to have done most of the original thinking in the fashioning of future policy.[3] Besides, the country

---

1. Cited in Butt-Thompson, *op. cit.*, p. 133.
2. Ingham, E. G., *Sierra Leone after a Hundred Years* (London, 1894) p. 187.
3. Ingham, E. G., *op. cit.*, pp. 180–90: 'However great have been the Company's loss in a pecuniary view, the Directors are unwilling to admit that there has been a total failure in their main objects, or that their capital has been expended without effect. It must afford satisfaction to reflect that the Company should both have conceived and attempted to execute those plans of beneficence which led to the institution of the Colony; and that they should have continued to pursue them for so many years, in the face of opposition, disappointment and loss, in spite of severe calamities arising from European as well as African wars and much turbulence on the part of the Colonists ... The Company have communicated the benefits flowing from a knowledge of

lying some one hundred miles north and south of the river had been influenced for good by the Company's work in the Settlement. To the north, the Bullom country was, during most of the period, peaceable and prosperous. Beyond Bullom, the Mandingo tribe had established commercial links with the settlers. The Temne were increasingly employing themselves with work for wages, especially in the Timber trade, and the Mendes, to the south of the colony, were accepting the advantages of Freetown and making it their chief market. There were trading schooners on regular routes around the coast.

Recognising that the continuance of the slave trade would keep the Colony from the security it deserved and was intended to have, some of the directors of the Company, in the year they surrendered Sierra Leone, formed a new association called the African Institution. Its declared object was the final extinction of the slave trade by the improvement and civilisation of the people of Africa. Its birth coincided with the British Abolition Act of 1807 which made open slave trading illegal for British subjects. The first work of the Institution was to influence the establishing in Freetown of a court of law, the Vice-Admiralty Court, which had powers to condemn captured slave vessels, sell the ships so taken, punish the owners and masters, and set free the slaves found within them. For the purposes of capture and convoy, certain vessels of the Royal Navy were allocated to the West Coast. Through the original work of the Sierra Leone Company and its humanitarian directors had emerged a positive British African policy—the suppression of the slave trade, the civilisation of Africans through the encouragement of education, Christianity and commerce, which policy successive British Governments were to pursue, although with varying degrees of sincerity and diligence, for nearly half a century.

With the transfer of the Colony to the Crown new policies were bound to develop. A Liberated African Yard, The King's Yard, was soon established for the reception of recently arrived settlers—slaves recaptured from foreign slavers—who became known as 'recaptives'

---

letters, and from Christian instructions to hundreds of Negroes on the coast of Africa. . . . They have ascertained that the cultivation of every valuable article of tropical export may be carried on in Africa; that Africans in a state of freedom, are susceptible of the same motives to industry and laborious exertion which influence the natives of Europe; and that some African Chiefs are patriotic to comprehend and sufficiently patriotic to encourage schemes of improvement.'

or 'liberated Africans'. The first slaver brought into Freetown to be condemned by the Vice-Admiralty Court was the *Marie Paul*, captured November 10th, 1808. Two others were captured during that same month. The Governor was instructed to register all Africans recaptured and liberated by the Court and to send an annual return to London. Many registers survive in the Sierra Leone archives, showing name, age, sex, and sometimes a rough physical description including tatoo marks, with a note of how each was disposed of. Many of the returns were carelessly made out: often the mode of disposal and other relevant particulars were left out.[1] This carelessness is a major cause of the difficulties encountered when attempting to fix the exact numbers of liberated Africans involved in one of the greatest movements of the nineteenth century.

Sometimes, however, the entries in some of these old documents in the archives give a clear picture of the pathetic state in which these Africans arrived at Sierra Leone after 1808: reporting to the Governor of the capture of a slave ship in December 1828, the Superintendent of the Liberated African Department states:

> I received yesterday from slave vessel *Campeadora* 209 liberated Africans i.e. 75 men, 23 women, 81 boys, 40 girls, and from *Arcenia* 95 men, 52 women, 86 boys, 65 girls. Nearly the whole of the before mentioned people were landed from the vessels in perfect state of nudity, and I furnished them from the stores of this Department a duck frock for each man, and a wrapper of white calico for each of the women and the children. The deplorable and emaciated state of the people received from the *Arcenia* is shocking in the extreme, scarcely one of them was capable of walking from the waterside to the house, and as many of them are afflicted with ophthalmia and other infectional disorders I have appareled a separate building outside of the square at Kissy for the reception . . .[2]

Occasionally, before the slaves disembarked from a captured slave ship, the various colonial officials and law-court officers would first visit them on board. A medical officer recorded the scene on some of the slave-ships he visited at the Freetown harbour: *Elizabeth* of London, 602 slaves, 155 dead, most of the rest ophthalmic; *Young Hero* (Captain Molyneaux), 250 slaves, 132 dead, majority dysentery and ulceration; *Octavio*, captured only two days after sailing, 239

---

1. See Appendix VII.
2. Meyer-Heiselberg, Richard, 'Research Report No. 1: Notes From Liberated African Department in the Archives at Fourah Bay College, Freetown' (Uppsala, 1967).

slaves, 26 dead, 13 dying, 103 fever and dysentery. *Christina*, 384 slaves, 152 dead or dying of small pox and the rest infected.[1] Sometimes the visiting officers would succeed in making the slaves understand that they were free—and the scene on deck would change dramatically: shouting, leaping, frenzied crowds swarmed on every upper part of the ship, their fears, even their weakness and disease forgotten. Some knocked off their shackles with the billets of wood that had formed their beds, and threw them overboard, as in the *Paquetta de Rio*, in 1846, an incident reported in *The Watchman*, a Freetown newspaper of the time: others turned upon the crew and fought them until troops were brought in to quell them, as in the *Manzanares*, which was caught off the Gallinas Coast by the *Black Joke* in 1830.

The sick were at once hospitalised in a make-shift hospital. Those who were well were removed to the King's Yard, a huddle of wooden buildings situated to the east of Kru Bay, the gate of which bore the inscription 'Royal Hospital and Asylum for Africans rescued from slavery by British Valour and Philanthropy'. Here Dr Poole, long a medical officer to the Liberated African hospital, paid the new arrivals regular visits: Dr Poole has left a record of what he saw during some of his visits:

> In my visits, I have often watched these wild men. The whole scene was striking. These men, uncivilised, uneducated, and ignorant of the purposes of their creation, unclad, exhibiting frightful models of the human figure, irrational in their talk and gestures, apish in their laughter, fierce in their expressions of anger and resentment, devouring their food with the restless action of the animal, need be seen but once to be long remembered.[2]

Soon after their arrival at the King's Yard, a naming ceremony was arranged by the officers of the Liberated African Department. Some were registered under names suggested by countries: John England and John Spain, William Scotland; some by history: Roman Augustus, James Waterloo, Afric Charter; some were named after famous names: John Bright, Abolition Clarkson, Philanthropy Sharp; and some names were of a miscellaneous nature such as Wellington Heroe, Famous Festus, Sigismund Earl, John Bull Bathurst and Leone Leonard Lumpkin. The names of all the Governors, up to about 1850, were also given, and most of the prominent officials. Names of humour abounded: Ajax, Alabaster,

---

1. Cited in Butt-Thompson, *op. cit.*, p. 160.   2. *Ibid.*, p. 161.

Blackman, Bloodfirst, Kneebone, Root, Shirt (the man bearing this name became the first detective of the Colony). Even to-day, such names as Black Jones, Try John, John Bread, are still common in Freetown.

There were many re-unitings of families which had been broken up by slavery. The Chief Justice of the Colony in the 1820s remarked how a considerable number of the nearest kindred, 'husbands and wives, brothers and sisters, stolen at various times and put on board different vessels, have been unexpectedly restored to each other' in Freetown.

After undergoing the naming and the registration ceremonies, the liberated Africans were then removed from the Yard and sent in groups to the various settlement villages. The first such settlement to be built in Freetown was probably Leicester Village, the building of which opened to colonisation the high lands of the interior of the peninsula, which for so long had been guarded from intrusion by superstitious fears. Leicester Peak is about 2,000 feet high and the village built upon its slopes was about two and a half miles from Freetown. Governor Thompson allotted lands to those settlers who desired to live there, planning it as a farming district and giving in the name of his own birthplace, Kingston-on-Hull. The first house was built there in 1809 and in 1810 the village was called Leicester. Liberated African villages were established in districts called: Eastern district, Mountain district, Western or Sea district. Between 1809 and 1830, most of the villages had already been built: in the Eastern district were Kissy, Wellington, Allen Town, Hastings, and Waterloo; in the Western or Sea district, Kent and York were founded, with Dublin and Ricketts on the Banana Islands; while in the Mountain district, as neighbours to Leicester Village, arose Regent, Charlotte and Gloucester. In 1827 these settlements had an aggregate population of about ten thousand people: Waterloo, 1,200; Kissy, 1,000; Regent, 1,000; Charlotte, 900; Wellington, 800; Gloucester, 700; Hastings, 600; York, 600; Kent, 500; Bananas, 400; Allen Town, 150; Leicester, 100, and about the same number at Calmont and Grassfield Villages.

The liberated African Department consisted of a general superintendent, an assistant, three writers, a storekeeper and his assistant, and, in each village, a clergyman-superintendent and a schoolmaster. Probably because of the pressure of work—the Department was always complaining of shortage of staff—there was no attempt made to record the place of origin of the liberated Africans. If all the facts regarding every captured slave vessel had been collected and all the Africans brought ashore and liberated, it would certainly have furnished unique material for illuminating the slave trade in the nineteenth century and the history of Freetown.

From the source material available, however, some useful information can still be deduced about the Government's policy towards the liberated Africans in the period between 1808 and 1840.

By March 1808, the Privy Council established official regulations regarding the mode of receiving and employing all fit liberated Africans brought into Sierra Leone: enlistment in the West India Regiment, service in the Navy, or apprenticeship 'to respectable persons' in the Colony. The Collector of Customs was required to furnish annual reports to the Secretary of State, giving full particulars as to the numbers of liberated Africans landed in the Colony, enlisted, enrolled in the Navy or apprenticed to individuals.[1]

By 1814 figures furnished as to the number of liberated African recruits for the Navy and the West India regiment were 107 and

---

1. *Abstract of Acts of Parliament for Abolishing Slave Trade*, cited, Kuczynski, *op. cit.*, pp. 113–14. 'On receiving such negroes, the collector shall give notice to the Chief Officer of His Majesty's land forces in the Colony, or in the West Indies, to the Commander-in-Chief of the land forces in that part of the West Indies—of the number of male negroes fit for military service so received, to the intent that such officer or commander-in-chief may take any number of such negroes, as recruits for West Indian or African regiments, or to form new Corps, or as pioneers, according to such instructions as he may from time to time receive.' The Navy Officers will 'receive into His Majesty's naval service any number of such negroes that the service may want, and that may be fit for the same.'

Regarding those found unfit for the Army and for the Navy, the authorities will 'bind all such negroes . . . whether male or female . . . as apprentices to prudent and humane masters and mistresses . . . either in the same or other colonies, to learn such trades, handicrafts, or employments as they may seem most fit for, or most likely to gain their livelihood by, when their apprenticeship shall expire'.

See the following sources:
PP. 1829, Vol. xxv (275) 25, No. of slaves captured from 1808–1819.
PP. 1847–8, Vol. lxiv (116) 1, ·· ·· ·· ·· ·· 1810–1846.
PP. 1861, Vol. lxiv (359), ·· ·· ·· ·· ·· 1855–1859.
PP. 1865, Vol. lvi (527), ·· ·· ·· ·· ·· 1860–1684.

For numbers enlisted, PP. 1813–14, Vol. xii (356) 345; for numbers apprenticed, PP. 1821, Vol. xxiii (61) 119; for a long period the proceedings appeared to be either incorrectly recorded or not recorded at all; hence the annual records on these matters are not regularly available; Kuczynski, *op. cit.*, Vol. I, p. 11.

1,968 respectively. By 1816 military recruits had risen to 2,500 but no figures were given for apprenticeship or recruits into the Navy.[1]

The children were sent to one or another of the villages where the C.M.S. had agents to watch over them. Many of these children were put into households, dividing their day between serving their masters or mistresses and attending school. These were called 'protected' children. But there was no register kept of such, no personal super-vision by the King's Yard officials, no periodic visitation of the homes where they lived. There was no penalties and no punishments for those 'protectors' who failed to produce their charges when the protected period came to an end. 'Run away' was accepted as sufficient explanation. Little surprise that much secret slave dealing went on in the Colony itself, so much that Governor Kennedy even felt the liberated African residents themselves were deeply impli-cated in the illegal activities. Of the 33,595 Africans liberated and resettled in the Colony between 1808 and June 30, 1830, some 2,968 could not be accounted for during the 1830 census even after deducting one fifth of the total number as the number who died between 1808 and 1830.

Subsistence allowance was granted at the rate of about twopence per day to those too old or incapacitated to work. Unmarried women were granted rations for three months, by which time they were ex-pected to have gained employment or a husband. If the unmarried men of the village to which they were sent declined to marry them, the women were moved to another. It was during the time of Lieutenant-Colonel Dixon Denham, one of the ablest general Super-intendents that the Liberated African Department ever had, that much useful work and proper organisation were done in the De-partment. On taking office, in 1827 Denham soon found suitable sites for the cultivation of rice, sugar, coffee, ginger and indigo by the liberated Africans in their villages. He abolished the lax method of providing food for workers, substituting for this the sum of three-pence per day until the men, or women, were self-supporting. He also arranged for the establishment of local shops in every village, thereby doing away with the waste of time and the extra toil the journey into Freetown had entailed. Another improvement brought about by Colonel Denham was the division of the villages for purposes of administration, into groups—Eastern (the River

---

1. Kuczynski, *op. cit.*, pp. 114–17.

district), Central (the Mountain district) and Western (the Sea district).

Managers, responsible to a district superintendent, were appointed to each village, to foster the progress of the people, control their conduct, and protect them. Gradually these managers were chosen from the black settlers themselves, with happy results.

By no means all the liberated Africans continued to live on Government subsidy. While many owned only what the Department had given them, there were others who ultimately established themselves in the Colony and successfully entered into business or other occupations. One peculiar feature was the ease with which these people, of many languages and of differing date of rescue, and therefore differing social position, merged during the years and with splendid cooperative spirit helped each other to prosperity. The many organisations and cooperative societies which flourished in the Colony at this time were proof enough of the vitality of their comradeship. In the Old Native Association, the Kissy Defensive Association, the Council of the Seventeen Nations, and a host of others, was manifested the spirit in which the liberated Africans were facing the new life in the new land.

The love of trading was particularly strong among them. At the sale of prize goods—goods seized from captured slave ships—many of them would club together to purchase large lots of unbroken bales. Soon the liberated Africans were taking control of a large part of the shop-keeping of the town, and many rose to positions of influence through their frugal and industrious habits. When the captured slave ships began to be sold in the colony, the bidders were not all agents for slave dealers. Some of the liberated Africans had grown financially strong enough to purchase them. Harry Johnson, a Yoruba, who passed through the King's Yard about 1816, bought in 1830 the Schooner *Harriet*, of 140 tons, for the sum of £200, and soon after purchased another vessel—a felucca of one hundred tons. Another liberated African, Osoba, father of J. S. George of Lagos, was the owner of the *Nancy*, 159 tons, in which he and his family traded between Freetown and Lagos. The story of the Ibo recaptive, John Ezzidio, was typical. Brought to Freetown in 1827, like other recaptives penniless and destitute, Ezzidio rose to fame as a rich merchant by the turn of the century. Reporting in 1842 John Logan Hook, Collector of Customs, of whom we shall hear more later, remarked that 'there could not be less than fifty of these people worth five hundred pounds, and I know some that I have

reason to believe could muster three to five thousand pounds in hard
cash at any time'.[1] Perhaps there was some exaggeration in this, but
there seems to be little doubt that by the 1830s many of the older
residents were taking proper care of themselves and no longer depended on the meagre Government subsistence allowance of one and
a halfpence to twopence per day. What helped determine the industry and the economic future of any community was, of course, the
policy of its government. The Sierra Leone Colony had already become a visible and ever present reminder, to whichever Government
was in power at Whitehall, of Britain's humanitarian African policy.
To a very large extent its prosperity and the future of its inhabitants
depended on the degree of seriousness with which each successive
Government applied itself to the responsibility imposed by the noble
ideal and example of the English 'Saints' who had founded the
Settlement.

This was why some of the Governors, already impressed by the
industry of the liberated Africans and very hopeful of the Colony's
future, vehemently opposed the radical change which was already
occurring in official policy, from emphasis on agricultural and educational projects to emphasis on military and marine service or apprenticeship and later on labour emigration. Governor Thompson,
for example, frowned upon this shift in policy:

> This colony wants settlers, and many of them settlers who will live here
> and farm here and make the place prosperous.[2]

Thompson, appointed as the first Colonial Governor in 1808, tried
to reverse the provisions of the new Order-in-Council of that year.
By August he had passed an Ordinance which not only condemned
military enlistment of liberated Africans but declared the system of
apprenticeship illegal, and therefore null and void in the colony.[3] In
1809 he reverted to the Company's former policy on agricultural development, and re-introduced the award of premiums or bounties
to settlers who produced the largest quantities of produce from their
farm plots. In January 1810 Thompson passed a further measure
which made it possible for industrious farmers to be given freehold
titles.

Thompson's policy was short-lived. With the succession of
Governor Columbine in 1811, there was a reversal to the spirit of the

1. Cited in Butt-Thompson, *op. cit.*, p. 169.
2. *Ibid.*, p. 135.
3. Crooks, J. J., *History of the Colony of Sierra Leone* (Dublin, 1903) p. 75.

1808 Order-in-Council. Military recruitment appears to have been the most popular policy with subsequent Governors up to 1840. One of the officials charged with these recruitments reported by 1837 that 'the whole of our African Corps, and a great part of our West India Regiments that serve in the West Indies, are supplied from the liberated Africans at Sierra Leone'.[1] Judging from the figures of military recruitments by 1816, the number of liberated Africans in the West India Regiment by 1840 must have risen to 12,000 or more.

The pronounced official emphasis on military recruitment led to conflict with the Dutch. By about 1836 the Dutch had also begun intensive military recruitment from St George d' Elmina on the Guinea coast, for service in the 'Corps des Guides' of the Dutch West Indies. The recruiting activities on the coast of the Dutch vessel, *Curaçao*, under the instructions of General Verveer, prompted the Foreign Office to protest to the Dutch Government in 1836 that recruitment for the Corps des Guides 'can only be considered as a deviation from the treaty of the suppression of the slave trade, and the example of this recruiting will encourage the slave-traders of all nations to revive the horrors of the slave trade under another name'.[2]

The Dutch Government replied tartly that the open manner in which military recruits were generally being obtained on the West Coast showed that 'the system not only has nothing in common with the slave trade, but serves, on the contrary, to make slaves . . . pass into the state of freemen'.[3] Just as the British Government claimed that it liberated the slaves at Sierra Leone before enlisting them, so the Dutch, and later the French, began to argue that the so-called 'certificates of manumission' which their officers handed out to the slaves after buying them from the Coast, sufficed as a sign of redemption or manumission. Yet many of these 'liberated' or manumitted slaves travelled sometimes in chains or under heavy guard, to Surinam in the Dutch West Indies, or to French Guadeloupe and Martinique. This initial Anglo-Dutch clash in 1836 foreshadowed the troubles to come in the course of the development of official policy towards liberated Africans.

The Government was led to investigate more closely its own system of military recruitment at Sierra Leone. Reports by officials

---

1. Cited Kuczynski, *op. cit.*, p. 120; see also PP. 1842, Vol. XIII: *Report of Committee on West Africa*, 1842, Part II, p. 363; *Minutes of Evidence*, p. 34.
2. Browe to Baron Verstolk (1836) cited in the *Anti-Slavery Reporter* of December 1st, 1841, pp. 258-9.
3. Cited, *ibid.*

seemed to reveal that some element of force or compulsion was in
fact applied.[1]

Instructions had gone out in 1834 in the historic year of the
abolition of slavery to avoid in future attempting anything like con-
straint in procuring recruits from the liberated Africans.[2] Yet it was
quite clear that Government policy towards its protégés in Sierra
Leone still needed proper definition.

The Superintendent of the Liberated African Yard stigmatised
the planlessness which he thought had characterised official policy
towards liberated Africans for much of the period between 1808–40,
when he lamented in 1827 that

> Every Governor has been left to follow his own plans, however crude
> and undigested; and no two succeeding Governors have ever pursued
> the same course. . . . Mr. Ludlam pursued the system of appren-
> ticing them; Mr. Thompson set that aside, and turned them loose in
> the Colony, without any other superintendence than its general police.

1. Major Ellis, *History of the First West India Regiment*, p. 16 'In former days,
   whenever the cargo of a captured slaver was landed at Sierra Leone, a party
   from the garrison used to be admitted to the Liberated African Yard for the
   purpose of seeking recruits amongst the slavers . . . though it must have been
   well known that they could not possibly have had any idea of the nature of
   the engagement into which they were entering'; once the recruits had been obtained they were marched into the church to christianise and baptize them,
   from which ceremony the recruits emerged a few minutes afterwards without
   their former 'heathen appellations' but with new, high sounding names such
   as Mark-Anthony, Scipio Africanus, etc.
   Kuczynski, *op. cit.*, pp. 120 ff.
   Thorpe, R., *A Reply to the Special Report of the Directors of the African Institution* (1815) p. 84 and *Letter to Wilberforce*, p. 23, cited Kyczynski, *ibid*.
   Thorpe, Chief Justice of Sierra Leone from 1811 to 1813, remained hostile to
   military recruitments:
   'I could not sanction the seizure of the poor ignorant captured negro the moment he landed as a free man, nor their driving a terrified Being to the fort,
   who knew not what was said to him, nor what was to become of him, and
   without his feelings, knowledge or consent being in the least consulted, making
   him a soldier for life.'
2. Hay, R. W., Under-Secretary to Lieut. Governor Temple, May 28th, 1834,
   C.O. 268, Vol. xxx, pp. 469–70, cited Kuczynski, *ibid*. The only other form
   of military service at Sierra Leone was laid down by the Militia Act which
   followed the Order-in-Council in 1808; military service under the Militia Act
   applied more to the old settlers, and became a source of trouble between the
   Government and the Nova Scotians and the Maroons who all protested against
   compulsory military service: Crooks, J. J., *op. cit.*, pp. 75 ff.
   Hoare, P., *Memoirs of Granville Sharp*, pp. 377–9.

Captain Columbine employed them on public works, or apprenticed them. Colonel Maxwell, after delivering over, to the persons appointed to receive them, all the men fit for His Majesty's Service, apprenticed a part of the remainder, and then commenced forming villages with those who could not be disposed of. Sir Charles MacCarthy gave up apprenticing them, except in particular cases, and adopted the plan of forming them into villages ... keeping the youths and children in schools, or making mechanics of them; neglecting perhaps too much, in his successful attempt to make them orderly and quiet citizens, the equally desirable object of making them industrious agriculturists and growers of exportable produce. . . .[1]

Military service, as a major method of finding employment for the liberated Africans between 1808–40, was liable to abuse because of the need to use coercion to obtain recruits. It needed either replacement or augmentation by a more progressive policy which provided opportunities for alternative employment.

As serious complaints of labour shortage began to be made in the West Indies by 1838, nothing seemed more natural than that the Government should seize the opportunity for ridding itself of embarrassing numbers of liberated Africans dwelling under its protection. Yet perhaps no single measure awaiting official decision seemed to be surrounded by so many formidable difficulties. Loopholes in the abolition of slavery in 1834, coupled with certain unhappy circumstances in the termination of apprenticeship in 1838, suddenly opened from 1840 onwards a highly important chapter for liberated Africans and for British policy.

Despite the embarrassments which the Sierra Leone Company had suffered through insufficient funds or through the character or conduct of some of its officials, its work and short-lived administration of the Colony under the direction of the 'Saints', probably represented the best example of real philanthropy in action. For with the transfer to Whitehall of control over the Colony from 1808, political calculations began to impinge upon policy, and British humanitarianism or philanthropy (in terms of labour without counting the costs or kindness without seeking rewards) soon became a thing of the past, as the 'voluntary' emigration policy was clearly to show.

---

1. Macaulay, Kenneth, *The Colony of Sierra Leone Vindicated from the Misrepresentation of Mr. MacQueen*, pp. 5–6, cited Kuczynski, *op. cit.*, pp. 113–14.

Chapter 2
The Origins of Liberated African Emigration

The abolition of slavery in 1834 and the compensation of £20,000,000 to slave owners by the British Government represented not merely a unique event in the history of the British anti-slavery movement since 1807; it was the act which above all others gave tangible proof of British humanitarianism and appeared to establish unequivocally the *bona fides* of the movement. Yet it was precisely at this time that the good faith of British policy was severely tested by the scheme for African Labour Emigration.

Because it appeared to perpetuate the slave trade in a new guise, African labour emigration supplied a powerful argument for other European powers to tolerate if not encourage the continuance of the slave traffic by their own nationals. Not that those powers might not in any case have refused Britain cooperation, given their powerful economic interests in the traffic and their jealousy of British naval and maritime supremacy; but for about a quarter of a century, in all her efforts to secure cooperation of these other nations, anti-slavery England was constantly reminded of the skeleton of African Emigration in her own cupboard.

The historical significance or importance of liberated African labour emigration—perhaps an insignificant movement when compared with other emigration schemes of the century—cannot be properly assessed merely in terms of its short duration (about twenty-one years), or in terms of the comparatively small number of people involved in the emigration (about 100,000 or more, if we consider those shipped from foreign stations immediately on recapture and about which no figures were furnished). The scheme had far more important and widespread repercussions on government policies, diplomatic negotiations, the anti-slavery movement, as well as a

significant influence, many years after, on the history of the West
African hinterland.

African labour emigration was the successor to the Apprenticeship
System which had been intended by the British Government to last
until 1840, but which, despite its protest, had been repealed by the
Colonies in 1838. The motives of the West Indian plantocracy in
abruptly ending a system which still supplied them with forced
labour were complex if not mysterious. Apprenticeship after 1834
had hardly worked well, since the period was one which saw the lash,
the goal and the treadmill still in the master's control; in the way of
managerial skill the planter knew no other expertise than coercion,
and was bitterly against the suggestion that he should dispense with
it. The plantation industry failed to prosper largely because of out-
moded methods of agriculture, the failure to adopt new techniques
of crop rotation and the use of the plough. Worse still, the evils
resulting from absentee ownership and inefficient and often corrupt
management of business by officials or deputies on the spot had all
contributed their part in ruining productivity and diminishing the
incomes of estate owners at home.[1]

The planter, however, had refused to examine or to see these problems in terms other than the supposed inadequacies in the quantity
and quality of their labour force, and came to the belief that the 'indolence' of the resident West Indian negro or creole could be over-
come by reopening a free market in imported labour. The hue and
cry for fresh 'free' and paid labour—especially because this demand
was raised at a time when the small measure of freedom of the apprentices irked the planters and when they were unprepared to pay
wage rates prevailing in a free but closed labour market—may not be
a true guide to the real cause of the West Indian crisis in the post-
emancipation period, nor an index of the magnitude of the alleged
labour shortage, much less a sign of candour or goodwill among the
plantocracy. For this demand for 'free' immigrant labour still leaves
unexplained why they should have decided on their own accord and
in spite of protests from the Imperial Government to dispense—two
years before the legal end of Apprenticeship—with the compulsory
labour they still had available to them. Men who had been so irked
that the apprentice labourer had been left a measure of personal freedom to work accordingly as the law of wages impelled him, would

---

1. Burn, W. L., *Emancipation and Apprenticeship in the British West Indies*
(London, 1937); Premium, B., *Eight Years in British Guiana* (London, 1848).

hardly be sincere in wanting a fresh labour force that would be, of all things, free or paid equitably.

The premature termination of apprenticeship in 1838, far from being a sign of goodwill on the planters' part, must be seen as a demonstration of the long existing impatience among the West Indian plantocracy against a system which they considered unsatisfactory compared with the system of labour before emancipation. It was a rash move to bring to an end the effects of their own action in 1807, when the mother country led them to acquiesce in great acts of justice through motives of self-interest.[1] They might, by forcing the hands of the mother country and returning to the old system of imported labour, forestall the growing politico-economic threats which an increasing number of a free and propertied black population posed to their own position.[2]

The absence of any goodwill between employer and employee, the manipulation of wages below the market price coupled with the proverbial 'indolence' of the West Indian labourer, all these make the labour problem in and after 1838 a very difficult question to assess.[3] Whilst the planters' Associations had remained bitterly against paying high wages, up 30 and 40 cents per task, to 'inefficient' apprentices, they had nevertheless paid even higher on *per capita* bounties between 1835–8, in order to divert or attract the labour force of other neighbouring colonies or countries; only to discover by 1839, however, that the fresh arrivals were even more difficult to manage than the ex-apprentices and 'less satisfactory' too as wage-labourers. The Imperial Government's disapproval of these 1835–6 migration schemes intensified the planters' annoyance, for unless fresh labour could be found to keep the lands fully cultivated, there was a real danger that the emancipated classes might themselves set up as landed proprietors with political rights.[4]

---

1. Ollivier, J., *Free Trade in Negroes* (London, 1849) p. 11; *C.H.B.E.*, Vol. II (1940) pp. 12–16.
2. Burn, W. L., *op. cit.*, pp. 356–7.
3. Laurence, K. C., *Immigration into Trinidad and British Guiana, 1834–70*, (Cambridge, Ph.D., 1858); PP. 1841, XVI, 147, Light to Russell, June 15th, 1840, No. 81; Burn, W. L., *op. cit.*, pp. 368–77; Mathieson, W. L., *British Slave Emancipation 1838–49*, pp. 104–6.
4. Laurence, *op. cit.*, p. 30–51; PP. 1839, XXXIX, 164–5: *Report on John Gladstone Coolie Emigration*, June, 1839. Unlike the small colonies, the three big plantation colonies were decidedly against the free negroes becoming land owners.

The planter thus saw himself as the victim of two forces. By the action of the Imperial Government he had been denied his old right to import labour; at the same time by the vigilance of the mother country he had been frustrated in his efforts, during the apprenticeship period, to exploit every means to maintain, at least socially and economically, a slavery that had come to an end legally.

Perhaps even more painful to the planters than the Act of 1834, was the failure of the efforts of the mother country to secure total international abolition. After the end of the Napoleonic wars in 1815, British diplomacy occupied itself for half a century in the task of inducing other nations to give up the importation of slave labour. As France and her allies during that war had been debarred by the British Navy from this traffic, which Britain herself had controlled thereby stocking her colonies with a large labour force by 1807, the British plantations would have been at a great advantage over their rivals if international abolition had been fully achieved or agreed to by the other nations immediately. As Mathieson points out, the West Indian planters were the only people who had anything to gain from international suppression.[1]

Partly because of these circumstances, British diplomacy was unable before 1840 to secure the full cooperation of the major powers in the general abolition of the slave traffic. France, her main rival, continued, in spite of treaties and conventions with Britain to restock her plantation colonies with slave labour.

Economic calculations or national interests with France, Portugal,

---

Bounties payable per head of immigrant, 1835–1838, Trinidad and British Guiana

about 6 dollars on each immigrant from Grenada and Tobago

··	8	··	·· ··	··	··	St Vincent
··	10	··	·· ··	··	··	Barbados and St Lucia
··	12	··	·· ··	··	··	Dominica
··	14	··	·· ··	··	··	St Kitts, Nevis, Montserat and Antigua
··	16	··	·· ··	··	··	Tortola
··	30	··	·· ··	··		Bahamas
··	25	··	·· ··	··	··	U.S.A.
··	30	··	·· ··	··	··	Canada

PP. 1842, XXIX, 453, Steward to Trinidad Immigration Society, July 20th, 1841; PP. 1842, XXIX, 195, Guiana Immigration Committee, August 10th, 1841; PP. 1842, XXIX, 309, Light to Stanley, December 7th, 1841.

1. Mathieson, W. L., *Great Britain and the Slave Trade 1839–1865* (London, 1929) p. 1.

Spain, as with the West Indian Planters[1] too, had counted for much
in the decisions for or against abolition. 'Perhaps there never was an
international agreement,' commented a famous historian in regard to
the international suppression effort, 'which so completely belied its
promise.'[2] For years France, Spain, Portugal and the United States
failed in their abolition promises in order to safeguard their interests.
But the great promise of a vast labour advantage over her rivals which
international abolition had held out to the planters largely explains
West Indian actions in 1807, when the colonies joined the mother
country in subscribing to the Act of Abolition; just as the failure of
this promise or expectation fully explains the attitude of the plantocracy over slavery questions and over the African Emigration scheme
a few decades after total international abolition had proved a failure.

Already by 1823 the planters' growing repentance of 1807 could
be seen in their attitudes towards the Amelioration Policy. Just as the
mother country had run into great difficulties with them over this
policy,[3] so also had she experienced an even stiffer opposition and
stubbornness over emancipation in 1834, and over passing the requisite legislation after 1838 which gave full rights of free men to the
emancipated apprentices. The unilateral action of the planters in
abolishing apprenticeship was thus perhaps a move to forestall the
further restrictions which the Imperial Government might herself
impose if the legislative provisions were left to Westminster.

The apprentices had hardly become free in 1838 when strict
measures against them began to reveal the spirit underlying the
termination of apprenticeship:

---

1. See, for example, Brougham, H., *An Inquiry into the Colonial Policy of the
   European Powers*, 2 Vols. (Edin., 1803) Vol. 1, pp. 520–40: Vol. 11, pp. 98–101:
   before the concurrence of the West Indian Planters to the Abolition Act in
   1807, an official Parliamentary Committee had revealed the superiority of the
   French Islands in fertility and productivity; the only way for the British West
   India Colonies to fight their rivals and offset this disadvantage was to make
   them agree to abolition and thus stop fresh importation of labour after the
   Napoleonic wars; and to do this, the British Colonies themselves had to set an
   example and hope with this to persuade a weak France, after the war, to adopt
   the same action.

   See also, for the Planters' anxiety to support the Abolition Act, Klingberg,
   F. J., *Anti-Slavery in England* (Yale, 1926) pp. 119–122; Wilberforce, R. I.
   and S., *Life of Wilberforce*, III, pp. 164, 304.
2. Mathieson, *op. cit.*, pp. 12–13.
3. Stephen, J., *England Enslaved by Her Slave Colonies* (London, 1826). Colonies
   refused to implement certain reforms recommended by the Imperial Government in 1823 which would have improved the condition of the slaves.

The action of the planters, in Jamaica particularly, made matters worse: first they tried to force the Negroes to accept wages below the market rate; then they took advantage of the fact that the Negroes' cottages and provision grounds were on the estates to charge them rent . . . as from the day of emancipation, and to regulate it according to the amount of plantation labour done.[1]

In England great disappointment was felt at the action of the colonists and, in rejecting a subsequent application by the planters for fresh importation of African labour, the Imperial Government expressed their lack of confidence in men of such tyrannical habits. To the first petition of the planters in August 1839, the Marquis of Normanby replied in blunt disapproval:

> more than enough has already passed to render her Majesty's Government decidedly hostile to every such project,

past experience having shown that no form of regulation or precaution against abuse and injustice could check the planters, or prevent any scheme of African emigration, in the existing circumstances of that coast, from giving a stimulus to the internal slave trade, or from bringing discredit on the sincerity of the anti-slavery effort in England.[2]

If the Imperial Government still sought to keep alive the Abolition effort, the absence of this intention in the thinking of the planters was only too clearly shown in the force of the materialist arguments embodied in their second petition of December 1839. The supply of tropical products such as cotton, tobacco and sugar, they lamented, was being monopolised by the slave holding countries, much to the detriment of the shipping and manufacturing classes in Britain, and to their West Indian Colonies abroad. Britain could, and should, they demanded, use her maritime supremacy to arrest this development by sanctioning a free and unrestricted importation of African labour.[3] The rejection of the second petition met with defiance from the colonists and dark threats of revolution. British Guiana talked of withholding the civil list[4] and in Jamaica the Assembly breathed secession.

---

1. Morrell, W. P., *The Colonial Policy of Peel and Russell* (Oxford, 1936) pp. 150-1.
2. PP. 1840, Vol. xxxiv, Normanby to Light, No. 70, August 15th, 1839.
3. PP. 1840, xxxiv, *Petition of West India Merchants of London to Lord John Russell*, December 17th, 1839, Enclosure I in No. 35.
4. *Ibid.*, Governor Light to Russell, No. 56, February 15th, 1840.

The immediate effect of the colonists' threatening stand was a sudden and dramatic change in the minds of the policy makers at home. As yet afraid, or rather reluctant, to bear the burden or responsibility involved in working out clear cut and definite colonial policies, the Colonial Office often had recourse to easy compromise, or even timid acquiescence in improper, if temporarily expedient, solutions. The West Indian plantocracy sought to exploit this official weakness when they manufactured[1] the policy of African emigration and used the threat of revolt to demand its immediate approval.

If official hostility or indifference[2] to the labour question in 1839 can be excused because of the planters' rashness in 1838, the root-cause of the whole problem must be traced back to the basic faults in official policy in 1834. The abolition of slavery was legalistic rather than a real social reform. A root and branch policy would have tackled the basic problem by breaking the economic stranglehold of the plantocracy, and giving the free negroes the opportunity to establish their own economic independence. Such a procedure in 1834 would have meant peasant proprietorship and land redistribution and could finally have brought a solution to the troubles caused by the unceasing demands of the plantocracy for cheap labour. But legalistic abolition simply removed the labour force from plantations, without reorganising the plantation economy. Hence the 'shortage' of labour; hence the Imperial Government's inescapable involvement later in the problems of West Indian plantocracy, liberated African emigration, and the need to make a clear distinction between true slavery, forced labour and voluntary emigration.

However, the policy of expediency or half measures was soon to be tried again. For by 1840 James Stephen was already counselling appeasement. Here is a legislature, he had minuted regarding Jamaica:

> which cannot be got rid of. . . . They cannot be destroyed or much enfeebled. . . . I believe we should do more good to the objects of our solicitude [the African labourer] by propitiating the goodwill of the Assembly, even at the expense of acquiescing in many bad measures, than we could do by the most inflexible exercise of the right of rejecting

---

1. PP. 1840, XXXIV, 125, 9, Light to Normanby, No. 105 and Enclosures June 26th, 1839, regarding Ordinance No. 13 of 1839, British Guiana; No. 14, April, 11th, 1839, Mein to Normanby regarding Trinidad Ordinance No. 19 of 1839. PP. 1840, XXXIV, 134, 5, Normanby to Light, No. 70, August 15th, 1839.

2. PP. 1840, XXXIV, 134, 5, Normanby to Light, August 15th, 1839, No. 70.

all such measures at the expense of one protracted quarrel with that House.[1]

The readiness to appease the planter interests was to involve the Colonial Office in increasing difficulties and embarrassments. It not only gave in to the demand for a regular emigration scheme from West Africa, but was prepared to leave the supervision and management of that scheme entirely in the hands of the planters themselves. The only major decision was that the colonies should be required to pass emigration Ordinances, conforming with certain requirements demanded by the Colonial Office.

Naturally, while these negotiations went on, the abolitionist and humanitarian groups in England scented the danger of a renewal of the slave trade under a new guise and raised a vehement opposition to the emigration scheme. They argued against the allegation of labour shortage in the Colonies, and maintained that the planters' ill-management or bad treatment of their labourers was the root of the problem.

An adequate labour supply, they contended, would be forth-coming once the labourers received proper and equitable treatment. The demand for immigrant labour arose not because the field was under-cultivated, but rather because the planters were desirous to extend cultivation and compete with the slave-holding countries in tropical produce. In thus rejecting the plea for more labour the abolitionists also denounced as hypocrytical and deceitful the contention that by removing them to the West Indies the African labourers would be enabled to better their moral and material welfare; the ex-apprentices, they observed, were still oppressed and cheated; but

> let it be known that the peasantry in Guiana are happy, and others will come without solicitation to share their good fortune.[2]

In addition they warned the Government of the embarrassment which would result from any scheme of African emigration:

> What shall we say to Holland, with which country we have lately remonstrated for going to Africa for labourers for Surinam? What shall we say again to France, with whom we have lately remonstrated also, for going to the same continent for soldiers to recruit a regiment for

---

1. Minutes by James Stephen, cited in Bell and Morell, *Select Documents on British Colonial Policy 1830–1860* (Oxford, 1928) pp. 418–21.
2. *The Anti-Slavery Reporter*, February 26th, 1840.

Cayenne? We hinder, and we have strained every nerve to make treaties to hinder, all other nations from going to Africa for labourers, and we go there for labourers ourselves.[1]

The Rev. Henry Townsend, with Samuel Crowther and a group of liberated Africans, had successfully penetrated Abeokuta and Badagry in the Niger hinterland with the Christian message in 1840–1.[2] The vehemence of missionary opposition to an official move which threatened the new evangelical experiment was understandable. But the difficulty which faced the Government was equally appreciable. Apprenticeship had ended too soon and too prematurely for them to have had any time to formulate a new labour policy for their Colonies; and the Colonial Office was hardly if ever prompt in framing rapid and decisive measures of this kind. While the danger of West Indian secession demanded immediate action, the rising prices of sugar in the home market threatened economic hardship at home. Under these pressures the Government of the day found itself with no alternative solution to the emigration scheme for promoting West Indian production and ending the political crisis. It can only be a matter for speculation whether the Colonial Office, in a situation of less tension and urgency, would still have sanctioned or recommended liberated African emigration, in the thick of the international abolition effort, as a solution to the West Indian problem. Emigration was however accepted as a measure of expediency rather than of sound policy. It needed only a humanitarian argument to make it the best policy, to salvage official consciences, and to palliate the outraged anti-slavery opinion in England.

One lay already at hand in the outcome of Sir T. F. Buxton's 'Remedy'.[3] The Government and the advocates of emigration quickly exploited the disastrous failure of the 1841 Niger Expedition and the Lokoja Farm settlement in order to demonstrate the futility of efforts or of any hopes to introduce modern agriculture, commerce and Christianity in West Africa. Here was the greatest proof that the African could only be civilised or evangelised in the West Indies:

---

1. Thomas Clarkson, *Not a Labourer wanted for Jamaica* (London, 1840) p. 15.
2. Ajayi, J. F. A., *Christian Missions in Nigeria 1841–1891* (London, 1965).
3. Buxton, Sir T. F., *The African Slave Trade and Its Remedy* (London, 1840). Once the hinterland was explored and legitimate commerce, agriculture and Christianity were introduced to the interior through the agency of the liberated Africans, the slave trade would end. This was the remedy with which the British Government was experimenting in the Niger Expedition of 1841.

The only chance that existed of introducing civilization into Africa, that large division of the World, was by the extensive introduction of Africans to the West Indies.[1]

Outside Parliament, the subject of African labour emigration had taken much of the headlines in the British press, and was viewed as the central feature of the West Indian question in 1841. *The Liverpool Courier* had yielded to none in admitting the expediency or the desirability of civilising Africa in 1841; but the encouragment of mass emigration to the West Indies was the only means 'of improving the habits, and stimulating the ambitions, and advancing the education of the native Africans', if they were to be rescued from the tyranny of their chiefs and the hostility of the tropical climate in West Africa.[2] It was on this humanitarian note that the Colonial Office at last sanctioned labour emigration from Sierra Leone in 1840, and recommended all liberated Africans and the resident population to avail themselves of the new measure with the slogan: 'A new epoch has arrived for the African race'.[3]

In the history of the British anti-slavery movement a new epoch had also only just begun.[4]

The official regulations which were supposed to guide the conduct of this scheme had been carefully prepared by the British Government, and adopted by the importing colonies of Jamaica, British Guiana and Trinidad. These regulations[5] conformed generally with the provisions of the British Passengers' Act, and contained in addition certain other provisions to meet with the peculiar circumstances of a delicate scheme. It was provided, for example, that no emigrant vessel was to embark emigrants at Sierra Leone except in certain proportions of the sexes; that emigration agents must not go beyond the Colony for emigrants, nor approach any local chiefs to procure emigrants; that no African was to be embarked who had not resided in the Colony for at least a period of six weeks; nor was he to emigrate without having previously given at least ten days' notice to the Government Emigration Agent who was to ascertain the free

---

1. *Hansard*, 1846, LXXXVIII, 91, Sir J. W. Hogg.
2. *The Liverpool Courier*, quoted from the *Anti-Slavery Reporter*, December 29th, 1840.
3. C.O. 268/38 No. 24, March 20th, 1840, Russell to Jeremy.
4. Pilgrim, E. I., *The Anti-Slavery Sentiment in England . . . its Decline and Fall, 1841–1854* (Cambridge, Ph.D., 1953).
5. In C.O. 386/123.

agency of the intending emigrant. In the quality of the transport vessels used, the provision of medical care and comforts, victualling, etc., the programme of African emigration was also to conform with the rules and regulations of the British Passengers' Act which guided many other schemes of emigration at that period. All these sound provisions became, however, mere formalities and had but very little bearing eventually on the actual conduct of the emigration.

Each of the three colonies, Jamaica, British Guiana and Trinidad, appointed an Agent at Sierra Leone. Competitive campaigning for emigrants began almost as soon as the British Government had given the green light to the importing colonies. The great advantages of the West Indies were represented in glowing language: plenty of work, wages varying from 1s. 8d. to 4s. 2d. per day, liberal allowances of food, gratuitous medical attendance, and no compulsory labour!

These representations and promises, reported the Governor of Sierra Leone soon after 1841,

> produced an electrical effect among our population; the public mind was violently agitated, ordinary avocations were neglected, distant visits were paid by persons anxious to canvass with each other, the whole merits of the new measure, and its probable results on their future welfare.[1]

It was no surprise that the first transport vessels obtained their full complement of emigrants with such rapidity that several hundreds of intending emigrants had to be put on the waiting list for the return of transport vessels. Within a few months some 1,169 souls had emigrated from the Colony and there was even fear that Sierra Leone might soon become a deserted settlement![2] The Colonial emigration officers and agents were thus fully occupied in Sierra Leone, as each transport vessel continued to obtain its full complement. By the end of 1841 Jamaica had received 663 liberated Africans from Sierra Leone; British Guiana 425; Trinidad 181.[3] By April 1842 altogether 24 ships had visited Sierra Leone, 11 from Jamaica, 9 from British Guiana and 4 from Trinidad; 1,343 emigrants in all had been collected. This success, however, was soon to suffer a serious decline with

---

1. PP. 1842, XIII, No. 35, January 30th, 1842: *Extract of a Report from the Officer Administering the Government of Sierra Leone* to Lord Stanley.
2. *Ibid.*
3. Laurence, K. O., *op. cit.*, p. 113.
   PP. 1842, XXIX, 175, Light to Russell, May 25th, 1841, No. 59.

the outcome of an experiment in the sending of delegates.[1] The idea of selecting and sending delegates from Sierra Leone to the West Indies on a fact-finding mission was devised between the Colonial Office, the importing colonies and the officials at Sierra Leone; and aimed at removing the suspicion among some of the residents, who still remained very cautious and doubtful about the new scheme and the propaganda about West Indian prosperity.

Many months after the first delegates were expected back in Sierra Leone, they still had failed to return with any reports. When at last those from British Guiana managed to come back, the circumstances of their return produced an exactly opposite effect from what was intended. The transport vessel *Superior* docked at Sierra Leone, with the delegates looking more prosperous than the residents thought was proper for ordinary labourers. The planters clothed them and sent them back as officers:

> in a uniform of fine blue cloth with scarlet cuff and collar, elegant forage caps, a scarlet waistband and fine cloth trousers.

These adornments, reported the Governor of Sierra Leone,

> proved, in the event, to be a very great mistake; intended, as they no doubt were, to allure emigrants, they had precisely an opposite effect; the scheme partook too much of artifice and delusion.[2]

This incident became one of the greatest draw-backs to a scheme that had started with amazing success.

But as if this was not enough, the planters embarked upon yet another action that brought emigration to a complete stop by the end of 1842.

In spite of the propaganda which the emigration agents actively kept alive in Sierra Leone, news was filtering through about unfulfilled promises and disappointments of emigrants with respect to wages and other conditions of service. Worse still, the Association of Planters had published, without Government sanction, 'New Rules and Regulations',[3] the main aim of which was to curtail the freedom of labour. By January, 1842, within one year of the commencement of the scheme, the planters were already virtually fastening the shackles of slavery round the necks of the newly imported labourers.

---

1. C.O. 318/155, April 20th, 1842, West India Committee to Hope, C.O.
2. PP. 1842, XIII, No. 35, January 30th, 1842.
3. *New Rules and Regulations for the Employment of Labourers on Plantations ... from and after 1st January 1842*, in PP. 1842, XIII.

The Governors of the three colonies took the side of the labourers against the planters. Governor Light of British Guiana deeply regretted the action of the colonists, and in his despatch to Stanley condemned the planters for 'attempting to impose on the labourers Rules and Regulations of so offensive and stringent a nature'.[1] One significant point about the labour strike which resulted was that it affected only those plantations in which these oppressive rules had been published, while in all other areas the labourers had continued to work under the existing labour conditions. Light doubted whether such an exhibition of calmness and quiet forbearance on the part of the labourers could be seen under similar circumstances in more civilised societies.[2]

The 'New Rules and Regulations' had produced their harmful effects only on a portion of the labourers in the West Indies, but in Sierra Leone they dried up the flow of emigrants almost completely and permanently. In the West Indies, the labourers affected had joined to petition the authorities for redress of grievances or, in default of this, for their passages back to Sierra Leone. A group of affected labourers first complained to the Governor:

> We do now wishful of ascertaining the case in its minute order [sic]. We feel this case too hard upon us and unless other measures are adopted, we will be obliged to send to her Most Gracious Majesty to justify us.[3]

The plea of yet another group of affected labourers was more revealing about the planters' new rules and regulations, as well as indicative of the stubborness of the labourers' resistance and jealousy of their freedom:

> We free labourers of plantation Walton Hall are already to work our liberty hours in putting hands and heart, providing in we getting what is right. As to say for taking one guilder per day, we cannot take it all all. ... We certainly thinks it to be very hard. ... During our slavery we was clothed, ration and seported in all manner of respects. Now we are free mens, free indeed, we are to work for nothing. Then we might actually say, we becomes slaves again [sic.].[4]

Liberated Africans in exile were already exhibiting that constitutional technique of petitioning over grievances, which was to be

1. PP. 1842, XIII, No. 4, January 16th, 1842, Light to Stanley.
2. PP. 1842, XIII, No. 9, January 13th, 1842.
3. Petition of Labourers of Plantation Affiance, to Governor Light, British Guiana, in PP. 1842, XIII.
4. Petition of Labourers of Walton Hall to Governor Light, in PP. 1842, XIII.

carried almost to excessive lengths in the West African hinterland many years later.

But Lord Stanley caught the important point—the sense, rather than the grammar—of the protest, and condemned the action of the planters as highly imprudent and unjust:

> I cannot but remark that, especially as related to the newly imported Africans, who had arrived in the Colony under a distinct engagement that they should receive a certain rate of wages, the attempt to lower suddenly was in itself unjust; and, as bearing on the effect which might certainly be anticipated, of checking the future supply from Sierra Leone, not less impolitic than unjust.[1]

In the meantime many of the planters had the sense to back out of the Planters' Association, and withdraw from the new measures. By the end of January many of the labourers had also withdrawn their requests to be sent back to Sierra Leone and had returned to the plantations.[2]

The whole incident of the labour strike and unrest in 1841–2 provides its own commentary on the disposition of the West Indian plantocracy; more than anything else, it became a vindication of the opposition of the humanitarian groups in England to the scheme of African emigration, in their contention that despite Parliamentary legislation a great change needed still to be effected in the temper and disposition of men of tyrannical habits—'before the West Indies can be made a fit place for free immigrants'.[3] But for the planters and the West India Committee in Britain, the whole affair, including the mismanagement of the delegates, justified a condemnation of the British Government for its 'indifference' and a demand for more positive measures to make labour emigration really work.[4] This embarrassment for the Government was heightened by the difficult questions which the Foreign Powers were already raising about the emigration scheme.

---

1. PP. 1842, XIII, No. 61, March 8th, 1842, Stanley to Light.
2. PP. 1842, XIII, No. 9, January 13th, 1842, Light to Stanley.
3. *The Anti-Slavery Reporter*, March 11th, 1842, p. 42.
4. C.O. 318/155, Hibbert (West India Committee) to Stanley (C.O.) October 26th, 1842; C.O. 318/155, Colvile (W.I.C.) to Stanley, November 15th, 1842 and the latter's memorandum on the same; C.O. 318/155, Colonial Office to West India Committee, December 19th, 1842.

Chapter 3
International Reactions

Although much historiography of nineteenth-century Africa has
dealt at length with the Atlantic slave trade and the problems
of mutual mistrust which bedevilled efforts for its international
abolition,[1] a serious gap seems to have been left by historians regarding the full significance of that absence of co-operation—its
causes, origins and nature.

True, general suspicion and hostility towards the chief abolitionist—Britain—had stemmed from extraneous factors: for instance, the international jealousy of her unrivalled naval and maritime
supremacy during the nineteenth century.[2] This however cannot
fully explain the general suspicion of her anti-slavery efforts during
most of that period.

As early as 1815, Prince Talleyrand had confessed to the British
Foreign Minister at the Treaty of Paris with respect to the suppression movement:

> I fully believe that you wish to get rid of the slave trade; I give you
> entire credit for sincerity; but I do not believe that there is another man
> in France who considers you to be sincere.[3]

---

1. Lloyd, C., *The Navy and the Slave Trade* (London, 1944); Coupland, R., *The
   British Anti-Slavery Movement* (London, 1933); Klingberg, F. J., *The Anti-
   Slavery Movement in England* (Yale, 1926); Mathieson, W. L., *Great Britain
   and the Slave Trade 1839–1865* (London, 1929); *British Slave Emancipation*
   (London, 1933); Mannix and Cowley, *Black Cargoes, 1518–1865* (London,
   1963; Mellor, G. R., *The British Imperial Trusteeship* (London, 1951); Soulsby,
   H. G., *The Slave Trade and the Right of Search in Anglo-American Relations,
   1814–1862* (Baltimore, 1933); Wyndham, *The Atlantic and Slavery* (London,
   1937); Bandinel, J., *Some Account of the Trade in Slaves from Africa* (London,
   1842).
2. Bartlett, C. J., *Great Britain and Sea Power, 1815–1854* (London, 1964).
3. Prince Talleyrand, French Foreign Minister, 1815, at the Treaty of Paris,

The heavy cost of a Liberated African Department at Sierra Leone, and the historic Act of Emancipation in 1834 at a cost of £20,000,000 to the British public, were all gestures by anti-slavery England and its Government, the undoubted magnimity of which could not fail to impress, or at least puzzle, the cynics, and reaffirm the sincerity of British abolitionism.

It was during the post-emancipation period in the 1830s that British diplomacy achieved its greatest successes since 1807. The United States, in spite of her intense suspicion of the right of search, had accorded the British Navy a measure of cooperation between 1836 and 1841.[1] France, in spite of her annoyance with British diplomacy, had signed the Anglo-French Conventions of 1831–3 which were to last until 1841.[2] Spain had also subscribed to anti-slave-trade treaties both in 1817 and between 1835 and 1839, and was also willing to cede her Island of Fernando Po to Britain as a second base for anti-slavery operations.[3] By 1839 Mixed Commissions had been established by Britain with other nations at various stations—Havana, Rio, Loanda, Boa Vista, St Helena—in addition to those at Sierra Leone.[4]

The inauguration of the African Emigration Scheme checked these early successes and revived the old suspicions against Britain.

From 1840 other powers came to see the leading abolitionist more as the Tartuffe who preached to them what he did not believe in; thus the whole act of West Indian emancipation with the new scheme of African emigration became that of the fabled Grecian Hygeia, which had strangled with one hand the snake which it was feeding with the other! Spain was among the first to protest in this tone:

Her Britannic Majesty's Government, the same who now demand the absolute emancipation in Cuba since 1820, have ... authorized [her

quoted by Lord Aberdeen during House of Lords Debates on African Emigration on February 22nd, 1848, *Hansard*, 1847–8, XCVI, 1046.

1. Soulsby, H. G., *op. cit.*
2. Gaston-Martin, *Esclavage dans les Colonies Françaises* (Paris, 1948) pp. 270 f.; Lytton, Bulwer, *Life of Viscount Palmerston* (London, 1870), Vol. III, pp. 90–8.
3. Dike, K. O., *Trade and Politics in the Niger Delta, 1830–1885* (Oxford, 1956) pp. 57–9.
4. Johnson, J. F., *Proceedings of the General Anti-Slavery Convention* (London, 1843); Lawrence, W. B., *Visitation and Search* (Boston, 1858); Lloyd, C., *op. cit.*; Mathieson, *Great Britain*; Bandinel, *op. cit.*; Leslie Bethel, 'The Mixed Commissions for the Suppression of the Transatlantic Slave Trade in the 19th Century', in the *Journal of African History*, Vol. VII, No. 1, 1966.

West Indian Colonies] to convey thither from Sierra Leone, thousands
of Negroes who, under the denomination of free labourers, for 14 or 15
years, will be real slaves, torn from their native country, and carried to
work in slavery; in consequence of this authorization, the Royal Navy
of England has already begun to convey negroes to Jamaica for a
slavery, which though temporary, is contrary to existing treaties; so that
it appears that England retrogrades to slavery for the advantage of her
colonies, notwithstanding all her resolutions with regard to the negroes:
Such is the force of facts.[1]

The British reply to M. Gonzalez, the Spanish Foreign Minister,
vainly sought to correct these impressions, pointing out the state of
British public opinion ruled out any possibility of a reversion to
slave labour.[2] But British protestations were powerless to prevent a
sharp change in Spanish policy. The British request for a renewal of
negotiation on Fernando Po met with a flat refusal.[3] In Cuba Spain's
action was even more clearly demonstrative of her reversion from
friendliness to open hostility. In 1831 it was Spain that begged and
persuaded Britain to relieve Cuba of the 1,000 or more *emancipados*
liberated at that island annually. Spain even undertook to pay the
cost of transhipping these labourers to the British colonies.

Worried that these *emancipados* might be enslaved again if left in
Cuba, Britain agreed in 1832 for Trinidad to receive and apprentice
them, with great care for their welfare and proper treatment.[4] In
June 1833 Trinidad received the first batch of 189 *emancipados*; in
1834 four ship-loads of 401; and in 1835 a further 564 arrived.[5] By
1835 it was thought that Trinidad could quarter 3,385 *emancipados*
yearly. The Anglo-Spanish Treaty of that year provided, among
other things, that the Spanish authorities at Havana should regularly
submit to the British representatives a list or certificate of all slaves
emancipated by Spain in Cuba. These arrangements had held good
until 1841.[6] After 1840, because British policy appeared to be no
more the function of pure philanthropy, the Spanish vehemence of

---

1. PP. 1843, Vol. xxxix, p. 617, and also 1845, Vol. xxxi. The Spanish Foreign
   Minister to the British Ambassador at Madrid, December 20th, 1841.
2. *Ibid.*
3. For the negotiations about the transfer of Fernando Po between 1831–41, see
   C.O. 82/4, Dillon to Goderich, July 25th, 1831; C.O. 82/5, 2004, Nicholls to
   C.O., January 30th, 1932, cited Dike, *op. cit.*, pp. 58–9.
4. C.O. 318/123, Minutes on Captured Africans in Cuba, October 24th, 1835.
5. Laurence, *op. cit.*, pp. 4–7.
6. See C.O. 318/140; 146; 149; 153; 155; 157; 159 and the heading: 'Removal
   of Liberated Africans from Cuba'.

opposition to the removal of the Cuban *emancipados* was matched by that of her plea to Britain in 1831 for their transfer to British colonies. The Spanish authorities would neither submit the usual certificates and lists, nor listen to British remonstrations regarding even proved cases of slave-trading by Spanish citizens.

When the British Commissioner at last complained to the Captain-General about this breach of treaty engagements, and the failure to produce 'any account as heretofore of emancipated negroes to whom had been given their certicates of freedom',[1] he was left in no doubt as to the deliberate intention of Spain to disregard for the future the provisions of the Anglo-Spanish Treaties. The Captain-General's official instructions from Madrid were that he was not 'in future to admit any denunciations made by H.M. Commissioners respecting disembarkations of Negroes' at Cuba; 'nor to enter into any answer with them on that subject'; furthermore, he was not to give them any 'further notices as have hitherto been given monthly of negroes to whom are issued their certificates of freedom'.[2]

The Spanish reverted to almost open slave trading, when a Spanish slave dealer, Don Pedro Blanco, formed his company to import what were termed *gangaes* or 'free labourers' for the *hacendados* or planters of Cuba. The British Commissionary Judge at Havana found it impossible to persuade the local Spanish authorities to condemn these acts of slave-dealing.[3]

The new Captain-General, O'Donnell, seems to have been appointed to obstruct and prevent all further Anglo-Spanish agreement at Havana over the Cuban slave trade.

While the short-lived Governor-Generalship of his predecessor, Valdez, had witnessed a great falling off in the importation of slaves, O'Donnell's strict obedience to his instructions from Madrid and his condonation of the slave traffic, no less than the general Spanish reaction to the African emigration scheme, had startling results. Within the first year of O'Donnell's regime, the Cuban trade had risen from its low figure of 3,000 at the time of Valdez, to 8,000 in 1843, and 10,000 in 1844.[4]

The Spanish proceeded to take measures to throw off the vestiges

---

1. F.O. 313/20, Enclosure 2 in No. 17, Havana, March 6th, 1844, H.M. Commissioners to Foreign Office.
2. F.O. 313/20, Enclosure 5 in No. 17, March 15th, 1844, same to same.
3. F.O. 313/20, Havana, November 18th, 1844, H.M. Commissary Judge to the Captain-General.
4. *Hansard*, 1847–8, XCVI, 1041 f.

of British surveillance, while at the same time taking their own measures to control the slave traffic. In 1844 a Commission was set up in Cuba[1] which, while tightening up the penal laws against Spanish slave dealers, called for an immediate end to the Anglo-Spanish Mixed Commission Courts at Havana and Sierra Leone—because it was discovered that some British officials in those Commissions were involved in secret and illegal transhipments of captured Africans to the West Indies.[2] 'How can we see with indifference', the Spanish Commission asked, 'the want of responsibility in cruisers, captors and judges; who may punish the members of those same Commissions in the case of their failing in their duties?'[3]

After 1844 the Cuban Government preferred to reassign the *emancipados* to Spanish planters,[4] rather than hand them over to Britain as before. However, Spain's indifference to the Mixed Commission Courts became, as we shall see, Britain's best opportunity in the running of the emigration scheme.

Until the late 1850s Spain's nearest approach to the British Government over the abolition question was when in 1858 Señor Don Jose Maria Lago, agent of a cotton Company at Cuba, wrote to the British Minister at Madrid to ask for British support for a project of African-Cuban 'free' labour emigration from West Africa.[5] In this, as in other questions during the nineteenth century, Spain had caused the British Government so much embarrassment and annoyance at Cuba to warrant Lord Malmesbury's lament and threat to that country in 1858:

> I must say that the conduct of Spain towards us on this question has been marked by the greatest ingratitude. It has always been the policy of England to support Spain, and defend her in the occupation of Cuba against hostile invasion. But if Spain continues to show that utter want of principle and that utter and base ingratitude which she has displayed towards this country, which has always been her friend, I don't hesitate to say that she must expect that indifference will be exchanged for amity; she must expect us to leave her to whatever consequence may ensue, whether proceeding from her present conduct or not.[6]

1. F.O. 313/20, Enclosure 3 in No. 13 of 1844, and enclosure in No. 36.
2. See Chapter IV.
3. F.O. 313/20, Report of the Spanish Royal Junta and Royal Tribunal of Commerce, May 29th, 1844.
4. F.O. 313/20, Enclosure 2 in No. 17, Havana, 6th March, 1844.
5. *British State Papers*, 1859–60, pp. 945 f.
6. Lord Malmesbury, during debate over Spain and Cuba; cited, Lawrence, W. B., *op. cit.*, p. 138.

The labour emigration question however was finally settled two years later, in 1860, when in lieu of labourers from West Africa, the British Government granted Spain permission to recruit labour from British possessions in India and China.[1]

The Anglo-French storm over African emigration was preceded by an official French investigation of the British scheme in 1841. M. Layrle, after visiting the various British West Indian Colonies, returned to submit reports of his findings to the French Government in a booklet form.[2] The new scheme of emigration, together with the recent oppressive regulations by the planters—in spite of the favourable impressions which M. Layrle had formed of those colonies—was strong evidence that the planters still regretted emancipation. France must, therefore, not attempt emancipation in her colonies—'unless at some distant period'.[3]

The major conflict did not come however until British cruisers had actually captured French slave-vessels operating on the West Coast under the new name of 'free emigration transports'. The French Government had entered into a contract with Victor Regis, a French merchant on the West Coast, to procure some 10,000 'free' African labourers for the French islands of Martinique and Guadaloupe. Regis established factories at Gabon and at Whydah (Dahomey) where a thriving labour recruiting business was carried on with the king of Dahomey.[4]

As the British Military Chaplain at Mauritius later wrote, 'France did not adopt this system till England had taken the initiative'; and the French Government 'in sanctioning the Regis contract did not overlook that England had taken the initiative in this matter'.[5] Indeed the 'free' emigration scheme destroyed what earlier cooperation there had been between England and France in the diplomatic efforts to secure international abolition, and saw both powers locked from 1841 onwards in mutual distrust and suspicion.

Serious trouble arose in 1841 when the French *Marabout* was captured by a British cruiser off the West Coast, and brought before

---

1. *British and Foreign State Papers*, 1859–60, pp. 86 f.; *Hansard*, 1861, CIXIV, 1659 f.; see also, for the objections of Stephen Cave on this issue, *Hansard*, 1861, CIXI, 953–8; See also Hargreaves, J. D., *Prelude to the Partition of West Africa* (London, 1960) p. 105.
2. *Précis de l'Abolition de l'Esclavage dans les Colonies Anglaises*.
3. PP. 1843, XXXIV, p. 618, Memo. from Stanley to Aberdeen, February 2nd, 1842, cited from M. Layrle, *op. cit.*
4. Lloyd, C., *op. cit.*, p. 202.
5. Rev. P. Beaton, *Six Months in Reunion*, Vol. IV (London, 1860) p. 45.

the British Vice-Admiralty Court at Sierra Leone for trial. The jurisdiction however belonged more properly to a Mixed Commission
Court. The trial of the case by a British court hurt the French more.

In the Chamber of Deputies the Duke of Fitzjames[1] thought the
diversion of captured vessels for trial by British courts was only
a clever device by Britain to monopolise the labour recruitment
scheme and provide her sugar colonies with all the proceeds of labour
of Africans recaptured. Has not monopoly always been the major
thread in British policy 'and will always be, the axis around which
British policy revolves'? Fitzjames became more anglophobic. In
fact the emigration scheme reopened the whole anti-slavery question
and the international abolition movement between both countries.
Duke Fitzjames proceeded to lecture the Chamber on the diplomacy
involved in the British abolition movement, emphasizing the suspicious suddenness and unanimity of opinion with which William
Wilberforce's motion had come to be passed in the British Parliament in 1807, after more than twenty years of continual rejection
by the same Parliament. This sudden change, Fitzjames concluded,
marked only the beginning of a new and immense secret plan of a
Government that 'had stopped at nothing less than the subjugation
of entire Europe, for the consumption of colonial sugar'.[2]

To the French in 1841 the British scheme of African emigration
was only the eventual inauguration of 'an immense secret plan' that
had long been suspected. It was believed to be a premeditated
scheme by which Britain hoped to recover what she had lost through
abolition and emancipation. British abolition diplomacy, therefore,
was only a trick to trap her rivals into the trouble from which she
herself had contrived to escape. This was why French national
opinion was so bitter about the *Marabout* incident, and saw the
Vice-Admiralty Court as merely a device for fulfilling the British
design.

A sarcastic congratulation hailed both British shrewdness and
French foolishness: '*Les officiers de la marine britannique*,' lamented a French journalist, '*étaient arrivés à leur fin, puisque la concurrence française était frappée l'operation commerciale anéantie*'.[3]
French commercial interests, colonial proprietors, private shipowners and others with vested interests in the French 'free'

---

1. See Gaston-Martin, *op. cit.*, pp. 273 ff.
2. *Ibid.*
3. de Maupassant, Jules, cited Gaston-Martin, *op. cit.*, p. 273.

emigration scheme joined in national propaganda calling for an immediate termination of the existing Anglo-French convention and treaty of 1833, which provided for naval co-operation and a mutual right of search. Thus in France, *'au debut de 1841, l'opinion nationale se trouvait à peu près toute derrière les adversaires de la politique de collaboration étroite avec Londres'*.[1]

The strength of this opinion compelled Guizot, apparently against his personal wishes, to reject the renewal of the 1833 convention and to back out from the ratification of the Quintuple Treaty of 1841. The action was condemned by Lord Palmerston in London as 'the most signal departure from a diplomatic engagement that has happened in Europe for a great number of years'.[2] By the end of 1841 Guizot was no longer prepared even to entertain any British comments on French slave-trading activities on the African coast, until the British Government could explain its own operations at Sierra Leone. Admiral Duperre had drawn up a memorandum for his benefit arguing, in effect, that French vessels on the African coast were only doing, at worst, exactly what the British emigration vessels were doing at Sierra Leone:

Le Gouvernement Anglais permet depuis quelque temps à ses Colonies d'Amérique d'enroler à la côte occidentale d'Afrique et spécialement à Sierra Leone, des traveilleurs qui, une fois rendue à Demarara ou à la Trinidad, y sont soumis à un engagement de 14 années pour le compte des planteurs auxquels leur services sont loués par les compagnies d'immigration. De quelle nature est cet engagement? Les Noirs qu'on énrôle en Afrique sont-ils bien réellement libres? Leur liberté, fictive ou réelle, n'est-elle pas dans tous les cas le résultat plus ou moins immediat d'un rachet de captivité, analogue à ce qui se passe dans nos établissements au Sénégal? Enfin les reglements coercitifs par lesquels les Noirs ainsi engagés seront maintenus à la culture, ne seront-ils pas de nature à faire penser que le travail force se trouvera rétabli dans ces colonies d'une manière deuissée, a l'égard de la population Noire immigrante? Toutes ces questions sont encore à éclaircir. J'ai pris des mesures pour m'en procurer la solution, et en supposant, ce qui semble difficile à croire, que dans ce système d'emigration Africaine, tout se passe d'une manière rigoureusement conformé au principe qu'invoque le gouvernement Anglais, il n'en importe pas moins de prendre acte, dès à présente, des distinctions que ce Gouvernement lui-même est obligé de faire, entre la Traite des Noirs et des opérations de recruitement effectuées à

---

1. *Ibid.*
2. Lytton, Bulwer, *Life of Viscount Palmerston*, Vol. III (1870) pp. 96–8.

la côte d'Afrique sont la garantie des autorités publiques, avec liberation préalable, des individus enrolés.[1]

As a reprisal for the *Marabout* incident a French warship in 1843 effected the capture of a British emigration vessel, *St Christopher*, which the Colonial Land and Emigration Commissioners had licensed and sent out to carry emigrants from Sierra Leone, and detained her on a charge of slave-dealing.[2]

By 1845 France was using her navy both on the West and the East Coasts to convoy her 'free' emigration vessels, and confessed that the purpose of her naval squadron on the coast was mainly 'to protect her commercial interests against the pretensions of Britain'.[3] Eventually, in April 1858, the French emigration scheme was threatened by a grave scandal when the supposedly 'free' emigrants on the *Regina Coeli* released themselves from their chains and attacked the French crew on board, killing some. The British Government made use of the case to re-emphasise their utter disapproval and condemnation of French proceedings on the coast. But the French press intervened: *Le Constitutionnel* argued:

> It is demonstrable that France, far from engaging in the slave-trade, which it abhors as much as any other Christian and civilized nation, takes the slaves from the coast of Africa to make free labourers of them; when an English cruiser captures a slaver, where does it take the cargo? Does it not transport them to an English Colony without their co sent?[4]
>   n—

On the East African Coast there was also a counterpart to these Anglo-French squabbles on the West Coast. A few years before, about 1840, a private French vessel, *La Conception Immaculée*, had carried a cargo of Africans for disposal on the French island of Bourbon.

When the French Governor prohibited the landing of the vessel, the Captain removed to the neighbouring British island of Mauritius, and easily sold off his cargo to the planters:

> 'Such was the eagerness among that highly respectable class to aid in spreading the light of civilization among the benighted sons of Africa'

---

1. *State Papers, 1842–1843*, Vol. XXXI, p. 410.
2. C.O. 268/38 (pp. 275–6). See also correspondence *ibid.*, dated July 4th, and September 6th, 1843.
3. Lawrence, W. B., *op. cit.*, pp. 46–8; 133–4.
4. Cited, *op. cit.*, pp. 165–6, as originating from the French Newspaper, *Le Constitutionnel*.

reported an eye witness of the auction sales, 'that, on the day of sale, they crowded the depot, and, inspired by a noble emulation, strove to outbid one another. The ancient vultures that had battened on the slave trade smelt the carrion from afar, and ventured forth from their places of darkness in quest of new prey.'[1]

The French planters of Bourbon were quick to profit by the Mauritius precedent. In their application to the French Government in 1846 they asked for permission to recruit and import labourers who would, 'as in the case of Mauritius, supply us with all the labour we require to make up the daily increasing deficiency in our industrial establishments'.[2] Very soon the French emigration scheme was flourishing on the East African Coast as its British counterpart continued in Mauritius and the Cape of Good Hope. In these remote regions the British scheme itself had not required many of the regulations elaborated for the West Coast. For instance, whilst the Government had taken over the supervision of the scheme from 1843 in order to check the abuses of 1841–2, it was decided in the case of both Mauritius and the Cape of Good Hope that 'in future the captured negroes should be at once dispatched' to those stations, as soon as captured anywhere along the Eastern Coast, or otherwise immediately 'forwarded to the West Indies'.[3]

In this way some 1,500 captured Africans had been dispatched to the Cape in May 1844, although the West Indian Colonies had been expecting to receive them.[4] The Emigration Commissioners considered this procedure to be much cheaper to the British Government, and deemed it unnecessary to 'continue the expense of employing an Agent at a fixed salary'.[5] Later this mode of proceeding was extended to other stations as the emigration scheme developed. As a result of anti-slave treaties with the Turkish Government and the Arab Chiefs of the Persian Gulf, the island of Mauritius was assured by 1847 of a cheap supply of African labour without the expense of emigration officers and agents. Under these treaties Britain obtained the right to take charge of all Africans captured in Turkish vessels or found in the vicinity of the Persian Gulf. The emigration

1. Beaton, P., *Six Months in Réunion*, Vol. II (London, 1860) p. 88.
2. Petition by Planters of the Island of Bourbon to the French Government, cited Beaton, *op. cit.*, pp. 44–5.
3. C.O. 386/48, Secretary, Colonial Land and Emigration Commissioners, to James Stephen, C.O., May 11th, 1844.
4. C.O. 386/48, same to same, *ibid.*
5. *Ibid.*

regulation here was quite simple. According to the official instruction:

> those captured off the coast of Africa in the neighbourhood of Mauritius, are to be at once carried to that island in the vessels in which they are seized; [and] those captured within or in the neighbourhood of the Persian Gulf are to be handed over to the British Civil or Naval Authorities to be forwarded by them to the Mauritius.[1]

The request by the Assembly and Governor of that island for permission to open up a scheme of emigration from Cochin and Abyssinia had earlier been rejected.[2]

Later on, in the 1850s, the Mauritius Government wanted to increase the number of immigrants obtained under the Anglo-Turkish Treaties of 1847. The Governor licensed a firm of shipowners, Hermans and Co., to import labourers from the neighbouring island of Madagascar. But Madagascar and Portuguese Mozambique were the seat of the French emigration scheme, and great care was needed on the part of the British if further conflict was to be avoided with the French. The Emigration Commissioners therefore advised the Colonial Office to sanction the Madagascar-Mauritius emigration contract of Hermans and Co., but with great caution.[3] As late as 1891 similar requests for liberated Africans from Portuguese Mozambique and other East African territories were being made by planters at the British island of Seychelles and were also approved.[4]

In East Africa, as on the West Coast, the French 'free' emigration scheme had proceeded apace with even greater vigour and much less scrupulousness, as French agents freely dealt with East African Chiefs and Arab slave dealers on the Mozambique coast.

In most cases the Portuguese and Arab merchants became the brokers between East African chiefs and French emigration officials. An eye witness of these proceedings described how very often the supposed free emigrants or *engagés libres* had been preceded and followed by soldiers with drawn swords, escorting the emigrants from the landing place to the depot.[5]

As in the case of the *Regina Coeli* on the West Coast, the French

1. C.O. 386/54, October 8th, 1847, Colonial Office to Emigration Commissioners.
2. C.O. 386/53, July 27th, 1847, Emigration Commissioners to Colonial Office.
3. C.O. 386/87, November 16th, 1850.
4. F.O. 84/2171, Petition of Proprietors and Agriculturists of the island of Seychelles to Administrator J. R. Griffiths; No. 85, May 9th, 1891, Griffiths to Lees; No. 34, Seychelles, May 26th, 1891, Lees to Lord Knutsford.
5. Rev. Beaton, P., *op. cit.*, pp. 99–100.

Government became exposed to an emigration scandal in the affair of *Charles et Georges* on the Eastern Coast. Under a new anti-French Portuguese Minister of Colonies, Viscount da Bandeira, Portuguese officials were instructed to lend no countenance to French emigration proceedings on the East Coast.

A conflict soon occurred when the French emigration vessel, *Charles et Georges*, was captured by Portuguese officers off the Mozambique channel early in 1859, the French captain being put into prison. This further scandal compelled the Government of Napolean III, in October 1859, to order an inquiry into French operations on the Coast and to investigate alternative sources of labour supply.[1]

Despite the Anglo-French Convention of July 1861, for the importation of Asians by France, the French 'free' emigration scheme in East Africa continued until the beginning of the present century, while Anglo-French cooperation against the East African slave trade still remained unattainable in the face of these recruiting operations.[2] As Lord Palmerston pointed out in 1864:

> Under the pretence of exporting from Africa free labourers, the slave trade was to all intents and purposes carried on under another name.[3]

In East Africa especially, these operations made Anglo-French cooperation against the Portuguese and Arab slave trade more difficult and gave direct encouragement to the traffic itself. For whether the English or the French agent called the scheme 'free' or 'voluntary' recruitment, made no difference to the African chief on the West Coast, or the Arab slave dealer in the East: 'No man will go for himself', a local chief had quite frankly told an emigration agent who had gone to negotiate for recruits; 'we shall buy them aslam we do that time slave tade bin [sic]'.[4] The Arab slave dealer on the East Coast put his own point with even more blunt indifference:

---

1. Beaton, *op. cit.*, pp. 104–5; Mathieson, *op. cit.*, pp. 168–9.
2. Mathieson, *Great Britain*, pp. 176–84; *Hansard*, 1862, CLXVI, 2180; 1864, CLXXIII, 1197.
3. Palmerston, *Hansard*, 1864, CLXXVL, 1385.
4. *Hansard*, 1857, CXLVI, 1666; 1675–77; 1679; CXLVII, 520, cited Mathieson, *op. cit.*, p. 147.
   Johnson, J. P., *Proceedings of the General Anti-Slavery Convention* (London, 1843). See p. 252–5 for Colonel Nicholl's account of negotiations with Duke Ephraim of Old Calabar for labourers to work at Fernando Po. Duke Ephraim would not provide the labourers unless Nicholl purchased them as slaves.

All same ting to me, old time you call it slavery, now you call it free labour; I go catch men, sell; you give [me] the money, all right.[1]

It was left mainly for Britain to continue the fight against the East African slave trade and, after the establishment of colonial rule over Zanzibar during the 1880s, to take the strictest measures against African dealers and Arab or Portuguese slave buyers in order to end the market in *engagés librés*.

For reasons which will become clearer later on,[2] the West African version of the voluntary emigration scheme, both of the French as well as of the British, was not allowed, like its East African counterpart, to continue after 1860. In that year a Convention bought off both France and Spain from the West African emigration with permission to recruit labour from British possessions in India and China.[3] At that time some British M.P's, Stephen Cave and others, raised the question why the West African emigration should not continue as that on the East Coast did; and asked why the African's blood should have become so much more important than that of the Indian or Chinese 'coolie' that the British Government should have thus sacrificed the latter to Spain and France in place of the African labourer.[4] The reasons for this official action lay largely in the change which occurred from the late 1850s in British economic policy in West Africa with regard to liberated Africans,[5] whose presence as commercial and political agents in the West African hinterland had become vital for the development of British trade and enterprise in that region.

Unlike Spain and France, the United States did not embark upon a scheme of free labour emigration as a counter to the British plan. Yet American reaction to the British action was as vehement and as productive of ill-feeling and lack of co-operation as the reactions of Spain and France had been. Perhaps the most critical and hostile among American Government officials was General Louis Cass, the American Ambassador to France, whose decided anti-British influence had worked very much against Britain in Paris, as well as in

---

1. Lloyd, C., *op. cit.*, p. 201.
2. See Chapter 7: British Commercial enterprise in West Africa required the agency of liberated Africans, as Laird pointed out after 1854, and Lord Palmerston in 1861.
3. *Vide supra*, p. 88, fn. 2.
4. *Hansard*, 1861, CLXI, 953–8; Hargreaves, J. D., *op. cit.*, p. 105.
5. See Chapter 7.

Washington, during most of the anti-slavery diplomatic negotiations.[1]

W. B. Lawrence was another American high official with similar views. His book,[2] virtually a petition to the American Government against any Anglo-American Treaty or naval cooperation in the suppression movement, dwelt at length upon the liberated African emigration scheme as the strongest proof of British insincerity.

This campaign was directed specifically against the existing Treaty with Britain, the Ashburton Treaty,[3] which provided for Anglo-American naval co-operation against the Atlantic slave trade. Lawrence also attacked the British Vice-Admiralty Court as calculated to undermine the working of the Mixed Commissions, since the existence of the former and the transfer of cases to them enabled the British cruisers to remove captured Africans without the intervention of the Mixed Commission Courts.[4]

Emancipation, Lawrence added, had become the greatest obstacle to the final extinction of the slave trade; because Britain and France, after achieving emancipation respectively in 1838 and 1848, had evolved other measures as objectionable to America as the slave trade itself 'to repair the consequences of the forced emancipation of their slaves'.[5]

In calling upon the American Government to cancel the Ashburton Treaty, Lawrence also persuaded the people of America to reject any idea of slave emancipation in the States: the French and English experience was strong proof that 'the immediate effect of the abolition of slavery here would be the disorganisation of the industries of the great producing states ... and other evils consequent upon a renewed importation of tropical labourers'.[6] The American Government, he stressed, could not rightly continue to uphold the Ashburton Treaty and keep her seamen and officers of the Navy on the Atlantic Coast, only to act as purveyors of labour for British planters, or as a decoy to bring within the reach of the British cruisers slaves

---

1. Soulsby, H. G., *op. cit.*
2. Lawrence, W. B., *Visitation and Search or an Historical Sketch of the British Claim to Exercise a Maritime Police over the Vessels of all Nations, with an Inquiry into the Expediency of Terminating the 8th Article of the Ashburton Treaty* (Boston, 1858).
3. See Soulsby, H. G., *op. cit.*, for a full historical account of the Anglo-American cooperation, or the lack of it, in the Suppression movement 1814–62.
4. Lawrence, W. B., *op. cit.*, pp. 83–4, 165–9; see also PP. 1865, Vol. LXVIII.
5. Lawrence, *op. cit.*, p. 142.
6. *Ibid.*, p. 169.

whose fate by the capture 'is simply changed by having their destination altered from Cuba to Jamaica'.

After making similar attacks on the French part of this scheme, Lawrence stressed the futility of hoping for effective international cooperation and the inexpediency for America to encourage any, since she did not need any of the extra agricultural labour which accrued to Britain and France from the captures:

> With the whole power of France directed to the protection of the trade of her colonies, while England is herself engaged in carrying on a more objectionable traffic in human labour, it would be absurd to attempt . . . to do anything which could bear sensibly on the great result; we abstain from what both the great European powers are doing; we do not invite wars among the barbarous Africans for the capture of prisoners to be sold to us under the name of Emigrants.[1]

Anglo-American co-operation was not to be achieved until the American Government saw it to be in its own interest at the outbreak of the Civil War in 1861, and under the Presidency of Abraham Lincoln, to join in full concert with Britain for the final extinction of the Atlantic slave trade.[2]

Professor Rose has observed with much truth that no great international movement for the uplift of mankind and the rescue of an oppressed people had ever suffered so sorely from national jealousies.[3] The British action had been severely arraigned before the tribunal of international opinion, and employed as an excuse for Spain, America and France to withhold their full cooperation and support for the abolition movement; the British anti-slavery effort had been interpreted by these powers merely as good business, rather than as an unprofitable work of philanthropy;[4] it must, however, be said that none of these powers had gained less when withholding their cooperation from Britain; nor gave it, when they did, without some hope for greater advantage for their own national interests.

National justice or righteousness, with regard to the suppression movement, lay not merely in doing no injury or injustice to the recaptives; but rather more in the endeavour to cooperate with others in an effort to do positive good. It might even be argued that British philanthropy, although swooning in the scheme of liberated African

---

1. *Ibid.*, pp. 175–6.
2. Soulsby, *op. cit.*
3. Rose, J. Holland, *Man and the Sea*, p. 242.
4. Lawrence, *op. cit.*, p. 166; Mathieson, *op. cit.*, p. 154.

emigration, had yet fallen while on active service; and fell perhaps partly from want of active international support.

We shall see in the next chapter how, although without much success in the end, the British Government, from 1843, tried to take certain steps in the face of these international criticisms to remove some of the abuses that existed in that scheme.

Chapter 4
'Voluntary' Emigration under Government Control, 1843–1846

In 1840–1, the West India Colonies were grudgingly allowed to recruit labour from Sierra Leone, the British Government remaining aloof from direct involvement in the scheme because, as James Stephen minuted, 'the direct intervention of the Government to bring about such removals [of liberated Africans] would seem to be obviously inexpedient'.[1] By 1843 however this position of aloofness could no longer be maintained, the Government itself having been more exposed to severe criticisms both at home and abroad than her colonies were.

Aware, therefore, that direct intervention could no longer be avoided, the Government took the first step later in 1842 by appointing two Select Committees, one to report on the West Indian economic problem, the other on the West African counterpart of that problem, African labour.[2] The reports of these two Committees are important in so far as they quickly supplied the courage and moral support which the Government badly needed to embark on a project that was manifestly as objectionable as it was detestable to them: government-controlled emigration. If criticism still came from die-hard humanitarians, Lord Stanley promptly drew their attention to the unanimous recommendation of two Committees that not only comprised many 'well-tried and undoubted friends of the African race' but had 'unanimously' advised that emigration would be the best means of affording 'the fairest prospects to the natives of Africa of an improve-

---

1. Cited Laurence, K.O., 'Immigration into Trinidad and British Guiana 1834–1870' (Cambridge, Ph.D., 1958) p. 118.
2. PP. 1842, XIII, Report of Select Committee on West Africa, July 25th, 1842; Report of Select Committee on West India Colonies, August 5th, 1842.

ment in their physical comforts, and an advance in the blessings of civilisation'.[1]

There was, however, another official report which held entirely different views about the emigration scheme and, unlike the two Select Committees, posed perplexing questions for the Government. This, the Madden Report, had appeared a little earlier, in July 1841.[2] How could the emigration scheme, the report asked, be supervised in a way that would preclude abuses, since past experience had shown the inadequacy even of elaborate rules and regulations to check excesses on the part of labour employers? Could the British Government establish further rules and regulations and, remaining so far away from the scene of execution of its orders in West Africa or the West Indies, expect proper observance of those regulations by persons who stood to profit by the violation of them? Moreover, Africans were noted for their nostalgic love of home and family; would emigration to the West Indies appeal to such people without some element of force being eventually applied? On these general grounds Dr Madden saw the ultimate failure of any emigration policy as a foregone conclusion.

Any official doubts which might have arisen from this pessimism of the Madden Report were erased by the famous shipwright, Macgregor Laird, who came out with many new ideas that could not fail to attract serious official attention. Shortly after the Government had had these three reports Laird launched his own views and recommendations in three separate memoranda, well written and argued with a mass of financial figures and statistics of trade returns. His memorandum on Sierra Leone first tried to impress on the Government how foolish and unnecessary was the costly expenditure incurred in keeping up the 'artificial population of the colony'. £100,000 was being spent on the establishment each year, the maintenance of the liberated Africans alone taking as much as £12,755 14s. 7d. annually.

Such expenditure, Laird complained, might have been excusable if the liberated Africans or the Colony itself were of any use economically to Britain. In population Sierra Leone with 50,000 was comparable among the West India Colonies only to Trinidad with 45,000. But economically Sierra Leone was not only inferior to Trinidad but a great liability to the British Government and people. The Trinidad

---

1. PP. 1843, xxxiv, No. 87, p. 605, February 6th, 1843, Stanley to MacDonald.
2. PP. 1842, xiii, No. 33, p. 603, July 31st, 1842, Dr R. R. Madden's Report.

population produced sugar, molasses, rum, cocoa and coffee, amounting in 1839 to £560,000 of exports, equal to £12 8s. 10d. of produce output per head; the import of British goods amounted to £327,000, equal to a consumption of British goods of £7 5s. 4d. per head. In Sierra Leone the picture was very different: £3,526 of annual exports, or equal to an output of 1s. 6d. per head; consumption of British goods was only equal to what Britain herself could afford to give the Colony as grant, £100,000, equal to £2 per head per annum!

> The value therefore of an African consumer at Sierra Leone to Britain is per head £2. Remove him to Trinidad and his value increases to £7.5.4. Keep him in Sierra Leone and he produces annually 1s. 6d. Remove him to Trinidad and his power of production increases to per annum £12.8.9d.[1]

The people of England, Macgregor Laird then emphasised, had a right to demand the benefits that were promised when they spent £20 million to emancipate the slaves in their sugar colonies, and when they supported the heavy expense of Niger expeditions in West Africa to open up the interior to British commerce. Six months after writing these ideas, he was expounding them more fully before the General Anti-Slavery Convention in London. The British consumer was already hard hit by the economic repercussions of his philanthropy: 'they really feel the cost of emancipation'. The Government should therefore no longer impose restrictions on African emigration but should fully encourage the scheme as a measure for cheapening for the British people 'that sugar which they so much desire, and which is now beyond their reach'.[2]

The 'wild idea' of Buxton's 'Remedy', the development of legitimate commerce and modern agriculture in West Africa as a displacer of the slave trade, should equally be discarded because experience had fully shown the impracticability of Europeans ever penetrating the continent:

> The enterprise of merchants, the zeal of travellers, the enthusiasm of the missionary, have alike failed to gain any footing in the interior. For fifty

---

1. C.O. 300/4, Macgregor Laird, 'Memorandum on Sierra Leone', London, June 7th, 1842, published in *Port of Spain Gazette*, October 14th, 1842.
2. Johnson, J. F., *Proceedings of the General Anti-Slavery Convention* (London, 1843) p. 253; C.O. 300/4, 'Memorandum on Emigration', *Port of Spain Gazette*, October 14th, 1842.

years we have been sacrificing life and money at Sierra Leone, with no good effect upon the surrounding population.[1]

After years of Niger commercial expeditions since 1832 Laird had turned, like many a practical man of business, to follow the line of the least economic resistance. He was now all out for emigration, even at the risk of being unscrupulous in the way it was to be conducted. Once the Government completely disregarded, as it ought to, hostile public opinion at home and international criticisms abroad, 'the slaves annually imported into Brazil and Cuba should be conveyed openly as emigrants, instead of covertly as slaves'.[2] In lieu of restrictive emigration rules and regulations the Government should promise all transhipped Africans free return passages to Africa after they had fulfilled their compulsory exile or industrial residence in the West Indies.

A shrewd man of enterprise, Laird did not forget to advertise ingeniously his own trade to the Government. Already a famous shipwright at a time when iron vessels were still suspect inventions in marine development, Laird tried to persuade the Government to patronise his own industry. A huge emigration scheme such as he advised might not only obtain for the British consumer cheap West Indian sugar, but might also win a shipbuilder rich contracts with the Government. After his two lengthy memoranda on Sierra Leone and on Emigration persuading the Government to take over entire management of the scheme, he submitted yet a third memorandum showing how the business could more properly be run by steamships.[3]

First, he reminded the Government that the emigration scheme would necessitate 'the establishment of a toll-free bridge both ways', since Africans would be enabled by the free return passage to move constantly between Africa and the West Indies; in short, a regular means of communication was necessary between the two regions and should be accomplished 'by a steam bridge, if possible'.[4] The memorandum then detailed other suggestions for the Government: two iron steam-ships each of 1,000 tons weight and each capable of carrying 1,000 emigrants should be despatched every month; the

---

1. Johnson, J. F., *op. cit.*
2. *Ibid.*, p. 252.
3. C.O. 300/4, 'Memorandum Shewing the Cost of a Monthly Steam Vessel Emigration Transport between West Africa and the West Indies', in *Port of Spain Gazette*, October 14th, 1842.
4. Johnson, J. F., *op. cit.*, pp. 238 ff.

transportation cost of 2,000 emigrants per month would then be just about £80,000; and within four years the steam-ships would have transported 48,000 Africans to the West Indies, the Government paying just over £288,000 for the transportation. There was nothing to be alarmed about in this cost, Laird warned; for the profit would be far greater, since at least some 1,200 out of this total of 48,000 emigrants would become effective labourers, equal to the production of 24,000 tons of sugar annually; which at the duty then existing of 24s. per cwt. 'would yield the Exchequer a revenue of £576,000'; excluding of course the amount of £100,000, the yearly expenditure on Sierra Leone and its population, which would as well have been saved through extensive emigration.[1] All forms of restriction on emigration, therefore, Laird finally advised, should be removed, and 'the Government should supply the steam vessels'.[2]

The Anti-Slavery Convention, where Laird found a platform to canvas these ideas in 1843, rejected his seven-point motion on the subject as totally subjective and unphilanthropic. Even his new idea of a free return passage had not impressed them, because its ultimate fulfilment seemed to depend, following his logic, on whether or not the attempts to explore and penetrate the Niger hinterland would eventually prove successful. An important delegate at the convention roundly condemned Laird's ideas:

> If the kind of emigration now called for involved no collateral mischief, would any West Indian, or other man, sugar manufacturer or otherwise, have thought of prefacing the proposition by a long rigmarole of resolutions? There is some art about this. It becomes evident that you want, under the name of free-emigration, what is not free emigration.[3]

Colonel Nicholls, Laird's father-in-law and ex-Governor of Fernando Po, revealed the impossibility of recruiting any labourers on the West Coast without approaching the local chiefs, who themselves would never agree to procure the labourers unless paid to purchase them as slaves. Under such conditions, added to the natural reluctance among Africans to leave their home, how could free emigration be really free? Nicholls asked, 'Let Mr. Laird or anybody else answer that question.'[4]

It was clear that Laird's conception of 'free emigration' was

---

1. C.O. 300/4, 'Memorandum on Steam Transports'.
2. *Ibid.*
3. Johnson, J. F., *op. cit.*, p. 253, Rev. J. H. Hinton opposing Laird's Motion.
4. *Ibid.*, Colonel Nicholls.

equivocal, involving the 'collateral mischief' not only of vested interest in the method of their transportation but also of coercion in securing emigrants. The 'free emigrants' were to be recaptured slaves from foreign slavers compulsorily transported to the West Indies. If the Convention rejected his motion, the Government however was to profit greatly from his new ideas. True, Laird received no contract to supply the emigration transports, with the cost of his iron-steam vessels so high. But his idea of free return passages, and that of compulsory and immediate transportation of recaptured slaves to the West Indies, immediately attracted official attention in a way that was soon to affect the course of the emigration scheme from 1843.

Some historians seem to have failed to view the African emigration project objectively, Dr Mellor[1] considering it a scheme largely of pure philanthropy, and Mathieson[2] as a short-lived idea borrowed from the French. Liberated African emigration entered upon a new phase from 1843 when, forced by the events of 1841–2, the planters' flagrant violation of the labour regulations and the international criticisms, the British Government took over direct control of the scheme, only to be influenced by some of Laird's ideas soon afterwards.

At first, however, official anxiety to ensure a proper organisation, free from abuse or irregularity, became manifest in the prompt transfer of the responsibility to the Colonial Land and Emigration Commissioners. It became the Commission's duty to charter or hire the three Government vessels with which it was decided to supply emigrants to Jamaica, British Guiana and Trinidad; the Commission had the responsibility also to see that no vessels were employed, as in 1841–2, which did not fully conform to the provisions of the British Passengers' Act regarding size and seaworthiness, adequate space and ventilation for passengers in the ships. Because of this, it was provided in the 1843 regulations that no vessels

---

1. Mellor, G. R., *British Imperial Trusteeship*, Chapter III.
2. Mathieson, *British Slave Emancipation, 1838–1849* (London, 1932) p. 152; *Great Britain and the Slave Trade 1839–1865*: 'That there was no compulsion is proved by the fact that not a few of them refused to emigrate and were readily picked up by the old residents as unpaid apprentices,' p. 125. Mathieson continued: 'Emigration from Sierra Leone began in April 1841 and was very brisk for a few months, when it entirely ceased', pp. 146 ff. Some others thought the Scheme was a new idea borrowed from the French: *The Times*, June 15th, 1857.

were to be despatched to West Africa by any other authority, not even by the Colonial Governors or legislatures, than the Commission itself, who had to see to it that every transport vessel, prior to its despatch, was thoroughly examined and approved by a Government surveyor. It was also stipulated that every vessel having up to fifty emigrants on board must, according to the provision of the British Passengers' Act, have a Naval Surgeon, that no vessel was to depart with emigrants without providing medicine chests on board, and that adequate food and water provisions were to be carried. Experience of other emigration schemes had shown the officials the essential safeguards against heavy mortality and other evils in a peculiarly delicate project.

As to the treatment of the emigrants, the old promises of fair treatment, good food, free medical care, freedom of labour, and good wages were repeated; Laird's suggestion of a free return passage came in as a great novelty in the new emigration project from 1843. Lord Stanley caused it to be widely circulated in Sierra Leone that those Africans who wished after some years in the West Indies to return to their home, would be enabled to do so 'free of expense to themselves, or with an amount of aid towards the cost of the passage'.[1] This promise, extended later also to 'Coolie' emigrants, appears to be a condition unique to the African and Asiatic emigration schemes.[2]

Full of optimism about the humanity of these new provisions[3] Lord Stanley could confidently inform the critics in 1843 of the Government's intention through the African emigration scheme 'to demonstrate to the world that the interest of religion and justice and humanity can be reconciled with the inferior but still important interests of commercial prosperity'.[4]

The Emigration Commissioners began in January 1843 to negotiate with shipowners: the *Arabian*, 391 tons, was chartered for British Guiana; *Senator*, 346 tons, for Trinidad; and *Glen Huntley*,

---

1. C.O. 268/38, No. 87, February 6th, 1843, Stanley to MacDonald.
2. Campbell, P. C., *Chinese Coolie Emigration* (London, 1923); Cumpston, I. M., *Indians Overseas in British Territories* (London, 1954); Jones, M. A., 'The Role of the United Kingdom in the Transatlantic Emigration Trade', 1815–75 (Oxford, D. Phil., 1953); Laurence, K. O., *op. cit.*, Chapters V and IX.
3. C.O. 386/123, Containing printed Copies of the Emigration Regulations. C.O. 386/33, May 5th, 1843 (see page 215) for Scale of Rations for Emigrants.
4. PP. 1843, Vol. xxxiv, Stanley, through the Earl of Aberdeen, to M. Gonzalez, Spanish Foreign Minister, February, 1843.

420 tons, for Jamaica.[1] The West India Committee was fully informed of every move taken.[2] A Government Emigration Agent soon arrived in Sierra Leone in addition to the three colonial agents already stationed there. Captain Leary, agent for Jamaica, and the Superintendent of the liberated African Yard, both began immediate campaigning for emigrants, obtaining eventually only 85 labourers for the *Glen Huntley* for Jamaica.[3]

The whole operation soon ran into troubled waters. The emigration agents complained of continuing suspicion among the liberated Africans, despite the new promises made. Worse still, the missionary societies and some employers of labour in the colony remained vehemently hostile to emigration, employing every means to discourage intending emigrants from coming forward.[4]

By October 1843 the situation had become so bad that Governor MacDonald even attempted the Pied Piper's artifice: a brass band to entice the occupants of the liberated African Yard into the emigrant transport, *Furia*, was badly frustrated by the eloquence of a Yoruba woman, who introduced a jarring note to the alluring music by reminding the marching troop of prospective emigrants of the danger of being too gullible or trustful. Immediately, as the Governor himself later regretfully reported, more than half of the emigrants were released from the hypnotic spell of the music and dispersed.[5]

The officials were puzzled and hurriedly took fresh steps to rescue the scheme from what looked like imminent failure. The regulations recently enacted were now modified, the rule about the proportion of the sexes was scrapped, enabling agents to recruit any emigrants available without having to keep them to the strict proportion of two males for every female. Also the requirements of six weeks' residence in the Colony, and of ten days' prior notice to the colonial authorities before emigrating were scrapped.[6]

Given the existing difficulty of obtaining emigrants, it would perhaps have been unwise to have left the regulations unrevised, while

---

1. C.O. 386/32, January 13th, 1843, The Emigration Commissioners to Shipowners.
2. C.O. 318/155, Memorandum by Stanley, December 18th, 1842; C.O. 318/159, January 14th, 1843. Emigration Commissioners to West India Committee.
3. C.O. 386/33, May 17th, June 2nd, 1843, Walcott to Burge.
4. PP. 1844, xxxv, No. 9, Enclosure 2, J. C. Cathcart, Agent-General for Immigration to Jamaica, February 4th, 1843.
5. C.O. 267/181, No. 69, October 10th, 1843, MacDonald to Stanley.
6. C.O. 386/48, May 3rd, 1843, Elliot to James Stephen.

also maintaining on foot the elaborate and expensive machinery of emigration agents and officials when practically no business was being done. But there was a danger that, having shown itself so sensitive to immediate pressures, official policy might constantly be subject to sudden, radical changes. There was no guarantee that it would not swing just as sharply to a much tougher treatment of prospective emigrants if the revised measures failed to attract them in sufficient numbers.

Already the West India Committee, annoyed by the slow progress made in the new arrangement since 1843, was growing dissatisfied and restless. The modification of the recent regulations had been already carried through, thanks to their impatience and demands for alterations. But furthermore, they had also begun to demand that the Government should employ more transport vessels, or allow more to be sent out for emigrants—by private enterprise, despite the fact that there had not been enough emigrants fully to occupy the three Government vessels engaged for the service.[1] But after amending the regulations, the Emigration Commission tried to adhere to the decision to keep the transportation wholly in Government hands.

It found this increasingly difficult. Private emigration merchants and members of the West India Committee were taking the law into their own hands in spite of the new regulations. Reports were coming in, by the middle of 1843, of vessels carrying excess passengers, of inadequate provision of food and water, of emigrants being improperly examined or exposed in the nude during medical examinations before embarkation, of a ship's Captain and his officers misbehaving promiscuously with the female emigrants during the voyage and so forth.

It appears distinctly in evidence that the emigrants were subjected to maltreatment proceeding directly from the master, and terminating even in death in the case of some persons who happened to be under medical treatment; and further that the master and persons belonging to the ship took part in the immorality which prevailed on board in regard to the female emigrants. There is the clearest evidence to show that the Dietary prescribed in this country for the use of the emigrants was not adhered to either in regard to the use of some of the articles of which it was to consist, or the quantity and the quality of others and though a Surgeon was placed on board, he was interfered with by the Master in his

---

1. C.O. 318/150, West India Committee (Malcom) to Stanley, July 11th, 1843.

management of the sick. The parties connected with the ship had clearly failed to perform their part of the engagement. . . .[1]

The Commissioners were loud in condemnation and regret but no other action was taken.[2]

By 1844 the continuing scarcity of emigrants and complaints from West India interests led to increasing relaxation in the enforcement of the existing regulations and the officials were also beginning to view the method of emigration in an entirely new light. A highly confidential memorandum had passed between the Colonial Office and the Emigration Commissioners late in 1843 which revealed that arrangements were already being concluded,

. . . if there be no objection on grounds of policy, at once [for] transporting captured negroes wherever they may be found to act as cultivators in the British Colonies.[3]

These arrangements were to include not only St Helena and Sierra Leone, but also the foreign stations of Loanda, Boa Vista, Rio and Havana. Clearly, since the promise of return passage had not sufficed, the other idea of coercion, suggested by Laird, might now be tried.

The chief difficulty lay in furnishing the British Officers in the Mixed Commission Courts in those foreign stations with clear instructions, which would effect this purpose and yet not expose or involve the British Government in diplomatic complications with foreign powers. It was a delicate business, as the Emigration Commissioners feared. Moreover the British Officers in those foreign stations were under the direct control of the Foreign Office, not of the Colonial Office; there was doubt, therefore, whether the Foreign Office, which was responsible for all diplomatic negotiations with other powers and was already finding agreement with them in the abolition effort very difficult, could agree and cooperate with the Colonial Office in the new project.

On May 4th, 1844, Lord Aberdeen was approached at the Foreign Office. His views were non-committal, but he remained doubtful

---

1. C. O. 386/48, May 17th, 1843, Elliot and Villiers to James Stephen, C.O.
2. C.O. 386/33, May 17th, 1843, Emigration Commission to Colonial Office; C.O. 386/48, May 3rd, May 17th, 1843, same to same.
   The ships involved in these irregularities were the *James Hay, Wasp, Herald* and *Chieftain*. The whole incident seems to reveal that even with the employment of three government vessels in 1843, private vessels had continued to engage in the emigration traffic, with or without government concurrence, or perhaps with official connivance.
3. C.O. 386/48, November 13th, 1943; February 1st, 1844, Elliot to Cox.

after studying the preliminary plan, 'whether it would be expedient to give to officers whose functions are those of a Judge, any interest however remote in the condemnation of slave vessels'.[1]

An alternative plan to hand over the business to the Registrars rather than the British Judges at those Commissions was also immediately discarded when it was discovered that the Registrars were in almost all cases subjects of the nation in whose territory the Mixed Commission was established, and could not, in the event of trouble, be covered by diplomatic immunity.[2]

However, Aberdeen agreed to pass on to his officers in the Mixed Commissions whatever instructions the Colonial Office might finally draw up on the matter—provided it was clearly understood that those officers were to perform this new task only temporarily until special officers could be appointed to take over the work. The Emigration Commissioners soon afterwards submitted a lengthy twenty-point Memorandum, to be communicated to the Foreign Office by the Colonial Department. This Memorandum containing the draft official instructions was to be forwarded in a confidential cover to the Consul at Boa Vista; the Junior British member of the Mixed Commission Court at Loanda, to H. M. Minister and H. C. Ouseley both at Rio, and to the Superintendent of Liberated Africans in Havana.

Paragraphs 4, 5, 7, 9, 11, 13 and 20 of the Memorandum are of particular interest. In the 4th instruction the officers were ordered to 'forward all captured Africans with the least possible delay, in order that they may not longer than necessary remain a burden to the British Treasury', nor be detained from reaching places where they can earn their own subsistence. This clause, in effect, was in perfect agreement with Macgregor Laird's views on emigration. The other instructions were a virtual violation of the existing regulations on African emigration. The 5th clause or instruction allowed the conveyance of the captured slaves, the emigrants, in any vessel, including the foreign ones in which they were captured. The 7th, 9th and 11th clauses respectively referred to scales of food rations, victualling, medical comforts, carrying of excess passengers, and the employment of surgeons on board the transport vessels during the voyage. By discarding the legal provision of all these necessaries, the new Memorandum left the scheme of African emigration without any further proper supervision.

---

1. C.O. 318/162, May 4th, 1844, Slave Trade, Canning (F.O.) to James Stephen.
2. *Ibid.*

On reading the draft Memorandum Aberdeen immediately raised serious objections, and declined to communicate the instructions to the officers in the foreign stations without amendments to the Memorandum. To the 5th instruction he raised the objection that the shipment of the emigrants in foreign vessels would expose the Government to further criticisms or protests from foreign powers, with whom there had been anti-slavery negotiations. He therefore recommended an amendment to be incorporated in that particular clause to the effect that 'in places where British shipping can be procured for this service it is always to be engaged in preference to foreign'.[1] The argument of the Commissioners and the Colonial Office was that British shipping was very scarce in those out-of-the-way stations, and to wait for them might defeat the main purpose of the new scheme—prompt embarkation of those recaptured. However, they came to see the force of Aberdeen's objection, and so went even further than his amendment by altering that clause in the Amended Memorandum. The emigrants were to be forwarded 'in a suitable *British* vessel' only, the officer being warned at the same time that he should 'in no case forward them under the present instructions in any Foreign ship'[2] because 'we should have no confidence in the arrangement' if foreign ships were engaged 'expressly to meet the letter of this regulation'.[3]

Then came the 7th and 10th draft instructions to which Aberdeen also objected, because by their stipulations the legal provision for adequate medical attention in the emigration transports was discarded. Aberdeen also disallowed the 20th instruction because it stipulated that officers were to be paid for this service by 'head money' of 5s. per emigrant shipped or forwarded to the West Indies by them.[4]

Persistent objections by the Foreign Office on those points brought revealing explanations. Elaborate care about medical provisions, the Emigration Commissioners argued, might prevent the prompt despatch of all those recaptured and thus defeat the sole purpose of the new plan. It was more important, they argued, to transport liberated

---

1. C.O. 386/49, August 7th, December 11th, 1844, Emigration Commission to Colonial Office.
2. C.O. 318/62 and C.O. 386/49, September 20th, 1844: 5th Instruction of the Amended 'Memorandum for the Guidance of Officers who are to effect the removal of Liberated Africans from Foreign Stations to the West Indies.'
3. C.O. 386/49, September 20th, 1844: *Proposed Amendments of Memorandum for Guidance of Officers . . .;* Emigration Commissions to C.O.
4. C.O. 318/162, Draft Instructions: see Nos. 7, 10 and 20 of the Memorandum.

slaves at the first opportunity to the 'healthier' climate of the West
Indies and at the same time spare the British treasury from unnecessary expenditure in maintaining them. The Commissioners
even questioned the value of skilled medical attention: 'the profes-
sional skill [of a Surgeon] is comparatively less important in dealing
with uncivilised people with whom there can be almost no direct oral
communication'. Apparently here the official regulation[1] demanding
the employment of interpreters in every emigration transport had
been completely buried from sight. Under the new dispensation, the
legal provision of food rations, medical care, interpreters, even the
ascertainment of the sea-worthiness of emigration vessels, depended
only on one thing—on 'those general precautionary measures which
depend on the good sense and firmness of any person entrusted with
their enforcement'.[2]

The Foreign Office, however, continued to stress both the impro-
priety and inexpediency of a *carte blanche* Memorandum, giving up
all proper regulation, and leaving the scheme only to the discretion
and personal judgement of individuals charged with the duty of
running it. This objection became more stiff and prolonged because
of the provisions of clause 20 of the draft Memorandum, regarding
the remuneration of officers by 'head-money'. It was feared that
such a mode of payment might induce a more unscrupulous
or careless application by officers of their personal discretion or
tempt them, in response to the Colonial Office principle of 'earn as
you forward emigrants', to despatch 'as many recaptives as possible'
without due regard to their condition or state of health.

For several months, May till September, the two Departments
kept on exchanging revised drafts of the Memorandum. At last Canning of the Foreign Office wrote to James Stephen discussing the
matter at length. Lord Aberdeen, he said, was still worried, not only
about the mode of payment suggested by the Colonial Office, but
even more by the idea of involving British Judges in the Mixed
Commissions in the proposed scheme. Canning informed Stephen:

> I am to state to you that it appears to Lord Aberdeen that the mode in
> which it is proposed to remunerate the officers who are to undertake the
> duty of shipping emancipated Negroes to their destination in the West
> Indies (viz: by giving such Officers five shillings a head for all Negroes
> so shipped) renders [the Memorandum] objectionable.

1. C.O. 386/123. See Printed Regulations.
2. C.O. 318/162, No. 1545, West Indies, August 7th, 1844, Commissioners to
   C.O.

It was even more objectionable to Aberdeen 'that the British Arbitrator, an officer on whom the condemnation or non-condemnation of a captured vessel may sometimes depend, should be even temporarily appointed to execute such duty'.[1]

It was not that the Foreign Office was so strictly opposed to scrapping the former emigration regulations; or that they did not eventually concur with the Colonial Office and the Emigration Commissioners, in employing transport vessels without ascertaining the seaworthiness of such transports, as well as in promptly forwarding the recaptives without adequate medical provisions, food or clothing. Even the provision of a surgeon on board the vessels was shelved with Foreign Office concurrence. But Aberdeen remained quite adamant against British Judges being used to execute these plans. He feared the participation of such high officials in the Mixed Commissions might have graver consequences—since the provision of 'head-money' placed serious temptation in their path. The fact that the Spanish Tribunal, in May-June 1844, was already complaining of the scandal of British Judges being engaged in illicit transportation of captured Africans from Cuba, made Aberdeen's anxiety understandable. He was soon to insist on the immediate transfer of the duty to lesser officials in order to relieve the British Judges in the Mixed Commissions of any connection with the matter.

By September then, the disagreement between the two Government departments over the Memorandum was settled, the Colonial Office transferring these Instructions to other officials. Thus at Loanda the clerk to the British Judge of the Mixed Commission received the Instructions; at Boa Vista the British Consul took over; in Rio de Janiero, H. M. Ouseley of the British Embassy became responsible for that duty; while in Havana (Cuba) Hamilton, Superintendent of Liberated Africans, took over the execution of the Instructions.

It may be interesting to observe briefly what happened about the new Instructions, after the displacement of the emigration regulations which were feared to be 'tantamount to a prohibition against the [prompt] removal of the Africans'.[2] The lack of clarity in the new Instructions nearly perpetuated the delay which they were intended to remove in the prompt embarkation of the emigrants. Because of the

---

1. *Ibid*. Canning (F.O.) to Stephen (C.O.).
2. C.O. 386/49, August 7th and December 11th, 1844, Emigration Commissioners to C.O.

same fear of leakage of the proceedings to other powers, which might happen if, for example, the new Instructions got lost or mixed up in transit, the Emigration Commissioners had purposely couched many of the clauses in very ambiguous language. In fact one might still, without an awareness of this fact, greatly puzzle over some of the Instructions or misinterpret their real meaning. And the Officers who took up the new operations did puzzle for a long time over what they were really required to do in certain cases.

The 13th Instruction, for example, specified that the emigrants before being promptly embarked, should be provided 'with clothing furnished by the Public'. Which public? The Spanish planters in Cuba or the Portuguese in Rio de Janeiro—to provide clothing for British-colony bound recaptives? For many months the officers were puzzled and, after many delays had occurred while waiting vainly for the public to provide clothing, wrote home to ask for more clarification. The Emigration Commissioners replied through the Colonial Office, regretting the improper phraseology, but confessed this was used and 'calculated to mislead the officers on Foreign Stations who may be entrusted with the duty of providing the clothing'.[1] The Officers were expected to understand that in most cases they were not to wait for proper provisions, but should forward the emigrants as soon as captured, if possible in the very transports in which they had been recaptured.

Another clause in the Instructions of a misleading tendency was that which stated that the law of the British Passengers' Act 'does not extend to vessels sailing from foreign ports'.[2] If this were taken literally, the British Passengers' Act would have been reduced to an absurdity: if its application were confined to British vessels in home ports, the numerous Captains and ships' Officers would have had no case to answer, who were fined or suffered penalties in the Courts because of abuses or irregularities committed on the high seas or in foreign ports during the White Emigration of the period between Britain, Canada, U.S.A., Australia and New Zealand.

Since penalties were inflicted for abuses not committed inside the home port,[3] it is more correct to say that the law of the British

---

1. *Ibid.* Emigration Commissioners to Stephen, December 11th, 1844.
2. Memorandum and Instructions. See Appendix II.
3. In Canada (Quebec) in 1846, for example, legal proceedings were instituted in six cases for infringements of the British Passengers' Act. In five of these convictions were obtained: the Barque *Eleuthera* and the Brig *Hope* were each fined £5 for carrying excess passengers, the Barque *Triton* £1 5s. for im-

Passengers' Act applied equally to British vessels in foreign ports and that a Captain, Agent or Surgeon of an emigrant vessel was as justiciable for abuses committed in a home port as in a foreign station.

What then did that particular Instruction mean? Like the 13th Instruction about clothing, the clause regarding shipping was ambiguously couched and was very probably meant to convey to the officers that the employment of *any* type of vessel without observing the provisions of the Passengers' Act, about seaworthiness, for example, would not earn them any penalty; so also were they absolved from the penal laws of that Act, if they obeyed the new Instructions and proceeded with the new system of emigration which, under normal circumstances, would have earned them the penalties as laid down by the law of the British Passengers' Act. Without such assurances, officers who knew the normal laws of emigration might feel no sense of personal safety or security in proceeding with the new operations of immediate embarkation of emigrants in *any* type of vessel.

In the British settlements at Sierra Leone, St Helena, Cape of Good Hope and Mauritius, 'where the only question is of sending

---

proper construction of the deck, the Barque *Minna* £50 for failure to issue the proper allowance of water to the passengers, the Brig *Arab* £12 10s. for neglect to issue adequate provision and food rations. The *Elizabeth and Sarah* carried excess passengers, fever broke out on board and the Agent was obliged to charter another vessel at £200 to tow the emigrant transport into quarantine. Yet the Master of *Elizabeth and Sarah* was to be proceeded against, but died before he could be taken to court.

Infringements of the Passengers' Act for which legal proceedings were taken in New Brunswick against ships' Masters included the cases of the Brig *Danube* (sailing from Bally Shannon), fined £50 for having made use of temporary hold beams contrary to the requirements of the Passengers' Act; also for sailing without proper medicines, another £5 fine together with costs. The *Margaret Thomson* (from Donegal), fined £20 for supplying the emigrants with inadequate food and water as required by the Passengers' Act; the Barque *Renewal* (from Beerhaven), fined £10 with costs for the same offence, and another £5 fine with costs for carrying excess passengers. The Brig *Racer* (from Dingle) £5 with costs for excess passengers. Other vessels *Recovery*, *Alexander*, *Anne Wise*, were all fined for similar offences.

In 1846, while the Regulations on African Emigration had been replaced with the Memorandum and Instructions of 1844, the Emigration Commissioners took very strict steps to tighten up the provisions of the British Passengers' Act against violation by European Emigration Transport vessels.
Seventh General Report of the Colonial Land and Emigration Commissioners: PP. 1847, XXXIII, 809, 131, pp. 153 ff.

forward captured negroes recently landed from the ships of war',[1] neither the difficulties with the Foreign Office, nor the fears about giving definite or clear instructions had existed at all. These Settlements or Colonies were British and the officials servants of the Colonial Office. In fact by the middle of October 1844, there was no more need for emigration agents or officers at St Helena or Sierra Leone, the duty of 'forwarding' the emigrants to the West Indies having reverted to the Customs officials, under the Collector of Customs.[2] It was felt that the main object of employing Government transports in 1843, which was 'to restore confidence among the Africans who had almost entirely ceased to go to the West Indies' after 1841-2, had been accomplished.[3] Without any more Government regulation or restrictions on the scheme, there was no sense in continuing the employment of costly Government transport vessels, since private enterprise could take over the business on payment only of bounty to them, and was even anxious to do so.[4]

The indiscriminate rivalry and competition for emigrants which subsequently arose in Sierra Leone and St Helena between private enterprise and shipowners led to further complaints from the West India interests that not enough emigrants were procurable. But what else could the Government now do? Formerly, as already pointed out, the complaint was that emigration was being hampered or restricted by Government regulations; all the regulations or restrictions were then scrapped and private enterprise allowed to take over. By late 1844 the competition among private vessels was causing further trouble, the flow of emigrants failing to adjust itself to the indiscriminate and unregulated despatch of private vessels. It was hardly a problem caused by Government, or meant for them to solve, but rather for the West India interests and shipowners themselves to settle between them.

British Guiana and Trinidad took the first steps towards the solution of this new difficulty, and in July 1844 appointed respectively, the Butts and the Guppy Commissions of Inquiry in Sierra Leone, without the prior knowledge or permission of the Emigration Commissioners or the Colonial Office.[5] The Reports of these two

---

1. C.O. 386/48, May 11th, 1844, Emigration Commissioners to C.O.
2. C.O. 386/49, October 14th, 1844, Emigration Commissioners to C.O.
3. C.O. 386/48, May 22nd, 1844, same to same. Sixth General Report, PP. 1846, XXIV, 706.
4. C.O. 386/49, July 27th, 1844, same to same.
5. C.O. 386/49, July 27th, July 29th, 1844, Emigration Commissioners to C.O.

Commissions[1] are important in so far as they caused further action to be taken by the Colonial Office in the emigration scheme. The two reports had concluded that emigration could be sustained only if all incentives for settlement in the Colony were removed. In short, the Government was here again being reminded of Macgregor Laird's suggestion in 1843, that the Colony be wound up and financial support for its population withdrawn. Reporting the findings of these two Commissions to the Colonial Office, the Emigration Commissioners laid particular stress on that particular point:

> On the whole the conclusion of both gentlemen, seems to be that unless some change in the circumstances of the colony should materially diminish the Government expenditure and the circulation of money, no large emigration can be expected.[2]

Whilst the two Commissioners' criticisms of the indiscriminate despatch of vessels and the excessive rivalry that characterised private enterprise remained yet to be answered, the Colonial Office took immediate steps to improve the flow of emigrants. Governor Fergusson of Sierra Leone was instructed to issue a proclamation announcing that 'all allowances of whatsoever description heretofore issued to captured negroes . . . on their being landed in this Colony will discontinue and cease'.[3] The resultant chorus of protest[4] from the missionaries and their demand for the withdrawal of the proclamation proved unavailing. Even the objections[5] raised by the British Arbitrator in Sierra Leone, J. L. Hook, proved equally powerless to prevent the Government taking this radical step.

---

1. Fifth General Report, PP. 1845, XXVII, pp. 103 f., Appendices 13 and 14; Butt's Report to Governor Light of British Guiana, 7th August and Guppy's Report to Sir Henry MacLeod, Governor of Trinidad, October 18th, 1844.
2. C.O. 386/49, July 27th, 1844, Emigration Commission to C.O.; C.O. 386/50, February 18th, 1845, Emigration Commissioners to G. W. Hope (C.O.).
3. C.O. 268/38 (p. 332), Proclamation by Lieutenant Governor Fergusson, June 12th, 1844, PP. 1845, XXXI, No. 2, *Proclamation*.
4. PP. 1845, XXXI, p. 321, C.M.S. Protest Letter to Stanley, November 24th, 1844 and *ibid.*, pp. 326–7, G. W. Hope to D. Coates, C.M.S. Secretary, December 24th, 1844.
5. C.O. 386/49, Emigration Commissioners to C.O. (Stephen), 6th November, 1844. John Logan Hook, H.M. Arbitrator in the Mixed Commission Court in Sierra Leone regarded himself as an 'abolitionist in principle' of 30 years' standing; and his experience of the working of the new emigration scheme had 'led him to form an unfavourable opinion of the present regulations for the disposal of liberated Africans at Sierra Leone'. However, see Chapter V for Hook's subsequent role in the scheme after 1844.

The Emigration Commissioners turned for defence of the new policy to a wholesale attack on the Sierra Leone Settlement. It was enough only to draw attention

> to the frightful loss of human life which is here exhibited [in the Butts-Guppy Reports on Sierra Leone] as well as to the great disproportion between the number of Africans known to have been liberated in Sierra Leone, and the number of whom any account can now be given; the distribution of African women immediately upon their release from adjudication amongst any African men who apply for them, and the profanation in these cases of the marriage rite; the want of medical aid in the colony; the insufficiency of the food allowed to children in Government schools; the evils of the apprenticeship again resorted to under the sanction of the Governor, which state is described as being slavery without the protection which every code secures for avowed slaves.[1]

Why had the missionaries, even the Sierra Leone Government, come in for such a censure from the Butts-Guppy Commissions of Inquiry, and from the Emigration Commissioners as well? Guppy, Butts and the Commissioners were emigration enthusiasts, the missionaries and the Governors of Sierra Leone never were; because to them emigration policy was a contradiction of the long-established British African policy, the civilisation of Africa through the suppression of the slave trade and the full economic development of the Colony.

Early in 1840 Governor Doherty, in reply to instructions from the Secretary of State that he should encourage the liberated Africans to emigrate to the West Indies, had dwelt on liberated African grievances and the discouragements they had received in the Colony:

> They allege that in this colony they are retarded in the career of improvement, that no opportunity is afforded them of increasing their means and further ameliorating their condition; and certainly they receive little encouragement from the maroons and settlers, or from the Europeans themselves.[2]

After Lord Russell's reply in June, further instructing the Governor to encourage emigration, Doherty wrote another despatch in which he came out more plainly revealing his views about the whole project:

---

1. C.O. 386/50, Emigration Commissioners to C.O. (Stephen) July 8th, 1845; C.O. 386/50, Emigration Commissioners to C.O. (G. W. Hope) February 18th, 1845.
2. C.O. 267/159, March 20th, 1840, Doherty to Russell.

In regard to the liberated people the favourable opinion which I had occasion to express ... remains unchanged and has been confirmed since that time. After three years acquaintance with these people, I do not hesitate to pronounce them again to be, on the whole, an active and industrious and well disposed population. During visits which I recently made to the country districts I witnessed many proofs of their diligence and desire of improvement. Their crops, under all their disadvantages formerly stated by me, bore a full and luxuriant appearance; and the cultivation of vegetables and other market produce was sufficient to show how abundantly these would increase if an adequate demand existed for them, and they were adequately paid for.[1]

The Governor pointed out that among the agricultural population were also many other classes of liberated Africans: traders, river merchants, hawkers, craftsmen—all desirous and ambitious for progress and improvement:

If therefore there be any truth in the assertion so frequently made in England, that the object of British policy in founding this Settlement, the civilizing of these Africans, remains unattained, the failure is not to be ascribed to the people themselves. I have to repeat my former assertions that they have had to labour under great discouragements, peculiar to their position or to the colony.[2]

The Governor's faintly masked protests against emigration proved unavailing to deter the British Government. Later, whilst some of the Governors finally acquiesced in the reduction of the settlement in obedience to their official instructions, others covertly opposed the emigration scheme by defending the liberated African population in the Colony, or opposed the scheme openly by disregarding official instructions.[3]

The missionaries had declared themselves from the start staunch opponents of the emigration project. By their continued opposition and protest[4] in 1844, when so many powerful groups (from Butts

---

1. C.O. 267/160, No. 48, October 3rd, 1840, same to same.
2. *Ibid.*
3. See Chap. 5 for the Hook-MacDonald conflict.
4. C.M.S. Protest to Lord Stanley, November 24th, 1844; See PP. 1845, Vol. XXXI, p. 321 f. Up to December 31st, 1842, according to the protest, some 52,616 Africans had been emancipated at Sierra Leone; out of which number the C.M.S. claimed to have trained 35 native teachers, 26 seminarists; made 1,330 communicants and produced 4,974 school children attending 46 missionary schools. Then 'as to the children who form no inconsiderable portion of the liberated Africans', the C.M.S. protested against the proclamation stopping payment of Government allowances, 'how are they to provide entirely for themselves in Sierra Leone?' *ibid.*

and Guppy and the West India Colonies to the Emigration Commissions) were deeply committed to the project, they called down on themselves severe official censure which ultimately succeeded in silencing them.

It was one thing, however, for the critics to be beaten down, or for the Proclamation and other measures to be promulgated; it was a different matter to secure effective order and discipline in the emigration traffic. A change of organisation was vitally necessary by 1845 if the new scheme was to have any prospect of success. The Butts-Guppy Reports stressed the point. And the Emigration Commissioners concurred: 'We think the time has come', they reported to the Colonial Office, 'when some more general change should be made in the arrangement for the introduction of free emigrants from Sierra Leone.'[1]

The changes introduced in Sierra Leone between late 1844, after the Butts-Guppy Reports, and the beginning of 1845, had two aims in view: to increase the number of emigrants and to establish a better organisation in the despatch of emigration transports by private merchants. For the first of these purposes, the scheme was now extended to Gambia where permission for recruiting had earlier been refused to the West India interests.[2] Also a new form of assistance or 'subordinate agency' was to be employed in the Colony and its vicinity to help procure emigrants—the chiefs or leaders of the various settlements of liberated Africans in the Colony, and some school teachers. Both Butts and Guppy and the Emigration Commissioners had very high hopes of it:

> If this agency should prove as effective as may be hoped from the probable influence of the parties over the class of liberated Africans, it may supersede the use of delegates, respecting whom various complaints appear both in Mr. Butts' letters and in other places.[3]

Furthermore, the payment of 'head-money' of $1 per emigrant as allowance to the Chief Emigration Agent was instituted in addition to his salary of £300 per annum. A reduction in the number of

---

1. C.O. 386/50, February 18th, 1845, Emigration Commissioners to C.O. (Stephen).
2. C.O. 318/155 (Colville) West India Committee to Stanley (C.O.) November 15th and December 18th, 1842; C.O. 318/160 (Malcolm), W.I.C. to Stanley, July 11th, 1843; C.O. 386/49, July 27th, 1844, Emigration Commissioners to C.O.; C.O. 386/50, July 8th, 1845, same to same.
3. C.O. 386/50, February 18th, July 8th, 1845, Emigration Commissioners to C.O.

emigration agents was made. In place of the former three agents operating for the three West Indian Colonies, one Chief Emigration Agent was appointed from 1845 to serve the three colonies and was to utilise the new subordinate agency in place of the former three colonial agents.[1]

Then came the major question as to the method of controlling the despatch of vessels. Should the Government take it over once more, or ought private vessels to be left entirely free? This question had arisen because past experience had revealed the obvious difficulty of indiscriminate or competitive despatch of vessels under private enterprise. Between January 1841 and April 1842 the three West Indian Colonies had sent out 24 vessels to Sierra Leone with a combined capacity for 4,922 emigrants; their total recruitment was 1,343.[2] At one time three ships arrived in Sierra Leone simultaneously, two of which got four emigrants between them; on another occasion five ships arrived at the same place at the same time and got practically none.[3] There was clearly a strong case in 1845 for a complete reorganisation. The Emigration Commissioners, however, stopped short of radical reform in the measures introduced in 1845:

> It must depend on private parties to judge for themselves whether or not to send vessels to Sierra Leone under such circumstances on the chance of procuring emigrants.[3]

So the bickering and rivalry of private enterprise continued unchecked after 1845, except for the provision that the Governor of Sierra Leone, in conjunction with the new Chief Emigration Agent, Pike, was given authority to issue licences to private vessels arriving in the Colony to recruit emigrants, such licences being issued according to the order of the ships' arrival in Sierra Leone.[5] This decision or partial reform proved quite incapable of preventing the competition among private vessels and only its unforeseen consequences eventually obliged the Emigration Commissioners once more to intervene.

What were the results of this new arrangement before it was suddenly suspended at the end of 1846? First, British Guiana and

---

1. C.O. 318/164, June 25th, 1845, Emigration Commissioners to Stanley.
2. C. O. 318/155, Enclosure in West India Committee to Hope, April 20th, 1842.
3. *Ibid.*
4. C.O. 386/50, July 9th, 1845, Emigration Commissioners to C.O.
5. C.O. 386/49, July 27th, 1844 and C.O. 386/50, July 8th, 1845, Emigration Commissioners to C.O.

Trinidad, both very active in the emigration scheme, quickly established rates of bounty payable to private vessels and calculated on the numbers of emigrants received:[1] the Emigration Commissioners concurred, 'considering the necessity of holding out to shipowners some inducement to encounter the risk and uncertainty of the business'. With these 'high rates', as the Commissioners described them, the competition among the private vessels grew even more tense with the full encouragement of the West Indian Colonies and the West India Committee in England.[2]

Though it had been settled that licences to vessels should be issued only in Sierra Leone and solely by the Governor,[3] the West India Governors soon took the law into their hands and issued licences to vessels proceeding to West Africa. The Governor of British Guiana, for example, issued licences to the *Beatrice* and the *Louisa Baille*, both of which carried excess passengers, 7 and 23 emigrants respectively. He also licensed the *Roger Stewart*, a ship which the Emigration Commissioners themselves had earlier rejected as 'decidedly too old for the present service'.[4] Nothing, however, came of this early violation of the new arrangements.

The laxity evinced by the Commission even over rules which they themselves had recently laid down might have some connection with the state of public opinion during 1845–6 on the emigration question. Both in Parliament and outside it, popular opinion gave full support to unrestricted emigration. Sir J. W. Hogg in Parliament and Gibbon Wakefield both moralised on African emigration: 'the civilization of the Negroes in the West Indies', Hogg maintained, 'would have some good effect on the barbarism of Africa'.[5] William Hutt, a staunch defender of West India interests, urged the authorities res-

---

1.   Bounty payable per head of African Emigrant

Introduced from	Bounty payable per Immigrant in	
	Trinidad	British Guiana
Sierra Leone	£7 5s. 1od. or	35 dollars
	38 dollars	
St Helena	£8 6s. 8d.	35 dollars
Rio de Janiero	£8 6s. 8d.	35 dollars

C. O. 386/52, October 10th, 1846, Emigration Commission to C.O.
2. C.O. 386/50, August 13th, 1845, same to same; C.O. 386/51, May 29th, 1846, same to same.
3. C.O. 386/50, July 9th, August 13th, 1845.
4. C.O. 386/50, July 28th and August 13th, 1845, Emigration Commissioners to C.O.
5. Wakefield, E. G., *A View of the Art of Colonisation (1849)*, edited by J.

ponsible for emigration to 'throw open our West India plantations to the free emigration of the African race'.[1] The Emigration Commissioners agreed, re-emphasising their stand that 'the supply of immigrants from Sierra Leone must depend in a great measure on private enterprise'.[2]

In defying the new arrangement established in 1845 those with vested interests in the emigration scheme made it clear why officialdom must never intervene in any form: 'The day is gone', they warned, 'when men really aspired to achieve the emancipation of the negro race.'[3] Indeed the trend of public opinion appeared to support them. For while Bright and Cobden lectured in Parliament on the doctrine of free trade in 1845–6 and public opinion both in and outside that House absorbed its principles, those who applied the concepts of free trade to emigration stood to enjoy the advantage of popular approval of their proceedings.

'Public opinion on this subject', an abolitionist in Parliament regretfully pointed out during debates on the emigration, 'appears to have undergone a lamentable and disgraceful change. In works issued from the press there could not be found a single argument that did not bear tokens of alliance with the slave dealer.'[4] Another abolitionist, Bishop Wilberforce, observed how, even among members of Parliament, African emigration, a humanitarian question, had developed into a quite different logic and argument:

> The anti-slavery cause, from various reasons, had rather fallen to an argument of a different kind, and has become something of a political and sectional question.[5]

The abolitionists deeply lamented this development in public opinion. Officials in charge of the supervision of African emigration appeared to take early warning of the state of opinion, becoming more cautious in interfering with private enterprise. Private enterprise, delighted no doubt by public acceptance of the free trade doctrine,

---

Collier (1914), cited in G. W. Roberts *Immigration into the British Carribbean* (in Population Studies Vol. 7, 1953–4) p. 235.

Hogg, J. W., *Hansard*, 1846, LXXXVIII, 91.

1. Hutt, W., *Hansard*, 1845, LXXVII, 1197.
2. C.O. 386/51, November 29th, 1845, Emigration Commissioners to C.O.
3. *The Spectator*, December 11th, 1847.
4. Lord Denman, *Hansard*, 1847–8, XCVI, 1052.
5. Bishop Wilberforce, *Hansard*, LXXXVIII, 666, August 13th, 1846 and Debates by Lord Stanley and Lord Aberdeen, *Hansard*, 1847–8, XCVI, 1037 f. and 1048–9 f.

and by the state of public opinion in 1845–6, excelled itself in rivalry and competition for emigrants. The rest of the story until the end of 1846 provides its own commentary.

The first adverse report came early in February 1845 concerning the *Superior*, whose Captain embarked 11 men and 2 boys from Sierra Leone without formally entering their names in the ship's official documents; worse still, the boys were 'triced up' the vessel's rigging. This, admitted the Emigration Commissioners, was 'a most censurable proceeding'. But nothing could be done to the Captain, because 'the *Superior* is in no way under the direct control of the Government'.[1]

The *Rufus* case was even more serious. The Captain embarked 117 emigrants, mainly youths of ages between 6 and 14; food rations and water were inadequate: only 20 gallons of water per day for the whole 117 passengers, instead of rations of 1 gallon of water per adult per day and $\frac{1}{2}$ gallon per child per day, were provided; the food the Emigration Commissioners condemned as 'much worm eaten', and the ration of rice was severely cut, from $1\frac{1}{2}$ lb. per adult and $\frac{3}{4}$ lb. per child, to $3\frac{3}{10}$ ozs. per emigrant! The Commissioners called for severe action against the Captain. The incident, they confessed, deserved 'exemplary severity of penalty':

> Our impression is that the service was on the whole badly performed; and the emigrants not well treated, and on general grounds we think it very expedient that the Government [of British Guiana] should exercise the utmost stringency in superintending African Emigration.[2]

Powerless to ensure that the Captain of the *Rufus* was punished, the Commissioners merely regretted that he was eventually set free. The Court of Policy in British Guiana had decided: 'the non-issue of the proper allowance of water had taken place under extenuating circumstances; the omission to make proper issues of good provision had not been proved'. The recommendation made by the Commissioners of a £50 fine on the Captain was therefore rejected, the Captain, Thomas Pike, receiving his full bounty of £530, despite the fact that the *Rufus* had been involved in an earlier case of illegal proceedings.[3] 'We abstain from further comments', the Commis-

---

1. C.O. 386/50, Elliot and Wood to C.O. (Hope), February 10th, 1845.
2. C.O. 386/51, February 9th, April 20th, 1846, Emigration Commissioners to C.O.
3. C.O. 386/51, March 10th, 1846, Emigration Commissioners to C.O.

sioners remarked helplessly when the final decision on the *Rufus* became known.[1]

But further reports of abuse continued to come in, and the Commissioners were forced to comment. In May the *Roger Stewart* was involved in a case involving discrepancy in the numbers embarked from Sierra Leone and landed in British Guiana, 7 people being unaccounted for. 'The matter does not admit of being pursued further', the Commissioners concluded, and dropped the case.[2] Next came a report from Rio de Janiero. Eleven captured Africans became afflicted with sea blindness on board the *Crescent* and were abandoned. Dr Gunn, the British Officer in charge, asked for instructions whether to send them for treatment in the West Indies or in England, since they were no longer fit as emigrant labour. The Commissioners replied:

It probably will not be doubted that these poor people have strong claims on the humanity of the Government but as they do not fall within the description of persons to whom the measure of emigration applies, it would perhaps be beyond our province to enter further into this part of the case.[3]

Nothing more was heard of the matter.

These incidents, however, began to create such anxiety for the Commissioners that they were already contemplating banning private vessels from engaging in the emigration traffic:

There must always exist considerable risk of dissension and discontent so long as the present system shall continue of allowing Private Merchant ships to go from different places in quest of emigrants.

This system 'would require to be discontinued'.[4]

Meanwhile the case of the *Margaret* served to emphasize the need for an immediate change of system. That vessel was licensed from Berbice, British Guiana. It arrived in Sierra Leone and, defying the authority of the Sierra Leone Governor, proceeded outside the Colony to recruit emigrants. The licensing of the vessel by the British Guiana Government rather than by the Governor of Sierra Leone

1. C.O. 386/51, April 20th, 1846, same to same.
2. C.O. 386/51, May 19th, same to same.
3. C.O. 386/51, April 28th, 1846, Emigration Commissioners to C.O.
4. C.O. 386/51, March 10th, 1846, same to same.

was already an illegal procedure. The Captain's action in proceeding outside British jurisdiction on the coast for emigrants was not merely illegal but dangerous in that it could easily involve the Government with other powers on the coast. The Commisioners seized on the incident to stress

> The further evidence of increasing irregularities in the emigration by private vessels, which will not only justify, but demand, a prompt exercise of authority to prevent the growth of abuse.[1]

Immediately they put forward new proposals: no more vessels to be sent out to Sierra Leone except from England and with the full knowledge of the Commissioners; all licences for ships to be issued by the Commissioners; the Governor of Sierra Leone to be in full control regarding the movement and proceedings of vessels arriving in the Colony; a rotational system to be introduced in the sharing of emigrants between Jamaica, Trinidad and British Guiana, and in the despatching of ships to Sierra Leone; the West India Committee to cooperate in these proposals by taking on the responsibility for regularly nominating transport vessels to be licensed and despatched in rotation by the Emigration Commissioners.

'Provided the West India Committee would co-operate in one part of it' (the nomination of vessels and the rotational despatch of them for emigrants) the new proposals would solve the existing problems; so the Commissioners believed. But correspondence with the Committee dragged on for months, and eventually came to nothing. And the Commissioners had to admit the failure of the proposals because they 'could not be carried out without the concurrence and indeed the active cooperation of the West India Committee in this country'.[2] So the emigration traffic continued under private enterprise.

By November, 1846, the *Margaret* from British Guiana was again involved, this time in a case of heavy mortality among emigrants embarked from St Helena, 14 of them dying out of 351. These had been 'embarked in a sickly state and the journal of the medical officer was very imperfectly kept'.[3] The Commissioners took this opportunity

---

1. C.O. 386/51, April 20th, 1846, Emigration Commissioners to C.O.
2. C.O. 386/51, March 31st, 1846, Commissioners to C.O.; C.O. 318/167, West India Committee to Gladstone, June 17th, 1846; C.O. 318/169, West India Committee (Macgregor) to Gladstone, June 29th, 1846 and Minute on same.
3. C.O. 386/52, November 21st, 1846, Commissioners to C.O.

to pass observations on the proposals they made earlier, but which 'had fallen to the ground, in consequence of the West India Committee not joining in that part of the scheme which required their co-operation'.[1]

Finally the incident of the *British Tar* late in December brought a sudden end to the story of African emigration in 1843-6. Arriving in Sierra Leone early in December 1846, and failing to obtain any recruits, the *British Tar* proceeded, in defiance of the Governor, to recruit outside the Colony—only to embark as one of his passengers, Senor Potestad, the Spanish Commissary Judge of the Mixed Commission Court at Sierra Leone! Whether Senor Potestad boarded that ship as a *bona fide* passenger, or as a spy on a fact-finding mission for his Government, was never inquired into. The Captain of the *British Tar* was deprived of his bounty—practically the only penalty inflicted for illegal proceedings in African emigration since 1843! Private enterprise emigration was promptly declared suspended and prohibited 'until further notice'.[2]

The disagreement between the Emigration Commissioners and the West India Committee over African Emigration in 1843-6, was one of detail rather than principle; both parties had tolerated violations of the official regulations laid down in 1843; they had both equally encouraged the emigration to be run on the basis of free trade and private enterprise. But the incident of the *British Tar*, in producing so drastic and immediate a reaction from the authorities, would tend to indicate that official policy was much more sensitive to foreign publicity than to actual abuses of the scheme.

Thanks mainly to the vigour of private enterprise in implementing the official policy of 'free' labour recruitment, the West Indian planters were now full of hope for the future, and the Imperial Government appeared to feel a sense of relief from the planters' harassment. The question of numbers recruited must indeed continue to be a matter of intelligent guess, as it was even with the Emigration Commissioners. Because of the ebb and flow, the shifts and turns in policy as control of the scheme changed hands and methods several times, the official statistics about numbers are necessarily defective, perhaps on the side of underestimation, as the Commissioners several times stressed. The seven voyages made by

---

1. C.O. 386/52, December 3rd, 1846, same to same.
2. C.O. 386/52, December 24th, 1846, Commissioners to C.O.

the three original Government vessels between 1843–4 obtained emigrants as follows:[1]

Between 1845 and 1846 Jamaica received some 411 emigrants from Havana,[2] while British Guiana and Trinidad respectively received 2,076 and 1,006 from Rio de Janeiro during the same period.[3] The three Government vessels were together responsible for the removal of 2,187 emigrants: 512 to Jamaica by *Glen Huntley* ; 652 to British Guiana by *Arabian* : and 923 to Trinidad by *Senator*. Of the private vessels which went out for emigrants, seven reported their proceedings to the Commissioners and were together responsible for carrying 1,261 emigrants from Sierra Leone in 1845.[4] The report for 1846 merely mentioned the 'small numbers' obtained from Sierra Leone, after the *Louisa Baille* had recruited 115 and the *British Tar* '13 or 14' from the same place. It points out however that 2,014 emigrants altogether had been landed in St Helena in 1846 alone, 1,439 of these being despatched to the West Indies, and others to the Cape of Good Hope. About nine different vessels had been involved in this operation.[5] By 1846 some of the West Indian authorities could pay some measure of tribute to the new labour they were receiving: 'The Liberated Africans', Governor Macleod told Lord Stanley, 'are our best labourers'.[6]

After the incident of the *British Tar* in December 1846, a new and important plan was concluded to begin the following year, 1847. This was the H.M.S. *Growler* Emigration Scheme.

---

1. PP. 1846, xxiv, 33; PP. 1850, xxxix, 283. Returns of Liberated African Emigration.

Voyage	Glen Huntley	Arabian	Senator
1st	85	32	33
2nd	146	49	100
3rd	118	102	117
4th	121	23	92
5th	42	241	154
6th	—	205	243
7th	—	—	185

2. C.O. 318/161, McClure to Hope, September 30th, 1844; C.O. 318/164, same to same, May 29th, 1845.
3. Laurence, K. O., *op. cit.*, pp. 138–40.
4. *Sixth General Report*, PP. 1846, xxiv, 706.
5. *Seventh General Report*, 1847, xxxiii, 809, 131.
6. C.O. 295/147, Macleod to Stanley, No. 82, October 14th, 1845 and also *The Port of Spain Gazette*, September 15th, 1846, cited Laurence, *op. cit.*, p. 140.

Chapter 5
'Voluntary' Emigration
under Government Control:
The *Growler* Scheme and the
Hook-MacDonald Conflict
1847–1849

The importance of African emigration in British West India economic policy was further demonstrated in the 1847–8 Parliamentary
crisis over the West African Naval Squadron. Both to the advocates
and the opponents of the anti-slave trade Squadron, the topic of
emigration formed the central theme of debate. The expansion of
African emigration became the main interest of Hutt's group in
Parliament and led to many subtle arguments discrediting the work
of the Royal Navy and the anti-slave trade Squadron.[1] Hume and
Hutt, the leading opponents of the Squadron were the most voci-
ferous on the whole matter:

> If we allowed the British West India colonists to have as much free
> labour as they required to enable them to compete with the slave holders;
> if we allowed those colonists to obtain free labour at £4.10.0 a head, they
> would soon put an end to the system of slavery; the moment the plan-
> ters in our West India Colonies were enabled to reduce the cost of the
> Sugar they produced below that of Cuba or Brazil, there would at once
> be a cessation of the slave trade; on principles of humanity, this country
> ought at once to withdraw its squadron from the Coast of Africa. . . .[2]

Opposing these radical views of Hume and other West India
interests were Lord Palmerston and the Earl of Aberdeen, who
summed up the contradictions into which the Government had already been led in its policies on slavery and African emigration:

> Looking, then, at the state of our measures, our means and appliances
> for the suppression of the slave trade, next to our adoption of a course
> of policy tending directly to encourage it, and now to our proposal to

---

1. *Hansard*, 1847–8, XCVI, 1047, The Earl of Auckland, criticising the false
arguments made against the Naval Squadron on the African Coast.
2. *Ibid.*, 1111–13, by Hume, February 22nd, 1848.

withdraw our squadron altogether, must not any man say, either that we are the most egregious hypocrites, or that, if sincere, we must be mad ?[1]

The Naval Squadron continued its anti-slavery operations on the West Coast.

The great significance of the new emigration scheme, from 1847–9, was the attempt of the Government to meet, as far as possible, the desires of the planters without recourse to the extreme measure of withdrawing the Naval Squadron as had been demanded by the West India interests in Parliament. With this as background knowledge of Government policy, it becomes easy to follow the trend of events in the *Growler*[2] scheme and much easier still to understand the respective positions held in the new scheme by the new Chief Emigration Agent, John Logan Hook, and by the head of the Sierra Leone Colony—Governor MacDonald.

What were the essentials of the new plan ? In spite of the difficulties which had resulted from the activities of private vessels up to December 1846, it was still not intended to exclude private enterprise emigration; rather the idea now was to extend the boundaries or limits of recruitment on the coast, up to the Kroo Coast, in present day Liberia, and then allow private vessels as before to proceed up to those areas for emigrants. But until a government vessel, meeting in all respects the proper requirements and regulations for emigration, had been used first to restore lost confidence among Africans or others who might have become suspicious of the whole scheme, private vessels were not to be permitted to resume their operations as before. This, in brief, was the purpose of the *Growler* plan in 1847, which was underway by March of that year.

The new scheme needed not only an enthusiastic and zealous emigration officer on the coast to put it into successful operation, but also the active cooperation of the Governor of Sierra Leone. In John Logan Hook, British Arbitrator of the Mixed Commission and an 'abolitionist in principle' who had criticised the emigration scheme in 1844,[3] the Emigration Commissioners came to find the right type

---

1. The Earl of Aberdeen, *ibid.*, p. 1046.
   Palmerston, *ibid.*, p. 1123.
2. H.M.S. *Growler*, a warship, was to open up the 'free' recruitment on the Kroo Coast before private vessels were to resume recruiting operations; hence the *Growler* scheme.
3. C.O. 386/49, Commissioners to Stephen (C.O.) November 6th, 1844. John Logan Hook, British Arbitrator in the Mixed Commission Court at Sierra Leone, had notified to the Commissioners in 1844 his disapproval of com-

of person to take full charge of the *Growler* scheme. The new Agent soon established his headquarters in Sierra Leone. From the start Governor MacDonald was left in no doubt that he was to give his fullest co-operation.

> It will be of great importance that the Governor should give the benefit of his cordial co-operation to the measure, and that he should be fully sensible of the interest which Her Majesty's Government take in its success.[1]

Earl Grey instructed MacDonald accordingly.[2]

The policy of economic disincentive to discourage the growth of a resident population of liberated Africans at Sierra Leone was soon carried much further. An Ordinance was quickly passed for the summary ejection of 'squatters' on Crown and unregistered lands;[3] then later, came the imposition of compulsory hut-tax upon the peasant population in order 'to impose the necessity of some exertion on the rudest class of liberated Africans inhabiting the Colony'.[4] These, however, appeared to be the greatest limits to which MacDonald was prepared to go in support of the emigration scheme. His stiff opposition to what he felt or criticised as the 'inhumane ideas' of the Chief Agent, John Logan Hook, was to bring him hard up against the Emigration Commissioners and the Colonial Office.

As Chief Superintendent of the *Growler* scheme Hook was to receive a salary of £300 per annum and an additional allowance of one dollar per head on emigrants forwarded by him to the West Indies.[5] In return however, he was to bear in mind, the Commissioners clearly told him, that the success of the scheme depended very much upon him and his cordial relationship with the Governor. Hook in fact gave early proof of his enthusiasm and zeal for his new job. Once returned to Sierra Leone from his leave in England, he proceeded immediately to disregard his official instructions regarding

---

pulsory transportation of liberated Africans. The Commissioners reported this to the Colonial Office: 'The result of this gentleman's experience has led him to form an unfavourable opinion of the present regulations for the disposal of liberated Africans at Sierra Leone.'

1. C.O. 386/53, Emigration Commissioners to J. Stephen, March 8th, 1847.
2. C.O. 268/41, Sierra Leone, Grey to MacDonald, No. 122, November 15th, 1847.
3. C.O. 268/41, No. 10, January 6th, 1846, Gladstone to Governor Fergusson—when this Ordinance was at first rejected; and No. 48, January 1st, 1847, Grey to MacDonald, when it was approved by Grey.
4. C.O. 268/41, No. 380, November 30th, 1850, Grey to MacDonald.
5. C.O. 386/53, Commissioners to Stephen, March 8th, 1847.

the *Growler* project, replacing them with entirely new ideas which he drew up himself without consulting MacDonald.

In place of the 'few subordinate Agents' which he was instructed to select for the Kroo Coast only, he appointed as many as 28 sub-agents and one senior sub-agent for the Kroo Coast, and a further 15 sub-agents for Sierra Leone.

He also assigned to each of these agents a fixed salary of $10 per month, and additional 'head-money' of a half-dollar per emigrant, thus reinstating a measure that had earlier been criticised in Sierra Leone and discarded as a source of evil within the Colony. He also appointed a Maroon, Libert, as a senior sub-agent on a salary of £60 per annum in addition to the allowances of a half-dollar head-money, with a promise to increase this salary to £100 per annum if he worked hard! On the Kroo Coast, local chiefs became his emigration agents and they were authorized to explain to the natives that H.M.S. *Growler* 'is one of Her Majesty's vessels of war'.[1]

The sub-agents were told by Hook to keep in close touch with British cruisers and supply the latter with regular information about where they might effect captures on the coast. Hook tried to depart from his original instructions in other directions. He recommended for the Commissioners' consideration an extension of the emigration boundaries from Governor MacDonald's limit of 25 square miles on the Kroo Coast to a limit of 150 square miles; the bringing of all captured slaves from St Helena to Sierra Leone; and, finally, the detention of all liberated Africans in the Queen's Yard until they were afforded an opportunity to emigrate:

> This detention and the strict separation of newly arrived Africans from the residents in the Colony, are absolutely necessary for procuring emigrants from Sierra Leone; the younger Africans should be peremptorily sent to the West Indies, and none should quit the Yard till they have an opportunity of going; the Emigration Agent should be empowered to engage shipping for their transport, giving a bounty of £10.[2]

None of the original instructions from the Commissioners had made any such stipulations. On reading Hook's alterations, the Com-

1. C.O. 387/53, March 8th, 1847, *Instructions to Government Emigration Agent.* Again, this is another example of the dubious or ambiguous instructions by the Commissioners. Was the information of the *Growler* being a vessel of war meant to restore confidence among the natives, or to terrify them into emigrating?
2. C.O. 386/53, July 6th, September 14th, 1847 and C.O. 386/54, January 28th, 1848.

missioners first commented he should have sent them through the
Governor rather than directly; but their general reaction to these
changes speaks for itself:

> We will merely add that it appears to us a subject of satisfaction that
> the new agent should enter on his duties with zeal, and we hope that he
> may receive from the Governor every assistance which it may be in his
> power properly to afford.[1]

MacDonald was not to be so lightly thrust aside. He at once
weighed in with formidable objections showing how widely the
Hook plan departed from the official instructions and regulations
drawn up by the Colonial Office with the Commissioners themselves.
The number of sub-agents appointed by Hook was unwieldy, while
the payment of head-money constituted a violation of previous regulations at Sierra Leone and encouraged kidnapping and other illegal
means of obtaining emigrants. The employment of the agency of
African Chiefs on the Kroo Coast, the establishment of as many as
twenty Depot stations in areas outside British jurisdiction where the
slave trade still existed, the idea of indefinite detention of Africans in
the Queen's Yard and of separating them from their kith and kin in
the Colony until they agreed to emigrate, the immediate and compulsory embarkation of the younger ones among them—all these
were, in the Governor's own words, a 'pernicious mistake' on Hook's
part.[2] With his strong support of the original instructions Mac-
Donald felt almost too certain that Hook's violation of them would be
severely reprimanded, especially in the face of these serious objections. The Commissioners, however, turned upon the Governor:

> We regret to perceive that the Governor considers Mr. Hook as unfit
> for the appointment which he holds, and has disallowed every part of
> Mr. Hook's proposals.[3]

Not that MacDonald was wrong in his objections; the Commissioners admitted this, and even disallowed the idea of cooperation
between emigration agents and British cruisers which Hook had
recommended. The transfer of captured slaves from St Helena to
Sierra Leone was a matter for the Royal Navy and so outside the
power of the Commissioners and the Colonial Office. Beyond these

---

1. C.O. 386/53, July 6th, 1847, Commissioners to Stephen (C.O.); but see the
   original Instructions drawn up by the Commissioners, March 8th, March
   12th, April 26th, 1847.
2. C.O. 386/53, September 14th, 1847, same to same.
3. *Ibid.*

limits, the latter were not prepared to reject Hook's scheme, or entertain any criticism of it. Therefore, 'while the Governor of the Colony is at issue with the Government Agent on almost every point', the Commissioners would 'rely principally upon the judgment of the Agent immediately responsible' for the success of the new project.

Hook's scheme was finally approved,

> with an intimation, however, that he will be considered as strictly responsible for the good working of the scheme, in reliance on his discretion.[1]

To avoid 'the great embarrassments which might arise from the want of cordiality between the Governor and Mr. Hook', Lord Grey was prevailed upon not merely to reprimand the Governor, but to warn him to consider himself as little called upon to interfere with Hook's proceedings as could be done consistently with Colonial usage, bearing in mind that Hook was the Agent not of the Colony of Sierra Leone but of the West Indies, spending the West Indian revenue upon a service which was of great interest to the British Government.[2] When Grey at last wrote to MacDonald, it was not merely a warning, but a clear threat to relieve him of his appointment if he showed any further hostility to the scheme.[3] Thus MacDonald, at least for the moment, was cowed. For the *Growler* scheme, however, opposition and conflict had only just begun.

The Admiralty, owners of the *Growler*, became the stumbling block. Arrangements had dragged on between the Commissioners and the Colonial Office on the one hand, and the Admiralty on the other, since January 1847. In March the Admiralty was still sticking to its terms: the steamer could not be fitted out until the Admiralty was satisfied as to the adequacy of the regulations with which it was proposed to employ the *Growler* for the emigration scheme.[4] The issue of sufficient clothing, food rations, provision of medicines, and adequate supply of water—all the regulations which had practically been forgotten since 1844—now came up before the Emigration Commissioners for immediate revival. In addition, the Admiralty required at least 700 suits of clothing for the emigrants to be put on

---

1. *Ibid.*   2. *Ibid.*
3. C.O. 268/43, No. 353, September 7th, 1850, Grey to MacDonald.
4. C.O. 318/166, October 15th, 1846, Minutes by Lord Grey; C.O. 386/53, March 8th, 1847, Commissioners to Stephen (C.O.).

board the *Growler*, as well as at least 6,300 gallons of water, exclusive of that required for the crew.

The Commissioners quickly agreed to make all these provisions.[1] By May the Admiralty was demanding the provision of 'mess utensils for the emigrants on board the *Growler*'. The Commissioners excused themselves by reporting that they had written to Lieutenant Lean, one of the masters of the emigration vessels, 'to hasten the shipment of those articles';[2] then came another demand that all the 700 sets of clothes must be marked and badges provided for each African emigrant. The Commissioners demurred: 'As the badges may not be ready in time to admit of unpacking and affixing the numbers to the clothing previous to the sailing of that vessel', they proposed to send the badges out later as they could readily be fixed upon the garments at the port where the emigrants were to be embarked. They prevailed on the Colonial Office to persuade the Admiralty to assent to this suggestion.[3]

Yet the steamer could not proceed. The Admiralty desired also to see the substance of any instructions which the Emigration authorities or the Colonial Office might address to the Naval Commander and Surgeon of the *Growler*. Of the 12 point official Instructions to the Commander, and the 10 point official Instructions to the Surgeon, Nos. 1 and 2 of the Commander's instructions are noteworthy for a full understanding of the subsequent difficulties and conflicts that arose between the Chief Government Agent and the officers of the Navy:

> Instruction I stated: 'The Commander will see that the embarkation and disembarkation of the Passengers is effected in the manner best adapted for their safety and convenience.'
>
> Instruction II stated: 'No Passenger is to be received on board unless with the knowledge and approval of the Commander; nor is he to allow any passengers to be received except such as are duly reported to him for the purpose by the Emigration Agents. The Surgeon should inspect the emigrants as early as possible to ascertain that they are in good bodily health and fit for the voyage.'[4]

As we shall see, strict obedience to these rules by the Navy officers

---

1. C.O. 386/53, March 12th, 1847, Commissioners to Stephen (C.O.).
2. *Ibid.*, Commissioners to Stephen (C.O.) May 17th, 1847.
3. C.O. 386/53, same to same (C.O.) May 17th, 1847.
4. C.O. 386/53, April 26th, 1847, Nos. 1 and 2 of the *Official Instructions to the Commander of the* Growler.

was to interfere seriously with Hook's personal discretion in the running of the scheme; while more serious complications arose through the Commissioners' effort to enable the Chief Agent to exercise full authority, or have his way with the Naval commanders of emigration transports.

The Admiralty 'released the *Growler*, and when at last the vessel left for West Africa it was a virtually powerless Governor Mac-Donald and a triumphant Hook who welcomed it in Sierra Leone. It had not been necessary for the vessel to proceed as far as the Kroo Coast in order to open up the road for private vessels, for on Hook's orders the liberated Africans in the Queen's Yard were promptly embarked, the *Growler* departing immediately with its full complement of 476 emigrants for British Guiana. On this first venture 66 of them died.[1]

In the interval between the *Growler*'s first voyage and its return to the Kroo Coast the incident of the *Prince Regent* occurred. This incident is significant in illustrating the effects of the tardiness and protracted arrangements in fitting out the *Growler*. Apart from illustrating the impatience of the West India Committee, it explains the Admiralty's further hostility to the emigration scheme and also throws more light on the shifty policy of the Emigration Commissioners themselves. By May 1847 private vessels in advance of the *Growler* had proceeded to open up the Kroo Coast emigration contrary to the official arrangement. The Colonial Office and the Emigration Commissioners acquiesced in an embarrassed silence, even rejoicing that the *Prince Regent* had succeeded in obtaining some 108 passengers from the Kroo Coast. It was taken as a sure sign that the *Growler* scheme would prove successful on that Coast. On June 22nd, the Commissioners Communicated to Captain Pothury, Commander of the *Growler*, the knowledge of 'this promising commencement on the Kroo Coast' which the *Prince Regent* had achieved.[2]

By July 2nd, however, a query came from the Admiralty Office about the *Prince Regent*, asking whether it was part of the new arrangement that private merchant ships should proceed to the Kroo Coast in advance of the *Growler* and, as before, without proper regulations. The Admiralty warned that

---

1. PP. 1847–8, XXIII, 1, 829–30, Light to Grey, No. 158, May 13th, 1847.
2. C.O. 386/53, Commissioners to Stephen, June 22nd, 1847; C.O. 318/171, same to same, March 30th and June 22nd, 1847, on the departure and success of the *Prince Regent*.

If vessels without licence or permission proceed to remove emigrants from parts of the Coast of Africa out of the British Dominion it might expose the Government and might also raise very inconvenient questions if those vessels were seized by foreign cruisers.

The Commissioners immediately denied any knowledge of the *Prince Regent*; but agreed with the Admiralty that the vessel's proceedings had been 'a great irregularity'.[1] The Admiralty demanded that the *Prince Regent* be penalised and other private vessels debarred from coming up to the Kroo Coast without proper regulations and equipment.

When the Master of the *Prince Regent* arrived in British Guiana the Governor refused to pay him any bounty, on the grounds that private vessels had been banned since December 1846 from introducing any immigrants until the new *Growler* scheme had been put into operation on the Kroo Coast. The Master immediately petitioned the Colonial Office demanding full payment of his bounty.[2] A despatch was promptly addressed to the Governor of British Guiana criticising his refusal to pay bounty to the Master of the ship: .

Although the proceeding has been irregular, and the Governor will act rightly in refusing Bounty, I think it might convey some appearance of inconsistency if the occurrence [of the *Prince Regent*] should be noticed in any very strong terms of condemnation.

The Governor, the despatch continued, ought to have realised that

the only object of employing the Steamer [*Growler*] is to open the way for a large conveyance of emigrants by private vessels if the experiment prove successful; no one supposes that steamers of war could carry all the emigrants which it would be desirable that the West Indies might receive from the Coast of Africa; the only object of their employment is to inspire confidence and make a beginning.[3]

The Governor quickly paid the bounty.

Clearly the Admiralty's demands had not been met, and they could stop private vessels from recruitments on the Coast if they .desired to be so strict.

The knowledge that the Captain of the *Prince Regent* had not been

1. C.O. 386/53, July 6th, 1847, same to same reporting on the Admiralty's query.
2. C.O. 386/53, July 2nd, 1847, same to same.
3. C.O. 386/53, July 2nd and July 17th, 1847, same to same.

penalised obliged the Admiralty to press the Commissioners again. The latter turned on the Governor of British Guiana, after having forced him to pay the Captain, to criticise him:

> In granting bounty in the present instance, the Governor would ap-
> pear therefore to have exceeded his power under the existing arrange-
> ment.[1]

Official inconsistency in the case of the *Prince Regent* became un- fortunately typical of the whole *Growler* project. The Navy Officers remained 'unco-operative'. For the rest of that year, after the incident of the *Prince Regent*, no more private vessels were seen on the Kroo Coast: firstly, because by August even the *Growler* was finding it difficult to obtain its full complement of emigrants:

> Hook mentions that each Chief whom he saw on the Kroo Coast
> mentioned that he did not think the Natives would emigrate, until they
> had seen some of their countrymen return by the *Growler*.[2]

But if Government vessels failed to procure emigrants, private enterprise might do good business. This was true in 1844–6; it was also the plan meant to be adopted in the *Growler* scheme. In fact, following the 'promising opening' made by the *Prince Regent*, more private vessels had taken out licences from the Commissioners, who gave permission, subject to the vessels agreeing to go at their 'own risk', to proceed without Government Naval officers, surgeons, or other restrictive elements on board their vessels. Yet none of the licensed vessels[3] went to the Kroo Coast while H.M.S. *Growler* remained in the emigration service.

It was the Admiralty's manifest hostility to private vessels going outside British dominions that became the real scare that drove private merchants from the Kroo Coast after the *Prince Regent*'s en- couraging recruitment on that coast. Thus, in 1847–8, private ships were forced to return to Sierra Leone with fresh vigour to recruit

---

1. C.O. 386/53, July 17th, 1847, Commissioners to C.O.
2. C.O. 386/54, October 27th, 1847, same to same (B. Hawes).
3. C.O. 386/54, November 19th, 1847, arrangement concluded with the owner of the *Superior*; C.O. 386/54, December 30th, 1847, similar arrangements concluded with the *Una*, *Arabian* and *Helena*. By agreeing to go at their own risk private merchants denied themselves Government guarantee to pay a certain fixed amount of bounty as an insurance if they failed to procure any emigrants. But under this sort of arrangement the Government imposed no restrictions on them and placed no Government officers or Surgeons on board their ships, thus saving about £500–£750 on each unguaranteed voyage.

emigrants. Two major difficulties now awaited the whole *Growler* emigration scheme; at the Kroo Coast, outside British dominion, hostile and 'obstructionist' Naval Officers on board the *Growler*; within the Colony of Sierra Leone, a commandeering and over-zealous chief agent Hook, with an 'uncooperative' Governor MacDonald; then the problem of stiff competition among private emigration vessels at Sierra Leone.

Unstable policy started the actual trouble. The official instructions to sub-agents had authorized them to promise, on behalf of the Government, a free return passage to all Kroomen after five years residence in the West Indies.[1] But by 1848 Earl Grey had the Agents on the Kroo Coast announce that, like all liberated Africans from Sierra Leone, Kroomen emigrating to the West Indies could no longer expect a free return passage. At the same time they were to be subjected, like liberated Africans, to compulsory tax and indentured labour.[2] Kroomen refused to emigrate under those conditions.

Another cause of the failure of the *Growler* scheme on the Kroo Coast sprang from the conflicts and quarrels among the officials concerned. Already by the end of the first voyage of the *Growler*, Hook was involved in bitter dispute not only with Governor MacDonald in Sierra Leone, but also with the Navy Officers of the *Growler* on the Kroo Coast. The West India Committee cared little who was right or wrong in the disputes between Hook, Governor MacDonald and the Navy, but descended upon the Emigration Commissioners who had tried to mediate. The Committee alleged that MacDonald was being tolerated in checking Hook's plan of compulsory and im-mediate embarkation of emigrants from Sierra Leone, while at the Kroo Coast private vessels were being prevented by the obstructive Navy. 'Extreme regret and disappointment has been expressed by Gentlemen interested in the West Indies,' complained Macgregor, Secretary of the West India Committee, writing to the Emigration Commissioners on the need to detain the liberated Africans in the Yard.[3] A month's detention was not enough; the liberated Africans should be detained indefinitely until a vessel was available to remove them. The Committee was siding with Hook only and demanded

---

1. C.O. 386/53, Instructions to the Chief Government Emigration Agent, March 8th, 1847.
2. C.O. 268/43, No. 244, December 19th, 1848, Grey to Pine; C.O. 268/43, No. 451, May 30th, 1848, same to same.
3. C.O. 386/54, October 27th, 1847, Commissioners to C.O.

that the Commissioners should remove every impediment from Mac-Donald or the Navy. The Commissioners first apologised,

> We never meant that the people might not be detained beyond one month; [because compulsory embarkation] is the course pursued by the Government in respect of liberated Africans landed at all other stations except Sierra Leone. But whether that place has such recommendations as to require that it should be an exception from the rule, is one of such magnitude that it is not for us to do more than point out as raised for consideration of higher authority.[1]

Having thus explained to the West India Committee, the Commissioners then returned to the attack:

> The fact however unwelcome it may be appears to be that the liberated Africans cannot be reckoned upon to emigrate spontaneously, in any large numbers from Sierra Leone to the West Indies. We sincerely regret this. But it is in vain for the West India Committee to suppose that anybody who testifies to this truth and difficulty—confirmed as it is by the result of a variety of experiments—must necessarily be biased or hostile. There appears nothing incredible in the fact that poor and uninstructed Africans, very recently liberated from extreme ill-usage by Europeans, should not be influenced by any nice calculations of a difference in the value of wages at Sierra Leone and in the West Indies; that if they find themselves able to subsist in the place where they are they should feel no inclination spontaneously to try the sea again under the care of White men.[2]

There were still the difficulties with the Navy regarding the Kroo Coast emigration. The Commissioners now returned to settle them. The case, briefly stated, was that Hook tried to 'impose' on Captain Pothury at the Kroo Coast, as he had done upon Governor MacDonald in Sierra Leone. He attempted to extend the Kroo Coast recruitment to an area 150 miles square, but Pothury in obedience to his instructions pinned him down to within 25 square miles, the area officially allowed by Governor MacDonald. The second Hook-Pothury clash occurred in the West Indies. In British Guiana Hook and Governor Light tried to fulfil the promise made to Kroo Chiefs about returning Kroomen who had earlier emigrated. But while many Kroos applied to return by the *Growler*, the Governor and Hook contrived to select and send back only those who could give

---

1. C.O. 386/54, October 19th, 1847, Emigration Commissioners through C.O. to West India Committee.
2. C.O. 386/54, October 18th, 1847, Emigration Commissioners through C.O. to West India Committee.

good reports about British Guiana. Pothury objected to the selective method and thought the *Growler* was being delayed unnecessarily by the details of selection. He revenged himself by returning to West Africa under sail alone, even with the wind against the steamer all the way.[1] On returning he reported Hook's proceedings to the Admiralty. The latter immediately wrote, criticising Hook and demanding explanations from the Commissioners about Hook's instructions. Pothury, the Commissioners replied, was blameworthy for 'unreasonable impatience', and for obstructing the selection of Kroomen returning as delegates from British Guiana:

> To collect and send back delegates is a proceeding which in the opinion of the Governors and also of all practical persons who have attended to this subject is considered of critical importance to the success of the service in which Commander Pothury is employed; the detention of the vessel a few days for this important object would have constituted no reasonable ground of complaint.[2]

If Pothury had appeared too strict, perhaps rigid, in observing his instructions as Commander of the *Growler*, Hook himself lacked that trained temper and tact which the superintendence of a very delicate scheme really required. One of the causes of the many difficulties and conflicts that occurred before the *Growler* was eventually withdrawn from the service, must be the Commissioners' belated discovery of the Chief Agent's quarrelsome temper and haughty disposition towards his co-officers in that service.

During the *Growler*'s second voyage, when that vessel again obtained its full complement from the Queen's Yard to Trinidad, Hook was once more complaining that the Commander had expressed an intention to interfere in the selection of the emigrants. Like MacDonald, Pothury had insisted on a strict observance of the official regulations and had maintained that all intending emigrants must, prior to their embarkation, be medically examined as well as vaccinated; he tried to resist or obstruct the embarkation of any liberated Africans from the Yard who appeared to him to be either unwilling to emigrate, or otherwise unfit to be embarked. Pothury's refusal to have any further dealings with Hook at Sierra Leone, except through the Governor, made matters even worse. Hook at last exploded and wrote a highly insulting letter to the Captain. It reads, in part:

---

1. C.O. 386/54, October 27th, 1847, same to same.
2. C.O. 386/54, October 8th, 1847, Commissioners through the C.O. to the Admiralty.

I have to express my regret and astonishment at such an assumption on your part. The gallant Commander commanding Her Majesty's Squadron on the Coast might with propriety assume such consequence, and, when requisite call upon the Government Chief Emigration Agent to address him through a *third* party; but for Commander Pothury, commanding Her Majesty's Steamer *Growler*, especially employed as a transport to convey volunteer emigrants from Africa to the West Indies, to assume an authority to which he has no right whatever, is highly inconvenient, and *seriously* injurious to the service in which he is engaged, and I believe, commanded to *promote* to the utmost of his power.[1]

By sheer defiance of the Captain he had managed, for his second voyage, to recruit some 445 more from the Yard, 46 of whom died before reaching Trinidad, while 34 others were rushed to hospital immediately on landing.[2] There was no query to the Chief Agent.

Hook continued to enjoy full official support against all other parties. As Her Majesty's Arbitrator in the Mixed Court at Sierra Leone, he appeared to be the only officer who had a real knowledge of the subject and whose energy and enthusiasm for the business might enable the Commissioners to escape the fury of West Indian indignation. They were determined to defend him not only against MacDonald but against the Admiralty Officer as well. So, since there already existed serious apprehension of failure owing to the dislike entertained for this service by the Navy',[3] it became the next task of the Commissioners to make the task more palatable to the Navy in order to smooth Hook's path: 'If a liberal allowance were made to the officers', the Commissioners confided to Grey, 'a more cheerful spirit might arise.'

Naval Officers on board emigrant vessels were thus to receive an extra gratuity of £150 in addition to their half-pay,[4] as a reward for full cooperation with the Chief Emigration Agent on the Coast.

To ensure that this cooperation was fully effective it was necessary to revise the official instructions issued to Naval Officers in April

---

1. C.O. 386/54, Hook to Pothury, enclosures in Governor MacDonald's despatches Nos. 128, 129, 131 and 133, November 3rd to 13th, 1847, and Emigration Commissioners to C.O., January 28th, 1848.
2. PP. 1947–8, XLIV, 586–7, Harris to Grey, No. 103, December 8th, 1847.
3. C.O. 386/54, October 27th, November 30th, 1847, Emigration Commissioners to C.O.
4. *Ibid.*

1847. Clauses 1, 2, 3 and 7, both of the former[1] and of the new[2] instructions, are the most relevant here. In clause one, formerly, the Naval Officer was responsible for seeing that the embarkation and disembarkation of the passengers was effected in the manner best adapted to their safety and convenience; the corresponding clause in the new instructions merely required the officer to 'wear the uniform established for his rank agreeably to the practice of Her Majesty's Navy'. Clause two of the former instructions placed the whole responsibility on him of seeing to the free agency of prospective emigrants: 'no passenger is to be received on board unless with the knowledge and approval of the Commander'. The corresponding clause in the revised instructions merely required him to inform the officers of any foreign cruisers that might be met on the West Coast that the emigration transport was 'proceeding with the sanction and authority of Her Majesty's Government'.

In the former instructions, clause three placed on the officer the duties of berthing and of dividing the emigrants into proper messes. His duty in the new clause required that on the Kroo Coast, but only if the Chief Agent was not present, the Naval Officer was to 'make himself sufficiently acquainted with the proceedings'; in Sierra Leone he was clearly to understand he was 'not to be held in any way responsible for the selection of the emigrants to be put on board'. The 7th clause of the revised instructions was practically a re-emphasis of where authority now resided. Whereas the 7th Instruction previously held him responsible for the general management and preservation of cleanliness in his ship, the Naval Officer, by the corresponding clause in the present instructions 'is in no way to interfere in the management or navigation of the ship'.[3] With all the power thus transferred to Hook, to recruit and embark emigrants where and how he pleased, the stage was now well set for the real *Growler* crisis.

Hook took the *Growler* to the Kroo Coast and then went off in her to British Guiana in defiance of Governor MacDonald's instructions to return to Sierra Leone after supervising the recruitment of passengers in the vessel. Once arrived, he sucessfully embroiled

---

1. C.O. 386/53, April 26th, 1847, Elliot and Rogers to Stephen: *Instructions to the Commander of the* Growler; C.O. 386/53, March 8th, 1847, same to same: *Instructions to the Chief Emigration Agent for the West India Colonies.*
2. C.O. 386/54, November 30th, 1847, same to B. Hawes (C.O.): Heads of *Instructions for the Naval Officer on board the African Emigrant Transport.*
3. C.O. 386/54, October 27th, 1847, Revised Instructions, 7th clause.

Governor Light and MacDonald over the question of emigration boundaries on the Kroo Coast:

> Mr. Hook considers that the whole of the Kroo Coast (Light complained to Grey) an extent of 150 miles should be included in the scheme of emigration. It appears that Governor MacDonald is disposed to limit it to a distance of 25 miles; but on this I do not presume to give an opinion.[1]

The Chief Agent next moved to Trinidad and there set Lord Harris, Governor of Trinidad, at odds with MacDonald over the question of returning delegates. MacDonald, it appeared, still remembered the old idea of a 'toll-free' Afro-West Indian bridge which, as Laird had earlier promised, 'shall be free for every negro to traverse'. But while MacDonald insisted that no African labourer in the West Indies should be hindered who wished freely to return to Sierra Leone, Lord Harris regarded his colleague's idea as 'useless if not mischevious', maintaining on his part that the return of delegates should be regulated, as Hook had suggested, on a strictly selective basis. Like Governor Light, Harris also complained to the Colonial Office of MacDonald's activities.[2]

With such ample evidence flowing in from all corners of MacDonald's hostility towards the emigration scheme, Hook's triumph seemed complete when the Emigration Commissioners pronounced their verdict against his foe:

> With regard to the propriety of offering a free passage to Sierra Leone to such Negroes as may wish to return to Africa in the capacity of delegates or otherwise, Governor MacDonald especially recommends that all persons who are disappointed with the West Indies should be sent back to Africa. Lord Harris on the contrary thinks the sending of Delegates useless if not mischievous; we should ourselves be inclined to think that a few carefully selected delegates would probably be useful in dispelling prejudice among their country-men. But we should most urgently deprecate the adoption of a proposal so much calculated to destroy all hopes of a voluntary emigration as that of offering a free passage to Africa at the public expense to all persons disappointed with the West Indies. And we are very much surprised that this recommendation should be made by Governor MacDonald. The report of one dissatisfied person will do more to stop the scheme of emigration

1. *Ibid.*, Light to Grey.
2. C.O. 386/54, October 27th, 1847, Commissioners to C.O. reporting on Lord Harris's views.

than the reports of ten others to encourage it. We concur with Lord Harris in thinking that those persons should be sent back by preference who could give a good report of the Colony.[1]

This verdict was clearly at variance with the Commissioners' own instruction earlier in 1847, when it had been expressly laid down that:

> The different Agents will inform all emigrants from the Coast of Africa, whether from Sierra Leone or elsewhere, that they will be entitled to demand a free passage back after five years from their arrival.[2]

When the *Growler* scheme began in 1847, it had been found necessary to repeat this promise which was first made in 1843. By 1848, the fulfilment of it was being replaced instead by forced labour and compulsory taxation at Sierra Leone as well as in the West India Colonies, although many petitions poured in to the West India Governors from liberated Africans and others entitled to benefit under the promise.[3] When later some of these emigrants were permitted to return, it was only because of the reports from the Emigration Agents at the Kroo Coast and at Sierra Leone that the non-return of those people was 'presenting a great bar to emigration both from the Kroo Coast and from the African Yard'. The Governor of Sierra Leone was then authorized 'to assure the Chiefs of the Akoos at Sierra Leone that the stipulation of furnishing a return passage after five years shall be adhered to'.[4] In spite of these reassurances, it was still the Commissioners' decision and the Hook plan of careful selection that operated for a very long time.

Despite continued official support for Hook, his personal wrangling brought about his downfall. He was foolish enough to pursue

---

1. C.O. 386/54, January 28th, 1848, Commissioners to C.O., communicating to the Colonial Office their verdict on the returning of Emigrants or Delegates.
2. C.O. 386/53, March 8th, 1847, *Instructions to the Chief Emigration Agent for the West India Colonies.*
3. C.O. 386/55 June 19th and September 26th, 1848. See the Commissioners' observations on the Petitions and Memorials of certain liberated African emigrants demanding their free passage back, without sucess: 'The appearance of bad faith in furnishing them return passages may materially weaken the emigrants' confidence in the Government and to the same extent injure the prospects of future emigration.'
   Jamaica had refused the grant of return passages by the Jamaica Act No. 3784 of 1847; British Guiana by Ordinance No. 3 of 1848; and Trinidad by Ordinance No. 9 of 1847; and all were approved by the Colonial Office.
4. C.O. 386/55, Commissioners to Merivale (C.O.) November 17th, 1848.

his quarrel with Pothury to the extent of instituting an action against him in the Sierra Leone Courts. At the same time he published, without MacDonald's permission, a public notice concerning emigration. MacDonald, who had doubtless been biding his time, now struck. He at once dismissed Hook as Chief Agent and replaced him by Fisher.

The Commissioners immediately went to the rescue of their man. Even before going into the details of the affair, they maintained that no fault on the part of Hook should have warranted or 'required the extreme measure of immediate suspension to which the Governor has proceeded'. They persuaded Grey that Hook and MacDonald should each state his case.[1] By February MacDonald had sent in a marathon despatch, covering both the Hook *versus* Pothury and the Hook *versus* MacDonald conflicts.[2] It forced the Commissioners to reverse their judgement and opinion of the Chief Agent.

In the court case instituted by him in Sierra Leone against Pothury 'the decision of the Magistrates appears satisfactorily to show that these complaints were groundless, and that Mr. Hook had acted injudiciously and vexatiously towards Captain Pothury in bringing them forward'; and his addressing an insulting letter to the Naval Officer 'is the least capable of being excused or explained'.[3] Also in publishing an emigration notice without MacDonald's permission, Hook had 'acted irregularly' and had 'aggravated his negligence in giving currency to an exaggerated and inaccurate statement, by which the good faith and candour of the Government might have been compromised'.[4] The Commissioners now had to acknowledge that they had mistaken their man:

> Mr. Hook does not possess the temper or discretion which is necessary for carrying on the difficult service with which he is charged.[5]

It was a belated discovery.

MacDonald's appointment of Fisher as the next Chief Agent at Sierra Leone was confirmed, with the Commissioners hardly concealing their discomfort at Hook's dismissal. Hook received a

---

1. C.O. 386/54, January 28th, 1848, Commissioners to Grey (C.O.).
2. C.O. 386/54, February 29th, 1848, Commissioners to Grey and enclosures Nos. 128, 129, 131 and 132.
3. *Ibid.*, Commissioners to Merivale (C.O.).
4. *Ibid.*, same to same.
5. *Ibid.*, same to same.

quarter's salary of £75 and another significant sum of £99 3s. 4d. as 'head money' on 476 emigrants last forwarded by him, and was gone.

Yet enough of Hook's ideas remained to exercise a powerful shaping influence on the emigration scheme. The Commissioners' fresh plans for emigration in 1848 centred mainly on the return of delegates on a selective basis, on indefinite and compulsory detention of liberated Africans in Sierra Leone until they agreed to emigrate to the West Indies. MacDonald on hearing this promptly denounced the 'double illegality of compulsory detention and compulsory embarkation of Africans'. 'This emigration', he now suggested, 'can only be conducted properly in or under the convoy of a man-of-war'.[1]

1848–9 was one of the peak years of African emigration. Before discussing its leading events and the reasons why Hook's ideas triumphed over MacDonald's, it is necessary to glance at the Anglo-West Indian relationships. They were far from cordial. Despite the *Growler* emigration scheme since 1847, the West India economy was still tottering on the brink of ruin, thanks mainly to the Imperial Sugar duties in 1846. The cost of producing a hundredweight of sugar had been calculated at $4 to $5; the average selling price in the latter half of 1847 was $2·50 as against $3·83 in 1846.[2] Forty-eight English estates had calculated their liablities at £6,300 in 1847 as a result of the sugar duties in 1846.[3]

Fearful lest the ruin of the planters might come to discredit emancipation and the whole anti-slavery cause, public opinion, even anti-slavery sentiment, had begun to turn in genuine sympathy to planters. The Glasgow Emancipation Society could write to Grey in May 1847 pleading the planters' cause; anything that African emigration could offer ought to be exploited to rescue the suffering planters. By 1848 Grey was being besieged with petitions from all sections for more vigorous action on emigration.[4]

An angry West India Committee informed Grey, late in 1847, that 'disastrous consequences for the negroes as well as for the planters'

1. *Ibid.*
2. PP. 1847–8, XLV, 217, 275–6, Harris to Grey, Nos. 27, 31, March 23rd, April 5th, 1848; PP. 1952–3, LXVII, 400, Harris to Grey, No. 69, September 6th, 1849; PP. 1847–8, XXIII–i, 839, Light to Grey, No. 7, January 10th, 1848.
3. Cumpston, I. M., *Indians Overseas* (London, 1953) pp. 127–8. Laurence, *op. cit.*, p. 209.
4. C.O. 318/173, Glasgow Emancipation Society to Grey, May 12th, 1847; PP. 1847–8, XLIV, 560–525, Harris to Grey, No. 81, September 18th, 1847, No. 14, February 2nd, 1848.

would follow, if the Imperial Government failed seriously to tackle the problem of high production costs of sugar by stepping up African emigration.[1]

We have already discussed how the *Growler* scheme, the direct response of the British Government to earlier threats, was ruined by the wrangling and persistent conflicts between the officers charged with responsibility for that project. By 1848 the West India interests were again using the language of threat to the Imperial Government and made a near impossible demand—a return to colonial protection!

The Government had however, in 1846, taken an irrevocable step. Grey, while warning that 'the Imperial Government would not again be coerced into acting against their own deliberate judgement or at the expense of the common good of the empire at large', was, nevertheless, fully prepared to consider how to obtain more labour for the planters.[2]

In fact, West Indian animosity towards the Imperial Government in 1848 attained the same height of defiance as it had in 1838. The Select Committee on Sugar[3] met in 1848 to give full consideration to these economic problems. Among the major charges against the Government was 'the imposition of vexatious restrictions as to immigration'.[4]

In default of a return to sugar protection, the Imperial Government adopted a conciliatory attitude all along the line. In addition to continuing African emigration, Asiatic emigration from India and China was to be stepped up as well; a generous loan of £500,000 was immediately offered to cover the costs of importation.

Yet it took more than another year before the big colonies sulkily agreed to avail themselves of the loan.[5] It ought to be pointed out at

---

1. C.O. 318/173, Macgregor (W.I.C.) to Grey, September 14th, 1847; C.O. 318/173, Cave (W.I.C.) to Grey, October 26th, 1847.
2. PP. 1847–8, XLVI, 636, Grey to Harris, Nos. 239 and 243, May 23rd and 30th, 1848; PP. 1847–8, XXIII–iii, 261, Light to Grey, No. 25, February 11th, 1848; PP. 1847–8, XLV, 236–7, 239, same to same; Nos. 41 and 49, March 6th and 18th, 1848; PP. 1950, XXXIX, 253–4, Barkly to Grey, No. 177, December 5th, 1849; PP. 1847–8, XLVI, 605, No. 1, Grey to Barkly, June 17th, 1848.
3. PP. 1847–8, XXIII–iii, 416–18, 453–9, *Report of Select Committee on Sugar and Coffee Planting*, May 29th, 1848 (Lord George Bentinck, Chairman).
4. C.O. 318/179, *Memoranda on the Charges brought against the Home Government by Witnesses before the Recent Committee on Sugar Duties* (1848).
5. C.O. 386/57, Commissioners to Merivale, November 20th, 1849: The loan was made available on September 15th, 1848, the colonies sulkily accepting it a year later, see PP. 1850, XXXIX, 136, 150, 209, Nos. 111, 119, 141, July 18th, August 3rd and September 19th, 1849, Barkly to Grey.

this juncture that the idea of Asiatic immigration—with Chinese and Indian 'coolies' remaining more costly to introduce, more difficult to manage on the Estates, more prone to drunkenness, idleness, vagabondage and ill-health[1]—never really appealed to the West India planters as much as did the liberated African emigration scheme. After 1847 liberated Africans no longer involved the obligatory expense of a return passage and 'in the West Indies liberated Africans are preferred to every other class of similar immigrants'.[2] Whilst it cost on an average $35 or about £7 to import a liberated African labourer, the cost of each effective coolie was calculated at £54 in five years, after allowing for the cost of their return passage.[3] For this and other reasons official opinion even in the Colonial Office was not favourable to coolie emigration: 'There are peculiar difficulties in keeping them in the labour market or turning them to good account', Henry Taylor at the Colonial Office told Elliot of the Emigration Commission; and the latter agreed. The Emigration Commissioners recommended in 1848 that rather than allow long coolie contracts, it was better to abandon Indian emigration entirely.[4]

From the West Indies Governor Light informed Grey that the planters continued to apply for coolies and Portuguese labourers only because enough African labourers had not been forthcoming.[5] Trinidad appeared even more hostile towards 'so costly and unsatisfactory an enterprise' as Asiatic immigration.[6] 'The colonies will

---

1. PP. 1847–8, XLIV, 527–8, No. 121, Harris to Grey, December 28th, 1846. 'After deducting the value of their labour at the average rate, there is a dead loss on every coolie—man, woman and child for this year 1846. I think it is time to pause, to look matters thoroughly in the face, and to have the affair rigorously investigated before larger debt is incurred.' Lord Harris proposed to concentrate on the much cheaper African immigration. See, for further complaints about poor quality of coolies, PP. 1847–8, XLVI, 629, Harris to Grey, May 10th, 1848, No. 45; PP. 1847, XXXIX, 218, No. 72, April 16th, 1847; PP. 1847–8, XLIV, 556, 560, Nos. 78 and 81, Harris to Grey, September 4th, 1847; PP. 1847–8, XLVI, 645, same to same, No. 71 and enclosures June 19th, 1848. See also the Report of Official Inquiry set up in 1847 by the British Guiana Government to investigate the quality, health and habits of the various racial groups of labourers—Africans, Coolies, Portuguese: PP. 1847–8, XXIII–iii, 246–9, No. 10, January 11th, 1848, *Dr Bonyun's Report on Hospitals and Immigrants, January 6th, 1848.*
2. C.O. 386/54, October 27th, 1847, Commissioners to C.O. (B. Hawes).
3. C.O. 318/182, November 16th, 1849, West India Committee to Commissioners (Elliot).
4. Laurence, *op. cit.*, p. 20.
5. PP. 1847–8, XXIII–iii, 247, Light to Grey, January 11th, 1848, No. 10.
6. *Port of Spain Gazette*, October 29th, 1847.

be no losers on financial grounds', Lord Grey concluded at the final decision to terminate or discourage further Indian coolie emigration.[1]

For similar reasons of cost the West India planters felt no great enthusiasm for Chinese labour immigration where the bounty rate remained high ($76 per head in 1843).[2] Although in 1846 the Emigration Commissioners had dismissed Chinese labour as of 'very doubtful expediency',[3] in 1848 the British Government again concluded arrangements with the Hong Kong Government to recruit labour.[4] Yet in general no planter agreed to import on the terms agreed unless the Imperial Government was prepared to bear the entire burden of paying $100 bounty on every Chinese imported. By 1855 complaints were constantly made about high passenger freight rates. Like the local recruiting agents in India, the Chinese 'crimps' or local recruiting officers availed themselves of every opportunity, not only of defrauding their fellow countrymen, but of cheating the planters for whom they did the recruiting.[5] Given such 'considerable expense and risk', Asiatic immigration never really appealed to the planters until the springs of Liberated African labour dried up entirely.

From 1848, after the *Growler* scheme, until about 1860, it was to African rather than Asiatic emigration that both the Imperial Government and her West Indian colonies chiefly turned with redoubled effort in order to solve West Indian economic ills.

In fact the official memoranda after the Select Committee's Report in 1848 lifted all blame from the sugar duties and held labour emigration responsible for the planters' difficulties:

> If the experiment of free labour has not been fairly tried in consequence of an insufficient supply of labourers, or of impediments offered to the effective use of their services, the Act of 1846 is so far exonerated from the charges made against it as the sole cause of the distress of the sugar planters. The supposed impediments to sufficient

---

1. PP. 1847–8, xlv, 278–9, No. 228, April 15th, 1848, Grey to Harris; PP. 1847–8, xxiii–iii, 255, No. 319, March 29th, 1848, Grey to Light.
2. C.O. 318/160, November 24th, 1843, West India Committee to Stephen and C.O. minute, Hope to Stanley, November 25th, 1843.
3. C.O. 318/167, November 28th, 1846, Emigration Commissioners to C.O.1; C.O. 318/171, November 20th, 1847, same to Merivale (C.O.).
4. C.O. 318/178, September 20th, 1848, Nixon to Grey; PP. 1851, xxxix, 387, No. 392, February 1st, 1850, Grey to Harris.
5. Campbell, P. C., *Chinese Coolie Emigration to Countries within the British Empire*, p. 95–103; PP. 1852–3, lxviii, 380, Bowring to Malmesbury, December 27th, 1852, *ibid.*, 436, same to same, January 5th, 1853.

immigration offered by the Government form a more important matter for investigation.[1]

Refusing the demand for protection the Imperial Government agreed to the planters' demand for a 'renewal of large scale immigration'.[2] Grey immediately directed that bounties should be paid on African immigrants only in view of 'the superior capabilities of the African labourer'.[3]

The *Growler* and its obstructionist Naval Officers had to be wound up at once. Its last voyage had ended in April 1848 with no less than 135 deaths out of 441 emigrants. As the Emigration Commissioners themselves observed in their report, another 168 were ill and could not be immediately engaged for labour, while yet another 28 were in hospital and were expected to die.[4]

'Consonant with precedent when private vessels used to go to Sierra Leone for emigrants', private vessels had begun to be sent out even before the *Growler*'s last voyage. The *Una*, *Amity Hall*, *Arabian*, *Helena*, *Superior* were all despatched without Government officers on board.[5] The Naval Officers were out of the show.

By June 1848 the results began to arrive: the *Helena* embarked 133 at Sierra Leone, emigrant mortality 12; the *Arabian* embarked 266, emigrant mortality 22; the *Amity Hall* got 277, number of deaths 37; the *Una* embarked 240, number of deaths 52. From St Helena other reports arrived. In the *Vanguard* only 18 died out of 216; in *King William* 18 out of 311; *Reliance* lost 20 out of 230; *Euphrates* 46 out of 309; and the *Rhyn* 54 out of 334 emigrants. There was real alarm everywhere. Official investigations were set on foot both by the West India Colonies and by the Emigration Commissioners, the latter collecting all these reports for a full study.

Their various reports concur for the most part in ascribing the sickness to the state of debility or incipient disease in which liberated Africans are shipped for the West Indies and which is traceable to the previous suffering on board the slavers from which they have been

---

1. C.O. 318/179, *Memoranda on the Charges brought against the Home Government by Witnesses before the Recent Committee on Sugar Duties.*
2. PP. 1850, XXXIX, 136, 150, 209, Barkly to Grey, Nos. 111, 119, 141, July 18th, August 3rd, September 19th, 1849.
3. Grey, cited Roberts, G. W., *Immigration into the British Caribbean*, p. 238; *Eighth General Report, 1848* (June), PP. 1847–8, XXVI, 21–2, 22–3, 245.
4. C.O. 386/54, April 19th, 1848, Commissioners to C.O.
5. C.O. 386/54, November 19th and December 30th, 1847, Commissioners to C.O.

taken; many of these Africans when taken on board were so weak that it was necessary to lift them over the bulwarks of the vessel, [and] some could hardly stand.

The absence of interpreters on board the vessels, inadequate diet, compulsory embarkation of children; in short, the total absence of 'proper vigilance . . . in excluding unhealthy emigrants', completed the tale.[1]

The new Chief Agent, Fisher, was asked to explain why emigrants were embarked in such a sickly state. 'The Africans were all that way in the Yard', he replied.[2] It began to occur to the Commissioners that the payment of 'head-money' to Emigration Agents, a practice which not only the Foreign Office but Governor MacDonald had opposed, might be 'operating as a temptation to the Emigration Agent to fill the ships without sufficient regard to the eligibility of the emigrants'.[3] The failure to provide adequate checks over the health of prospective emigrants was partially attributable to the head-money inducement offered. MacDonald's opposition to this evil was now seen as fully justified.

But the Commissioners were not prepared to give him the credit but instead charged him with responsibility for the absence of proper supervision! For the first time the Commissioners voiced complaints about 'underfeeding' of the occupants of the Queen's Yard at Sierra Leone and advised Grey to institute 'a strict inquiry into the mode in which these unfortunate people are treated in the Establishment'. MacDonald replied sarcastically, inquiring whether the Commissioners had forgotten to appoint Surgeons or Naval Officers on board their transport vessels, so that they should at least have discharged their duty by rejecting all 'underfed' and unhealthy emigrants—in case the Governor forced these on the private vessels!

These fresh wrangles continued between the Governor and the Commissioners until August, the latter still maintaining 'Mr. MacDonald's letter has not removed the unfavourable impression which we have been led to form respecting the state in which the emigrants are embarked at Sierra Leone'.[4]

Yet the Commissioners fully recognised that the emigrant mortality had been caused by other factors for which they themselves

---

1. C.O. 386/55, *Report on the Morality on Board the Emigration Transport Vessels*, 1848–9, April 27th, May 5th, June 13th, 1848.
2. C.O. 386/55, June 13th, 1848, Emigration Commissioners to C.O.
3. *Ibid.*
4. C.O. 386/55, August 17th, 1848, Commissioners to Grey.

were fully responsible. The whole trouble lay in the 'present mode of proceeding by which Surgeons are not engaged by us but selected by the owner of the vessel subject only to our approval'.[1] By September this confession was growing into real anxiety and the Commissioners now confided to Grey

> ... our anxiety that every vessel employed on this service should carry an officer selected by ourselves or by some Government authority exclusively responsible to us for the execution of his duties and charged with enforcing the performance of the stipulation of the Charter Party. This hitherto has not been the case, the Surgeon being appointed and paid by the Owner though approved by us, while the only duty of the Naval Officer, when such an officer was placed on board, was to see that no emigrants were embarked from prohibited parts of the Coast. We propose that the Surgeons of these vessels should be placed on the same footing with those employed on the Australian Emigration, that is to say that they should be appointed and paid by this Board and entirely removed from the control or influence of the ship owner.[2]

Emigrant mortality had explained itself, behind MacDonald's back.

The new proposals met with little response from private shipowners and emigration merchants who were not prepared to tolerate such a close and minute Government supervision of their activities. The Government tried other palliatives, such as the Guarantee System by which the Government placed supervising officers on board a private vessel and in return compensated a ship owner with up to £500 for failure to obtain a full complement of fit emigrants. This plan had but a short life, as it never appealed to private enterprise, while Grey himself thought it too costly to be maintained by the Government and stopped it.[3]

Another alternative was for the Admiralty to supply steamers to run the entire business, but this proved equally expensive.[4] For the hire of H.M.S. *Growler* alone, for instance, the Admiralty had submitted a claim for £9,190 on account of some 920 emigrants despatched in that ship, in addition to a further claim of £423 as gratuities due to the Naval Officers manning her. In June 1849, the Commissioners raised serious objections and with difficulty agreed

---

1. *Ibid.*
2. C.O. 386/55, September 6th, 1848, Commissioners to Grey.
3. C.O. 386/56, April 11th, 1849, Commissioners to C.O.
4. C.O. 386/55, October 6th, 1848, same to same.

to pay only £8,560. To be forced to pay such a huge sum on a service that was, for the most part, badly conducted, many of the emigrants dying on the voyage before they could be usefully employed, was painful enough. A new and vital question was now raised by the Commissioners: whether transport vessels ought to be paid bounty on the number of African emigrants *embarked*, or rather on the number *landed alive*.[1] With such vital questions occupying the Commissioners' minds in 1849, emigrant mortality became a problem to be genuinely and conscientiously faced, as the next chapters will show.

Because 1847-9 marked the peak of labour emigration (about one-third of the total recruitment was obtained between 1847-9) as well as the peak of emigrant mortality (compared with other years of the emigration scheme) it is necessary to say something more about mortality rates and about the various methods of recruiting emigrants during this period.

---

1. C.O. 386/56, June 26th, 1849, Commissioners to Grey.

Chapter 6
Labour Recruitment Techniques:
The Coastal Squadron and the
Vice-Admiralty Courts

A review of the large number of 'voluntary emigrants' recruited at this time, or rather recaptured from foreign slavers, involves some discussion of the respective roles of the Mixed Commissions, the British Vice Admiralty Courts and the Royal Navy in the recruiting operations.

It has already been shown how, because of the Government's anxiety to procure labour in large numbers for the colonies, the emigration scheme degenerated into almost open slave trading after 1843. The consequences of the secret memorandum of 1844[1] were bad enough for the health and welfare of the Africans recaptured on the high seas and promptly despatched to the plantations, but the emigration scheme probably had its most harmful effect on the work of the anti-slavery Squadron on the West Coast.

British policy after 1841 became more interested in capturing foreign slavers on the high seas and making 'voluntary emigrants' of their cargoes than in preventing the slave dealers from embarking the slaves from the coast. The abandonment of the Denman strategy of inshore cruising by the Royal Navy, which we shall presently discuss, indeed destroyed the highest hopes which that strategy had raised by 1841 of exterminating the foreign slave trade in a matter of months, and it also largely explains the success of the labour recruitment scheme as well as why the West African slave trade lingered on for many decades after 1841.

Captain H. J. Matson, Captain E. H. Butterfield and Captain the Hon. Joseph Denman were clearly the most outstanding officers in the Royal Navy's work of suppressing the West African Atlantic slave trade. The officer who probably did more than anyone else

---

1. C.O. 386/48, November 13th, 1943; February 1st, 1844, Elliot to Cox.

to improve the efficiency of the squadron was Captain the Hon. Joseph Denman.

In 1843, after many years' service on both sides of the Atlantic, he was put on half-pay and during this period of retirement he drew up the Instructions for the use of Naval Officers engaged in the suppression of the slave trade. In all his efforts and campaigns against the slave trade Joseph Denman was helped by his father, Lord Chief Justice Denman, an enthusiastic abolitionist.

Captain Denman first became interested in the suppression of the trade when he was serving as a lieutenant off the coast of Brazil in command of the *Curlew*, in succession to Captain Trotter. In that year he captured the first slaver ever taken off the coast of South America. He was told to take his prize, with its human cargo of 550 miserable African slaves, across the Atlantic to Sierra Leone.

Denman was 46 days on that voyage, during which time he witnessed how dreadful the sufferings of slaves were across the Middle Passage. At Sierra Leone Denman failed to secure the condemnation of the slave-ship because she was a Portuguese vessel captured south of the line. The wretched slaves had therefore to make a third passage back to Brazil. The ruthless methods which Denman subsequently adopted against foreign slavers on the West Coast clearly owed their origin to this experience of the unnecessary cruelty involved due entirely to the regulations governing the capture of slave vessels. If other European nations were reluctant to grant the Royal Navy the right of search on the high seas, surely the Naval Officers, with the approval of the Home Government, could secure anti-slave trade treaties from African chiefs and on the basis of these, check the slave trade from the port of embarkation. In 1839 Lord Palmerston at the Foreign Office had actually launched the anti-slave trade treaty-making policy with African chiefs. In that same year the energetic Captain Denman was appointed to command the *Wanderer*, an armed schooner of eight guns.

In 1840, on the basis of an anti-slave trade treaty with the King or Chief of Gallinas, Denman made his name by the destruction of the Gallinas slave factories, the barracoons.

The Gallinas estuary, situated about 150 miles south of Sierra Leone, had achieved widespread notoriety through the slave trading activities of Pedro Blanco, Theodore Canot, Senor Buron and other foreign slave dealers. By the autumn of 1840 these men were in desperate straits as a result of Denman's four months' close blockade. Unaware of the new inshore cruising tactics, their employers at

Havana kept on sending vessels full of goods with which to barter for slaves. The stocks of goods kept piling up, the slaves insisted on dying by the hundreds in the barracoons, and not one of the nine slave vessels there dared to embark them. Day after day the *Wanderer*, or her tiny consorts, the *Rolls* and the *Saracen*, sailed to and fro outside the estuary.

As soon as the Chief of the Gallinas had signed the treaty with Denman, the burning of the barracoons began by firing incendiary rockets into them, the slaves having been removed to the ships out at sea. Eight hundred and forty-one slaves were thus liberated on the spot and the work of destruction lasted three days. The foreign slave owners, meanwhile, trembled for their lives as the local people of Gallinas began to exult over their downfall. They begged to be taken with the slaves to Sierra Leone in order to escape with their lives.

When Captain Denman's action was reported to the Governor of Sierra Leone, to Lord Palmerston at the Foreign Office, to Lord John Russell at the Colonial Office as well as to the Admiralty, a great sensation was created. For the first time a definite step had been taken to strike at the root of the trade. As the Governor of Sierra Leone jubilantly pointed out:

> One opinion only, as it seems to me, can be entertained respecting the decisive measures adopted by Commander Denman; nor does it seem possible, in any view of the subject, to estimate too highly the services which that very intelligent and active officer has rendered by them to the cause of the suppression. The slave traffic has undoubtedly sustained a greater blow by what has been done now on shore, than it has received during my administration of this Government, by any of the numerous and important captures which have been effected at sea. Gallinas was the most celebrated mart and stronghold of the Spanish Slave Trade on the whole line of the African coast. As such it had long maintained itself in insolent defiance of this colony, its immediate neighbour; and as such it may be said for the present, to have ceased to exist.[1]

By the destruction of the slave factories the export of between 12,00 and 15,000 slaves a year had been checked at a spot which was long regarded as the heart of the trade. Consternation reigned among the merchants of Havana at the loss of both slaves and goods. Naval Officers were as jubilant as the traders were depressed. At last an

---

1. Governor Doherty to Lord John Russell. Quoted in *The Friend of Africa*, April 19th, 1841. See C.O. 267/160 No. 67, December 7th, 1840; C.O. 267/163 No. 2, January 4th 1841, enclosed in Jermie to Russell.

example had been set which all could follow: Captain H. W. Hill, who had been at the Gallinas raid, did the same thing at the mouth of the Sherbo river; in 1841 Captain Nurse destroyed the slave factory at the Pongos river north of Sierra Leone; in 1842 Captains Matson and Foote destroyed the slave factories at Kabinda and Ambriz, south of the line, liberating 1,074 slaves at Kabinda and 240 at Ambriz.

Palmerston, overjoyed at the actions of these zealous officers on the coast, immediately recommended that 'similar operations should be executed against all the piratical slave trading establishments which may be met with in parts of the coast not belonging to any civilized power. The course pursued by Captain Denman seems to be the best adapted for the attainment of the object in view.' Denman was soon rewarded with a captaincy and he and his men together received special grants to the sum of £4,000.[1]

Unfortunately, Palmerston was soon out of office and by 1842 Lord Aberdeen, who took a different view of Captain Denman's work, became the Foreign Secretary. Encouraged by the views of Lord Aberdeen, Senor Buron, the slave dealer whose factories had recently been destroyed at the Gallinas and who had saved his skin from the infuriated natives at Gallinas by begging a passage in Denman's ship, now sued him for trespass and the seizure of 4,000 slaves and goods to the value of £180,000. Other actions pending in the Court of the Exchequer amounted to claims totalling £370,000 against Denman and £80,000 against Matson and Foote.

The Foreign Office under Aberdeen must have been aware of what slave dealers on the coast would be likely to make of any official disapproval of the Denman strategy; it is, therefore, surprising that the Foreign Office disapproval of the action of the Naval Officers could not have been kept secret but was, on the contrary, publicised.

On May 20th, 1842, Aberdeen wrote informing the Admiralty that his Advocate-General

> ... cannot take upon himself to advise that all the proceedings described as having taken place at Gallinas, New Cestos and Sea Bars [Sherbro], are strictly justifiable, or that the instructions to Her Majesty's Naval Officers are such as can with perfect legality be carried

---

1. Lloyd, C., *The Navy and the Slave Trade* (London, 1949). Much of this analysis is based on the account given on pp. 92–100 of Lloyd's book and in C.O. 267/167, F.O. to C.O. March 27th, 1841, and Admiralty to C.O. April 8th, 1841.

into execution. The Queen's Advocate is of the opinion that the block-ading of rivers, landing and destroying buildings, and carrying off per-sons held in slavery in countries with which Great Britain is not at war, cannot be considered as sanctioned by the law of nations, or by pro-visions of any existing treaties.[1]

Yet Aberdeen well knew that the action of the Naval Officers at Gallinas was fully protected by Denman's treaty with Siacca, the King of Gallinas. Nor, as happened over the question of right of search, did any European power protest against the destruction of the barracoons or contest the right of British Naval Officers to do so once the yobtained the consent of the local chiefs on whose soil the slave factories were erected.

The Aberdeen letter appeared to create the false impression that the British action against the slave trade applied only in respect to countries with which Britain was at war; while the interception of foreign slavers and seizure of their property on the high seas, an operation which the foreign powers always resisted, and often by force, was now more legitimate than the destruction of the slave factories or barracoons on the coast, which actions the anti-slave trade treaties with African Chiefs fully allowed, without opposition from any of the foreign powers. As Captain H. D. Trotter later pointed out,

> The destruction of barracoons and slave factories is a question with the native African rulers or governments and not with those of which the miscreant slave traders are the subjects who, in every case, are violating their own laws, so far as they extend. In the several instances that have occurred of destroying factories, no complaint has been made by the government of the country to which the slave traders belonged.[2]

Now, if no foreign power ever so much as raised a protest against the destruction of the barracoons, if the Naval Officers and therefore the British Government, by their treaties with the local chiefs, were already legally protected in whatever action they might take against the slave factories at the point of embarkation; in short, if Captain Denman's strategy was demonstrably so effective against the slave trade while not exposing the British Government to any difficulties with any of the foreign powers, why did the Foreign Office under

1. Cited, Lloyd, C., *op. cit.*, p. 97. See App. III, however, for Treaties with African Chiefs.
2. Wilson, Rev. J. L. and Trotter, Captain H. D., *The British Squadron on the Coast of Africa* (London, 1851), footnotes on pp. 9–10.

Lord Aberdeen so hurriedly and promptly secure the abandonment of a new operation that gave a sudden and certain promise to destroy the foreign slave trade almost immediately in 1840–2 ?

The harmful effect of Aberdeen's letter to the Admiralty was three-fold: on the one hand the exertions of the Naval Officers engaged in the suppression of the slave trade were greatly diminished by the fear of the legal consequences which might ensue. In fact by 1843 reports coming from Sierra Leone stated that at the Gallinas the slave trade establishments had been restored and were in active operation once more. Because of the fear which the Foreign Office under Aberdeen had infused, deliberately or otherwise, into the Naval Officers, the more timid type of officer found it an excuse for doing nothing at all. On the other hand, the slave dealers were encouraged because they imagined, and the Advocate-General or the Foreign Office allowed them to do so,[1] that Lord Aberdeen's letter of warning to the Naval Officers virtually legitimised the activities of slave traders on the coast. Hence Senor Buron and his men now proceeded to sue Captain Denman, claiming damages for their factories and slaves at the Gallinas. The effect produced on the West Coast after Aberdeen had frightened the Naval Officers into inactivity was both ludicrous and disastrous: ludicrous, because the native Chiefs who hitherto had been co-operative enough in signing anti-slave trade treaties with the Naval Officers to enable them to destroy the barracoons, now thought 'that a revolution had broken out in England, that Aberdeen had overthrown Palmerston's government by cutting his predecessor's throat'.[2] The effect was disastrous because, while the cruisers retired to the high seas, there to await the 'voluntary emigrants', the slave dealers resumed full operations on the coast.

We have already discussed in the previous chapters Lord Aberdeen's or the Foreign Office approval of the secret memorandum of 1844 and the deliberate attempts made by the Colonial Office to buy over the Naval Officers employed in the H.M.S. *Growler* emigration scheme in 1847–9. The hurried abandonment of the Denman strategy, at a time when no risk of international complication was involved and when the local African chiefs were even anxious to co-operate,[3] probably had something to do with the official anxiety over

---

1. Lloyd, C., *op. cit.*, p. 98.
2. *Ibid.*
3. Under Lord Aberdeen the Foreign Office after 1841 was responsible for the breakdown of many of the Anti-Slave Trade Treaties which Lord Palmerston

the emigration scheme, the success of which depended directly on the freedom of the slave dealers to embark their slaves from the slave factories on the coast.

Indeed the emigration scheme, together with the abandonment of the most effective naval strategy ever devised against the slave trade, did much more to promote the foreign slave trade than the Sugar Duties Equalisation Act did between 1841 and 1846. The Sugar duties only encouraged foreign slavers to come out for more slaves; the abandonment of the Denman strategy by the Navy enabled them, the slavers, to succeed in embarking their cargoes. The advocates of free trade and unrestricted emigration soon over-reached themselves when they began to criticise the work of the Naval Officers on the West Coast.

The attack on the 'inefficiency' of the 'costly' Squadron which had 'failed' to suppress the slave trade obliged many of the Naval Officers to speak up and make important revelations, during the 1848–9 Parliamentary Committees on the African Squadron, about the changes which had been made in their cruising methods and instructions since 1841–2. One of the officers interviewed, Captain E. H. Butterfield, had answered the following questions before the House of Commons Committee:

Question 605: You have stated that you considered that the Slave Trade was nearly suppressed on that part of the coast where you commanded in 1848?

Answer: Yes.

Question 606: To what do you attribute its increase since that period?

Answer: To putting Loanda and Ambriz, and I think, generally, the Portuguese possessions, under charge of the Portuguese Government. I think that that revived it during the time it was under their charge, and enabled the slave factors to continue it, but before that [1842] they could not continue buying the slaves, from not being able to embark them.

Question 611: Did you ever hear that in consequence of the difficulties in prosecuting the slave trade, from the vigilant guarding [in shore cruising] of the English cruisers, the slave trade had been given up?

Answer: It was given up at Ambriz certainly.

Question 612: Was it afterwards resumed?

Answer: Yes.

Question 614: To what do you attribute that resumption?

---

had encouraged with African Chiefs. Dike, K. O., *Trade and Politics in the Niger Delta* (Oxford, 1956) pp. 81–6.

Answer : I suppose it must have been from its being almost thrown open at Loanda by being under Portuguese authorities.

Question 282 : And the Portuguese Squadron was employed to watch the Portuguese possessions ?

Answer : Yes, the British Vessels were removed.

Answering one of the questions (Q. 3686) another naval officer stated:

> If there was nothing else to account for the enormous increase in the trade from 1843 to 1846 and 1847, the inefficient and unsuspicious reliance that was placed on the efforts of the Portuguese authorities for so long a period at Loanda and its neighbourhood, were quite enough to account for it. From that period till January 1847 no vessel was stationed between Congo and Cape St. Bras . . . [embracing an extent of coast] so notorious beyond all other places in Africa.[1]

Whatever the reasons or circumstances behind the decision, the withdrawal of British cruisers from the most notorious slaving spots, and the abandonment of inshore cruising to the Portuguese squadron, not only made nonsense of the hard-won Anglo-Portuguese Equipment Treaty and other anti-slavery conventions by which Britain after 1839 had acquired the right to patrol and seize foreign slavers in Portuguese territories south of the Equator; that decision or arrangement certainly enabled both the foreign slave trade and the emigration scheme to thrive together.

It is significant that while in the twenty years between 1819 and 1839 the British Squadron had captured 333 slavers, in the ten years between 1840 and 1849, the peak years both of liberated African emigration and of the foreign slave trade, the Squadron captured more than 740 slavers on the high seas.[2] Had the Denman strategy of inshore cruising been allowed to continue, both the slave trade and the emigration scheme would probably have ended soon after 1841–2. It remains to see how another anti-slavery establishment on the West Coast, the British Vice-Admiralty Courts, came in very useful for the recruitment of this type of labour.

First, the Mixed Commission Courts. These were jointly estab-

---

1. Wilson, Rev. J. L. and Trotter, Captain H. D., *op. cit.*, pp. 10–20; PP. 1849, Vol. XIX, House of Commons Committee on the African Squadron Questions, 605 ff.; PP. 1850, Vol. IX, House of Lords Committee on same, evidence given by witnesses.

2. Wilson and Trotter, *op. cit.*, p. 15, footnote.

lished by Britain and other powers from 1819, and the *de jure* existence of some of them lasted until 1871.[1]

Together, these Mixed Commission Courts[2] were responsible for the trial of over 600 slave vessels,[3] and the liberation of some 80,000 slaves, 3,000 in Rio de Janeiro, while the Sierra Leone Mixed Commission Courts were responsible for the liberation of nearly 65,000. These were the hot centres of the slave traffic. Until about 1845, the Mixed Commission Courts in those regions remained fully occupied with captured cases.

After 1845, however, the British Vice-Admiralty Courts practically monopolised the capture and trial of foreign slavers. The Vice-Admiralty courts had tried by far more than 100 slavers by 1845,[4] and were soon to take over almost completely from the Mixed Commission Courts. We have seen in Chapter III how by 1841 Spain, France, America, even Portugal, had come to suspect both the emigration scheme and the Vice-Admiralty Courts as yet another device by which their rival contrived to monopolise this source of emigrant labour. From 1841 France insisted that French vessels should be tried in French courts alone. In Cuba, in 1844, Spaniards called for the abolition of the Mixed Commission Courts; the United States used the role of the Vice-Admiralty Courts as an excuse for refusing all co-operation with Britain; in 1845 the Anglo-Brazilian Mixed Commission Courts at Rio and Sierra Leone were dissolved. Whatever remained of the Mixed Commission Courts in other stations, many of the member-nations regarded them as a farce, 'completely useless', in the presence of the Vice-Admiralty Courts.[5]

Indifference to the Mixed Commission Courts after 1845 enabled the British Vice-Admiralty Courts to establish a monopoly in the judging of captured cases. In 1847 only one case appeared before

---

1. Bethel, Leslie, 'The Mixed Commissions for the Suppression of the Transatlantic Slave Trade in the Nineteenth Century', *Journal of African History*, Vol. VII, No. 1, 1966, pp. 79–93.
2. F.O. 315, Freetown Mixed Commission Court, Sierra Leone; F.O. 312, Cape of Good Hope Mixed Commission Court; F.O. 314, Spanish Town Mixed Commission Court; F.O. 313, Havana Mixed Commission Court; F.O. 128, 129, 131, Rio de Janeiro Mixed Commission Court.
3. Bethel, *op. cit.*
4. *Ibid.* For lists of captures taken before British Vice-Admiralty Courts at St Helena, the Cape of Good Hope, Sierra Leone, up to 1845, see respectively F.O. 84/748; F.O. 84/824, August 1839 to September 1849; and F.O. 84/556, 1840–4, enclosures in Melville to J. Bandinel, January 1st, 1845.
5. *Ibid.*

a Mixed Commission Court; while between 1845–71 only seven cases were tried by the Mixed Commission Court in Sierra Leone, compared with over 500 cases between 1819–45. But during 1846–50 the British Vice-Admiralty Courts alone tried 320 captured slavers thus liberating some 20,000 or more slaves.

Before discussing in more detail how the British cruisers and the Vice-Admiralty Courts actually became the real backbone of a highly successful emigration between 1847–50, a point must first be made about the attitude of the foreign powers over the Mixed Commission Courts.

Their indifference to the Mixed Commissions or pretended annoyance with the British courts only implied one thing: the slave-trading nations never really wished the international anti-slavery operation much success. Just as the emigration scheme had enabled them to acquire a plausible excuse for maintaining a policy of non-cooperation, so the role of the Vice-Admiralty Courts provided a similar excuse for remaining indifferent to, or backing out from, the international Mixed Courts. The best line of action, had the powers been genuinely anxious for the success of the Mixed Courts, would have been to insist that they be given a complete monopoly of all slaving cases. Such concerted action would seriously have affected the role of the British courts in the liberated African emigration scheme.

As to the Vice-Admiralty Courts, though their subsequent role appeared to lend great weight to the suspicions raised against them, it is difficult to agree that their establishment originally had anything to do with liberated African emigration. The British Government was still bitterly opposed to any emigration scheme when the first Vice-Admiralty Court appeared in Sierra Leone in about 1808. British anti-slavery operations had necessitated not only a new policy of treaty-making with African Chiefs, but also the establishment of a *bona fide* British legal machinery on the West and East African Coasts for dealing with such cases.

By allowing the Mixed Commission Courts to be displaced, the foreign powers only enabled the Vice-Admiralty Courts to become 'collectors of emigrants' for the West Indian planters. Portuguese, Spanish, American, as well as French slavers, rather than be caught and brought for trial in the international courts, with more severe penalties if convicted, preferred to be caught by British cruisers as 'stateless' slave vessels. They even often assisted the cruisers in this sort of capture by throwing their national identity, their documents, papers and national flags, overboard, as soon as a British cruiser was around!

By catching slavers as 'stateless' vessels British cruisers became in the first place freed from the risk of paying heavy indemnities in the case of an 'illegal' seizure or capture. By electing to be tried as stateless vessels before the Vice-Admiralty Courts, the foreign slavers themselves got away with lighter penalties and the cruisers and the British courts were able to bring more liberated slaves within the 'care and protection' of the emigration agents and authorities. The foreign slavers were easily 'dealt with more summarily as stateless ships in British Vice-Admiralty Courts',[1] where British Arbitrators, some of them Chief Emigration Agents, presided. About ten slavers were captured at Sierra Leone in 1847–8, with 3,910 slaves on board. 2,319 of them emigrated, 1,204 to Jamaica, 906 to British Guiana, 211 to Trinidad. At St Helena eleven ships were recaptured with 2,798 on board, 1,772 of them emigrating, mostly to Trinidad.[2] In 1849, about 1,437 were similarly recaptured and forwarded from Sierra Leone, while St Helena despatched 1,738 emigrants.[3] Between 1848–50, the number of emigrants reaching the West Indies amounted to about 12,014, in other words about one-third of the total number of emigrants obtained during the whole period 1840–67. 'Stateless' foreign slavers, active cruisers, with British Arbitrators or Chief Emigration Agents in the Vice-Admiralty Courts, had made the period a peak one for the emigration.

Jamaica received 3,488 of the total for 1848–50, British Guiana received 3,027 and Trinidad 2,850. Four small islands—Grenada, St Vincent, St Lucia and St Kitts received altogether 2,649.[4] The returns furnished by the Emigration Commissioners in September 1847 showed that up to that year African emigration was the main source of immigrant labour in the West Indies. Intercolonial migration and the liberated African emigration scheme up to September 1847 had together given British Guiana, Trinidad and Jamaica respectively—'as far as known'—17,169, 15,011 and 3,899 African

---

1. Bethel, *op. cit.*, p. 91. Dodson, J., *Reports of Cases argued and Determined in the High Court of Admiralty*, Vol. II (London, 1828) pp. 236 ff.
2. PP. 1850, XL, 33, Statement of Liberated Africans captured in 1848, pp. 300–3, 360, 395.
3. C.O. 318/182, November 7th, 1849, C.O. 386/55, C.O. 386/57, November 7th, 1849, Commissioners to C.O.
4. Roberts, G. W., *Immigration into the British Caribbean*, p. 250.

labourers recruited from various British and foreign stations on both sides of the Atlantic.[1] This gave a total of some 36,079 African immigrant labourers up to the end of September 1847.

The large number recruited during the *Growler* scheme, 1847–9, the worst years of emigrant mortality, will be the only one to be taken into consideration in discussing mortality rates, since records of mortality in these years are practically the only ones available. It is not surprising that emigrant mortality during 1847–9 was the highest in the whole period of the emigration, in view of the relaxing of the regulations in those years. Between 1843–5 the three Government vessels *Glen Huntley*, *Arabian* and *Senator*, were together responsible for the conveyance of 2,187 emigrants to the West Indies. In the same period another 1,261 emigrants had been despatched by some of the private vessels which were already capturing the emigration traffic by 1845. Except in the case of two private ships, *Rufus* and *Margaret*, where the Commissions made mention of outbreaks of sickness on board, conditions in the private vessels in 1843–6 were generally described as 'creditable', while 'so far as regards the health of the passengers they were successful'.[2] But no figures for comparison were given about deaths occurring, if any, in private ships during that period.

Also, up to 1846, no returns or figures are available for St Helena, where at least nine private ships[3] had been responsible for the conveyance of 1,439 emigrants, out of the 2,014 landed in 1846 alone. While 4,045[4] was quoted by the Commissions as the total number known to have emigrated between 1840–2 in private ships, there is no means of knowing what the rate of mortality was, if any. In the Foreign stations of Rio and Havana, still less information was given about emigrant mortality.

However, details are available in the case of the three Government vessels employed during 1843–5, as well as for the *Growler* and

---

1. C.O. 386/54, *Returns of Immigration into British Guiana, Trinidad, Jamaica 1834—30th September 1847, as far as known.*
2. The *Superior, Roger Stewart, Margaret, Rufus, Louisa Baille, Arabian* and *Senator* were among these private vessels, with the *Superior, Arabian* and *Senator* despatched some times as Government vessels and at other times as private ships. *Fourth General Report*, PP. 1844, Vol. XXXI, 11; *Fifth General Report*, PP. 1845, Vol. XXVII, 617, 83; *Sixth General Report*, PP. 1843, Vol. XXIV, 706.
3. The *Mandarin, Nelson, Navarino, Standard, Margaret, Velox, Indus, British Tar, Arundel. Seventh General Report*, 1847, PP. Vol. XXXIII, 980, 131.
4. *Eighth General Report*, 1848, PP. 1847–8, Vol. XXVI, p. 21–5.

other vessels engaged in the scheme in 1847–9. During 1843–5 conditions in the Government vessels were good. In the first seven voyages, for instance, no deaths occurred. Even the *Arabian*, with an outbreak of smallpox on board, had only one death.[1] By the end of the fourteenth voyage with 1,519 emigrants already conveyed, only eleven deaths occurred in the three vessels; which gives a very low mortality rate of about ·07 per cent.

Even with the emigrants remaining suspicious of anti-smallpox vaccination, Government Surgeons on board the three Government vessels, in 1843–5, had still insisted on the vaccination of all emigrants before or immediately after embarkation.

Later, consequent upon the relaxation of the regulations, mortality rates began to soar and became so bad during 1847–9 as to cause the Emigration Commissioners themselves great anxiety. Mortality rates in many of the cases reached as high as 11 per cent or even more in some other cases. Much care however is needed in reading some of the figures furnished for Parliament in these matters. The *Growler*, for instance, had 66 deaths during its first voyage in 1847, when it carried 476 emigrants to British Guiana, but the report of the Commissioners showed only 20 deaths.[2] While the incidence of 46 deaths during the *Growler*'s second voyage to Trinidad was correctly recorded,[3] that of 135 deaths out of 441 emigrants in the *Growler*'s third voyage in April 1848 is missing in the returns on emigrant mortality in 1848–9.[4] On the other hand, the *Morayshire* whose mortality rate was the lowest in 1848, with only five deaths out of 159 embarked, had its low percentage rate counted more than once—first, in the returns for 1847; and again in the third voyage. However such mistakes and omissions came about, they no doubt have falsified the statistics and returns.

There is a remarkable significance when the mortality rates are compared between those vessels which were permitted to proceed to the West Coast for emigrants at their 'own risk', without the Government placing any supervising officers on board such ships or

---

1. *Fourth General Report*, 1844, Vol. XXXI, 11.
2. PP. 1847–8, Vol. XXIII–i, 829, 30; No. 158, Light to Grey, May 13th, 1847. C.O. 386/55, *Report on Emigrant Mortality*, June, 1848.
3. C.O. 386/55, *op. cit.* PP. 1847–8, Vol. XLIV, 586–7, No. 103, Harris to Grey, December 8th, 1847.
4. C.O. 386/54, April 19th, 1848, Commissioners to C.O. reporting the case of the 135 deaths on board the *Growler*; but see the *Returns of Emigrant Mortality* in C.O. 386/55 and C.O. 386/57; also in the *Eighth General Report*, PP. 1847–8, Vol. XXVI, 961, 41, where no record of the 135 or more deaths was made.

guaranteeing them against loss or failure to obtain emigrants (Class A vessels), and those vessels with Government Officers placed on board, after such guarantees against loss had been promised (Class B vessels). The following tables show this clearly:

Mortality Rates 1847–49 (Sources C.O. 386/55, 56, 57)

(In 1847 H.M.S. *Growler* was the main transport vessel, an official emigration transport with government officials in full control.

Ship	Class of Vessel	Total Embarked	Deaths	Approximate Mortality Rate
H.M.S. *Growler*	Govt.	476	66	16%
H.M.S. *Growler*	Govt.	445	46	11%
Prince Regent	Private— probably class A	108		(not recorded in the returns)
Morayshire	A	159	5	4.5%
H.M.S. *G owler*	Govt.	441	135	34%

Sierra Leone: 1848

Class A Vessels—Government Officers on Board				**Class B Vessels—No. Government Officers**			
Ship	Total embar-ked	Deaths	Approx. mortality rate	Ship	Total embar-ked	Deaths	Approx. mortality rate
Persian	211	5	2%	*Helena*	133	12	11%
Clarendon	266	8	3%	*Arabian*	266	22	11%
Glasgow	255	2	1%	*Amity Hall*	277	37	13%
Ethelred	267	2	1%	*Una*	240	52	25%
Simon Taylor	248	5	2%				

Sierra Leone: 1849

Class A Vessels				**Class B Vessels**
Una	367	2	less than 1%	
Clarendon	250	2	·· ·· 1%	
Amity Hall	236	2	·· ·· 1%	
Agnes	257	2	·· ·· 1%	NIL
Ethelred	281	3	1%	
Conservative	96	3	1%	

St Helena: 1848

Class A Vessels—Government Officers on Board				Class B Vessels—No Government Officers			
Ship	Total embarked	Deaths	Approx. mortality rate	Ship	Total embarked	Deaths	Approx. mortality rate
Seapack	90	5	6%	*Vanguard*	216	18	9%
Zephyr	203	3	2%	*Reliance*	230	20	10%
Emma				*Euphrates*	309	46	15%
Eugenia	390	10	3%	*Rhyn*	334	54	18%

St Helena: 1849

Ship	Total embarked	Deaths	Approx. mortality rate	Ship	Total embarked	Deaths	Approx. mortality rate
Tropic	210	4	2%	*Eliza Moore*	140	10	9%
Bathurst	319	4	1%	*Janet*	254	12	6%
Reliance	179	4	3%	*Levinside*	171	11	10%
				Tuscan	154	11	11%
				King William	311	18	6%

A simple comparison of mortality rates in Class A vessels and Class B vessels easily shows why the Emigration Commissioners had begun to express such anxiety in 1849 about reversing the whole system and taking back full responsibility for the appointment of surgeons on board emigration transports. Of all the transport vessels despatched between 1847 and October 1849, the *Growler*, a Government vessel, had the worst mortality rates of 16 per cent, 11 per cent and 34 per cent respectively during its three voyages. Official anxiety to procure as much labour as possible, with the consequent replacement of the original regulations by the Hook plan, largely explains the high mortality rate in the *Growler*. In 1848, compare mortality rates in Class A and in Class B vessels going to Sierra Leone for recruitment, and also make a similar comparison for St Helena. In both places, Class A vessels were infinitely better, emigrant mortality remaining very low compared with the Class B vessels. Again, compare the mortality rate in 1849 Class A vessels at Sierra Leone, with the Class B vessels in St Helena in the same year: Class A vessels were still better in all cases.

But one should also compare mortality rates in African emigration with other emigration schemes of that period: Even in its worst years, 1847–9, the rate of mortality among African emigrants was nothing extraordinary when compared with the high mortality occurring on board some of the Chinese or Indian 'coolie' ships in the same decade.[1] Also in the more properly organised white emigration of the nineteenth century, cases of irregularity, even of high mortality among emigrants, occurred.[2] The difference, however, between the liberated African emigration scheme and all other types of emigration was that, whilst the authorities responsible for the Asiatic or the European emigration schemes exerted themselves always to check all forms of abuse committed either by Captains of emigration transports, or by recruiting agents and emigration brokers, African emigration did not enjoy such strict official supervision or vigilance against abuses. On the contrary, irregularities committed by private emigration traders on the African Coast often took their origin from official policy.

However, as the next chapter will show, events in the *Growler*

---

1. Cumpston, I. M., *Indians Overseas* (London, 1953); Campbell, P. C., *Chinese Coolie Emigration* (1923); Laurence, K. O., *op. cit.*, Chapters V, IX. Examples of Indian Coolie Mortality on board some of the transports 1856–7 were:

The Bucephalus embarked 380, lost 45. Mortality rate about 15%					
Sir Robert Sepping	··	291,	·· 61	·· ·· ··	20%
Roman Emperor	··	313,	·· 88	·· ·· ··	29%
Adelaide	··	310,	·· 25	·· ·· ··	8%
Sir George Seymour	··	348,	·· 36	·· ·· ··	11%
Eveline	··	380,	·· 72	·· ·· ··	23%

    See PP. 1859–i–xvi, 156, 365, 325, April 7th, May 4th, May 28th, No. 21. Keate to Labouchere, 1857.
    Mortality average in Coolie ships had risen from 3·61 per cent in 1850–1 to 17·26 per cent in 1856–7. But see the Mouat report of July 1858, which completely exonerated the Management, PP. 1859–ii, xx, 426–47, Calcutta, May 10th, 1858.
    C.O. 318/225, Commissioners to Merivale, August 25th, 1859.
    Examples in Chinese emigration mortality were:

The Glentanner embarked 305, lost 43. Mortality rate about 14%					
Lord Elgin	··	154,	·· 69,	·· ·· ··	68%
Samuel Bonnington	··	352,	·· 52,	·· ·· ··	13%

    C.O. 318/202, Commissioners to Merivale and Minutes on same, January 7th, 1853; PP. 1852–3, LXVIII, 649, 637, No. 4, December 26th, 1852; No. 41, March 12th, 1853, Barkly to Pakington; PP. 1852–3, LXVIII, 551, 559, No. 8, January 24th, 1853, Barkly to Pakington; No. 15, Barkly to Newcastle, January 8th, 1853.

2. In 1853, for instance, 269 British and Foreign Emigration ships carried to the U.S.A. and Canada a total of 128,882 emigrants, 1,556 of them dying on the voyage; cf. Jones, M. A., 'The Role of the United Kingdom in the Transatlantic Emigration Trade', 1815–75 (Oxford, D. Phil., 1955) p. 511.

scheme, 1847-9, were destined to influence official policy—for good. With the problems of heavy mortality very much on their minds, the Emigration Commissioners and the Colonial Office began very seriously to search for a more proper and efficient method of running the scheme. The contract firm of Hyde, Hodge and Company seemed to hold the answer to these problems.

Chapter 7
The Hodge Contract and the End of Emigration Policy

The emigration contract of Messrs. Hyde Hodge and Company marked a turning point in the scheme of liberated African emigration. Not all abuses were stamped out, but the mortality figures together with complaints or reports of irregularities showed a sharp decline compared with the period between 1843 and October 1849. This achievement was the more remarkable because by the time the contract came into force many other colonies apart from Jamaica, British Guiana and Trinidad, had been included in the share of imported African labour[1]—a fact that might have led to further rivalry and competition between the various colonies, and probably too to more irregularities in the whole scheme. Another improvement which came through the Hodge contract was the knowledge of the exact numbers emigrating or dying between November 1849 and 1854. The returns on these points no longer depended on being 'as far as known' to the Commissioners.[2] The Hodge contract was in

---

1. A new principle of apportionment of immigrants was devised between the various colonies, viz: one ship-load of immigrants for every 100,000 cwt. of the average export of sugar. The ratio of apportionment was as follows: Jamaica 7; British Guiana 6; Trinidad 4; Grenada 1; St Lucia 1; St Vincent 1; St Kitts and Tobago 1. The actual apportionment did not, however, always conform to these exact ratios. St Lucia, for example, received 379 African immigrants more than its due share by 1850, while Trinidad, a bigger colony, received 344 less than its due share. C.O. 386/57, November 20th, 1849, Commissioners to C.O. (Merivale); C.O. 386/88, June 7th, 1851, same to same.

2. C.O. 386/54, February 19th, 1848, *Returns of Immigrants into British Guiana, Jamaica and Trinidad*; C.O. 386/55, *Returns of Immigrants* from August 1st, 1834 to September 30th, 1847; C.O. 386/57, *Returns of Immigrants* from January 1st, 1841 to November 6th, 1849.

In most of the above returns the statistics furnished by the Commissioners were covered with 'as far as known'. There were obvious inconsistencies. Late in 1841, for instance, the Governor of Sierra Leone quoted the figures emi-

Bronze model, probably W. Nigerian c. 1860, of British sailors and an officer in a ship's boat. Pigtails, beard and the officer's haughty expression are finely observed. The style of the officer's hat was out of fashion by the end of the 18th century.

Boats from seven British warships, led by the Commodore in one of *Penelope's* cutters, crossing the bar of Gallinas River on an expedition to destroy slaving posts on February 2nd 1849.

'The burning of the slave establishments on Solyman River. The foliage on the banks is thick and luxuriant to the water's edge. The explosion was terrific; a constant fire of musketry was kept up from the bush, answered by volleys from the four boats, with grape from brass guns. The premises destroyed were the residence and factory of Don Jose Louis, a Spanish dealer.' — *Illustrated London News*, April 14th 1849.

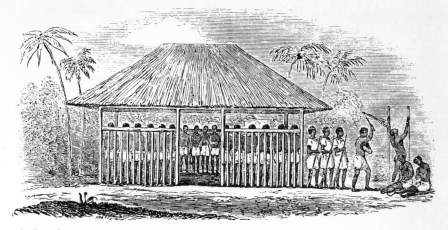

A slave barracoon

Capture of a large slave-ship by H.M.S. *Pluto*, reported on April 28th 1860

East Battery   Lower Commissariat   Freetown Church

Panoramic views of Freetown by Mrs Loetitia Jervis, 1852. H.

Queen's Yard for Liberated Africans
Watering Place

e lies in the bay.

The gates of the Queen's Yard as they appear today, part of the Connaught Hospital, Freetown. The inscription reads 'Royal hospital and asylum for Africans rescued from slavery by British valour and philanthropy. Erected A.D. MDCCCXVII. His Excellency Lieut. Col. MacCarthy Gov.'

The Court of the Mixed Commission (now demolished), Freetown.

Liberated African Department offices (now demolished), Freetown.

perfect agreement with the business spirit of the era, active participation of private enterprise even in Government projects.[1]

Early in 1849 the Commissioners conducted a full scale review of their work, preliminary to recommending the new system of contract agency.[2] The case for contract-emigration was very strong. Even if private vessels could easily be induced to engage in the emigration traffic the chances were that they would always seek to make their profits by irregular or illegal methods on the coast. The rate being paid as bounty ($£7$ to $£8$) to shipowners included of course not merely the actual and regular profits of the private shipowner but also a remuneration for the great risk attending the service; the risk, namely, of entirely failing to obtain a cargo, after provisioning the vessel and paying the officers. This had involved the Government in heavy expenditure. The irregularity which had attended the engagement of private ships and hence of the despatching of liberated Africans to the West Indies was a further problem which also called for a change of system.

The Commissioners came to the conclusion that if the whole conduct of the service was left solely in the hands of a single firm of shipowners, such a firm would be able not only to solve many of the existing problems but to offer, in addition, more advantageous terms to the Government than a private shipowner who only tendered his ship *pro hac vice* with merely an irregular knowledge of the circumstances of the emigration scheme and no command over the general despatch of shipping.

---

grating from the Colony within the first six months as 1,169. In September 1847 the Commissioners quoted the figure as 1,088—and this only for British Guiana and Jamaica and for the whole year of 1841. In 1848-9 the number emigrating was 3,810; but later the figure was given as 6,500—from Sierrra Leone (C.O. 386/107, January 18th, 1854, Commissioners to C.O.). The statistics for St Helena in 1848-9 also quoted the figures emigrating from that place as 3,510; but no separate figures were given for other stations such as Rio, Havana, Loanda, Boa Vista, supposing emigration took place from those places; or for the Gold Coast, Kroo Coast and the Gambia, supposing their figures were not already included in those for Sierra Leone. Also there were many returns of emigrants whose origins were 'not stated' or 'unknown'.

1. MacDonagh, Oliver, *A Pattern of Government Growth, 1800-1860*, cited, W. L. Burn, *The Age of Equipoise* (London, 1964) pp. 112-13; 165-6. MacDonagh, Oliver, *Emigration and the State; An Essay in Administrative History*, cited, Burn, *ibid.*, p. 228. See also, for the role of private enterprise in European emigration schemes of the nineteenth century, Jones, M. A., *op. cit.*

2. C.O. 386/56, April 18th, 1849, Commissioners to C.O. (Merivale); C.O. 318/181, April 18th, 1849, same to same.

Some of the final terms of the Hodge contract deserve mention. For a fixed period of one year the contract committed to the firm the sole right of management and conveyance to the West Indies of emigrants from Sierra Leone and St Helena. The Government remained chargeable with the maintenance of the liberated Africans at Sierra Leone and St Helena for a limited period of 3 and 6 weeks respectively. This meant that the Government's responsibility for their maintenance was limited to the period between their recapture and adjudication by the Vice-Admiralty or Mixed Commission Courts.

Further, it was agreed that if the contractor was able to embark the emigrants before the expiration of 3 and 6 weeks at Sierra Leone and St Helena respectively, he should receive a bonus equal to the estimated cost of their maintenance for every day during which he had thus relieved the Government from the cost of supporting them. On the other hand, if the emigrants remained in the Queen's Yard for more than the prescribed period, the contractor's pay would become subject to a corresponding forfeit calculated at the same rate; viz. 3d. per adult per diem and 6d. per adult per diem at Sierra Leone and St Helena respectively. The aim here, in short, was to give the firm a pecuniary interest in taking the emigrants out of Government hands not merely within the stated period but 'as rapidly as possible'. If this could be accomplished it would 'have a corresponding effect in enabling Government to reduce the cost of the establishment and other incidental expenses'.[1] Operating in its subsequent effect like the former system of 'head-money' payment, this particular provision was to become a major source of the difficulty—practically the only difficulty—which arose later.

However the Government was able through the new contract to solve many of the old problems which had been a source of anxiety since 1843—the safety and welfare of the emigrants. Scales of victualling and medical comforts were no longer neglected but became entrenched in the contract agreement. In addition the Commissioners secured the right to conduct a thorough examination, previous to its despatch from England, of any vessel employed by the firm; a surgeon was to be appointed by the Government for each vessel despatched, but paid for by the firm; but above all, the Government secured the contractors' agreement to the payment of passage money or bounty on the basis only of numbers of African

---

1. C.O. 386/56, April 18th, 1849. Commissioners to C.O. (Merivale)

emigrants landed *alive* in the West Indies. For every emigrant taken from Sierra Leone and landed alive in the West Indies the Hodge Company was to receive £6 1s. 10d. per adult (i.e. above 10 years of age); or £3 0s. 11d. if the emigrant was a child (between 1 to 10 years of age); while for every adult emigrant or child removed from St Helena payment was to be at the rate of £6 14s. 10d. and £3 7s. 5d. respectively.

On the 15th November 1849 the contract came into operation. Five vessels, the *Glentanner*, *Brandon*, *Fame*, *Clarendon* and the *Atlantic* were immediately put into service. The whole scheme worked very satisfactorily at first. The firm found it good business. By August 1850 it had recouped over £1,000 from passages paid by emigrants returning from British Guiana. By the end of 1850 some 184 persons had been offered return passages in the Company's ships.[1] Many of the repatriates were 'wealthy'. The Kroomen among them, for instance, had deposited no less than $4,000 with the ship's captain. The Governor of British Guiana urged Governor MacDonald to establish a direct communication between Sierra Leone and the Kroo Coast, in the hope that their return to their homes with so much 'valuable property' would remove the check to emigration which their previous failure to return was alleged to have caused.[2] More about return passages later.

Meanwhile the Hodge Company began to experience some difficulties in the working of the scheme. A growing competition for Kroo labour was already becoming noticeable from the developing palm oil trade under the Liverpool supercargoes and European merchants on the West Coast. Worse still, the contract suffered a further shock through the fresh squabbles between the officials, this time between the Hodge Company and Governor MacDonald. The latter had insisted on the rigid observance of the regulations by the Hodge Company and would not permit the embarkation of any emigrants other than those selected by the Government Agent. Also, MacDonald insisted on the full payment of all tonnage and harbour dues by the Company's vessels. His action brought down upon him the wrath of the Emigration Commissioners:

We are quite unable to conjecture the grounds on which the Governor

---

1. C.O. 386/87, August 22nd, 1850, Commissioners to C.O. The *Glentanner* seems to have been reserved for return passages, having received by 1850 £285 15s. 0d. and a further £956 5s. 0d. on account of 236 emigrants returning from British Guiana.
2. C.O. 386/57, June 8th, 1850, same to same.

thought himself at liberty to enforce this prohibition. Our agreement with Messrs. Hyde Hodge and Co. contains no stipulation of this kind; we think that it is evidently desirable to encourage everything which may increase the communication between Africa and the West Indies or which may enable the contractor to derive profit from his contract without expense to the Government or detriment to the service.[1]

Grey followed up immediately with a tough despatch, a final warning to the Governor:

I have to instruct you on no account again to take upon yourself to interfere with the Orders which Messrs. Hyde and Hodge have under the direction of the Land and Emigration Commissioners given to the Commanders of their ships. I have to inform you that I cannot but fear that your whole proceedings in the matter have been prompted by a spirit unfriendly to an object in which you have been informed that Her Majesty's Government take a very deep interest, and I therefore think it right to admonish you that if I should have occasion hereafter to doubt the zeal and sincerity with which you endeavour to promote the success of this service, I shall have no alternative but that of advising Her Majesty to place the government of Sierra Leone in other hands.[2]

MacDonald determined to wash his hands of the scheme, leaving the Company to its own devices. But it was not long before the Commissioners and Grey himself, confronted with a case of high mortality on board the Company's ship and a heavy claim of indemnity by the Company, regretted that MacDonald had not intervened to prevent an improper embarkation of unhealthy emigrants! Practically the only serious problem that arose during the contract agency was in this case of the *Atlantic*, carrying smallpox-ridden emigrants to the West Indies.

The *Atlantic* incident had an important significance. Occurring in a scheme that was otherwise working satisfactorily, it came only as further proof of the obvious difficulties confronting the persistent official attempt to squeeze liberated African emigration policy in to one procrustean bed of philanthropic-*cum*-materialist motives. Indeed the sole responsibility of recapturing and of catering for the welfare of the slaves could not really deny the Government the corresponding power, in fact the right, of determining in what manner the services of their protégés ought to be judiciously and usefully employed. Yet the full discharge of this power or right had remained

---

1. C.O. 386/87, August 29th, October 4th, 1850, Commissioners to C.O.
2. C.O. 268/43, No. 353, September 7th, 1850, Grey to MacDonald.

because of international criticism and the opposition of the 'Saints' at home, a very delicate and difficult matter throughout the emigration scheme. If so, the profit-obsessed policy of *immediate* shipment with a view to avoiding costs or expenditure on their maintenance, seemed to be not merely impolitic but lacking in real virtue and philanthropy; it was indeed the source of many of the evils or embarrassments in the whole scheme of which the incident of the *Atlantic* in 1850–1 was one.

It is worth examining in closer detail. In 1850 the *Atlantic*, one of the Company's vessels, went to embark emigrants from St Helena. The medical superintendent of the liberated African Yard, Dr Rawline, retained nearly 200 of them on the sick list, and refused their immediate embarkation. But threatened with a charge of 'unnecessary opposition' to the embarkation of these emigrants and threatened, further, with a letter to the Colonial Office demanding his immediate dismissal from service, Dr Rawline gave in to his opponents—the Governor of St Helena and the Collector of Customs. About 138 of the recaptives were consequently removed from the hospital, issued with the usual certificates of fitness for embarkation, and at once embarked in the *Atlantic*, which then departed for Sierra Leone to obtain its full complement.

Meanwhile at Sierra Leone two foreign slavers, *Fleur de Maria* and *Caraman*, had been captured on the 24th June and on the 2nd July respectively, each with serious cases of smallpox on board. The *Atlantic* arrived in Sierra Leone early in July to pick up more unhealthy emigrants, embarking about 170 of those landed in the *Fleur de Marie*, and more than 260 of those released from *Caramarn*, according to the Commissioners' report, 'before it was at all clear that they had not themselves contracted the disease [or] while it was still to be expected that many of them would sicken of it'.[1] The *Atlantic* then departed for the West Indies.

A serious legal tangle arose later when the Hodge Company, on December 3rd, 1850, submitted a claim to be indemnified for £1,801 4s. od. as expenses incurred by them while the *Atlantic* was under detention in quarantine for 49 days in Trinidad. More than 70 of the emigrants had already died of smallpox. The Company's contention was that the Government Officers were fully responsible for the immediate embarkation of those emigrants at Sierra Leone and therefore for the heavy loss resulting. The vital question now

---

1. C.O. 386/87, April 15th, 1851, Commissioners to C.O.

before the Commissioners was to determine 'whether Messrs. Hyde Hodge or the Government are to bear the loss incurred by delay (quarantine) and otherwise from the appearance of smallpox on board the *Atlantic* and incidentally who, if anyone, is responsible for causing the misfortune'.[1]

MacDonald's neutrality in the *Atlantic* emigration proceedings had placed him above involvement or impeachment by Grey or the Emigration Commissioners. The latter now regretted that he had not intervened in the proceedings of the *Atlantic* since his intervention would have been the only way of avoiding the trouble and the Company's claims against the Government. The Governor was merely asked by the Colonial Office to narrate the case as he saw it. An effort to defeat or reduce the Company's claim involved the Commissioners in serious argument and apportionment of blame between the Hodge Company and the Government Officers. But the latter got the worst of it. Although the 13th article of the Charter Party empowered the Master of the Company's ship to reject any emigrants unfitted for immediate conveyance, the occurrence of smallpox on board the *Atlantic* was a case in which the Master could neither be expected nor was entitled to discover the real state of the health of the emigrants. This was the sole responsibility of the Surgeon and the Government Emigration Agent at Sierra Leone, and hence of the Government alone: 'For the selection therefore of emigrants the Government appears to us strictly responsible and we must say that we do not consider that selection to have been exercised with proper care. We cannot feel any doubt that such an immediate shipment was very imprudent.'[2] The Commissioners went on to state that the heavy mortality on board the *Atlantic*, with the financial loss resulting from it, had followed from an act for the proper performance of which the Government Officers were responsible and in regard to which they had neglected to exercise the caution which the circumstances demanded, and for the consequences of which the Hodge Company had a just claim to be indemnified. This was the Commissioners' final verdict. But there was yet another side to the matter.

It was only by the imprudence of the Government Officers that the Company had been enabled to escape a detention and a forfeiture that the *Atlantic* might still have been subject to in Sierra Leone. For what else would have happened, if Governor Mac-

---

1. *Ibid.*   2. *Ibid.*

Donald had intervened and prevented the immediate embarkation of those emigrants until the smallpox was over? The Commissioners began to re-examine the whole problem from a new angle. To the extent of such a delay, if MacDonald had intervened, the Company's ship, *Atlantic*, would have been equally detained at Sierra Leone, rather than in Trinidad, and would have been subjected to a forfeiture at the rate of 3d. per diem per adult for so long as the sick remained in the Yard at the Government's expense.[1] It was being implied, in short, that, with a view to escaping a forfeiture and at the same time receiving the stipulated bonus of 3d. per adult per diem, the Company's officials had tacitly acquiesced in the improper and immediate embarkation of unhealthy emigrants!

This was clearly a serious fault arising from a particular provision of the contract. The claim of £1,801 4s. 0d. for 49 days' detention in quarantine in Trinidad was seriously contested on this major ground, the Commissioners recommending that the Government should pay only £1,089 4s. 2d. instead of the Company's original claim. The case was finally settled, the Company accepting the Commissioners' decision.

The *Atlantic* incident was also remarkable in at once suggesting a detailed review of the existing contract and introducing the important question, especially after the payment of 'so large a compensation', of 'how far the contract with these gentlemen taken as a whole has hitherto acted for the benefit of Government' or of the Hodge Company.[2] The whole incident clearly underlined the one major fault existing in the contract agency, the idea of immediate embarkation, and hastened its removal in the second contract which was concluded with the Company in 1851.

A detailed review of the first year's contract showed many advantages in the contract agency, despite the large compensation paid in the *Atlantic* incident. During the first contract the Company had despatched 12 ships to the West Indies and conveyed 3,444 African emigrants from Sierra Leone and St Helena, the Government paying altogether £18,802 12s. 11d. for the service. The average cost per adult of passage-money or bounty paid to private vessels before 1849 was £6 0s. 1d. The average cost under the Hodge contract came to £5 18s. 9d. At a saving of 1s. 4d. per head the Government had saved through the Company about £99 19s. 4d. on the 1,499½ adults shipped from Sierra Leone. Also by immediate

---

1. *Ibid.*   2. *Ibid.*

embarkation of the emigrants the Company had reduced the normal length of detention at Sierra Leone by more than 10 days, thus saving the Government a great deal more on maintenance expenditure, which saving the Commissioners reckoned at £193 5s. 0d.

Government saving at St Helena had been even more substantial: the average cost per adult of passage-money before 1849 was £6 19s. 4d; the contract service had reduced this to £5 14s. 11d. thus showing a saving of £1 4s. 5d. per adult or £2,287 16s. 10d. on the 1,874 Africans despatched from that Island during the first year of the contract. Also by reducing the usual length of their stay or detention in the Queen's Yard from 48 days to 27 days and shipping them as soon as released from slave ships, the Company had saved for the Government some £996 9s. 0d. on the 1,898 souls landed at that place during the first year of the contract service. On the whole, then, Government profit was as follows:

Saving on conveyance
    £99 19s. 4d. + £2,287 16s. 10d.   =   £2,387 16s. 2d.
Saving on maintenance through prompt
    embarkation
    £193 5s. 0d. + £996 9s. 0d.   =   £1,189 14s. 0d.
Total saving at Sierra Leone and
    St Helena   =   £3,577 10s. 2d.

A study of the mortality rate showed also that the contract service had been much more efficient with regard to care of the emigrants than the private vessel system. During 1849 the mortality rate was about 8 per cent. Under the contract service this had fallen to 4·55 per cent by the end of 1850. From these general results of the first year's contract the Commissioners strongly recommended the renewal of the Company's contract.[1] The contract was renewed,[2] with minor changes, for 1852. The Company's service was extended to Rio de Janeiro; the return of delegates from British Guiana and Trinidad at a flat rate of £4 10s. 0d. per head was legally provided for, while the lesson of the *Atlantic* incident became evident in a new clause, Article XIX, which stipulated that in future questions of indemnity or compensation would be considered by the Government only if detention of the Company's ship occurred at the port of

---

1. C.O. 386/87, Commissioners to C.O., February 11th, 1851, April 15th, 1851; C.O. 386/88, see Printed Copy of the Renewed Contract Agreement.
2. C.O. 318/185, June 1st, 1850, C.O. Minutes.

disembarkation and was proved to be caused entirely by the fault or action of Government emigration officers. Immediate embarkation at the port of recruitment was thus clearly out of consideration. The *Atlantic* incident had also the effect of causing Grey practically to eat his own threatening words to Governor MacDonald, the latter being now required in future to intervene, if the emigration proceedings appeared to him to be irregular![1] The new contract was to last for another year ending June 30th, 1852.

The falling off of the foreign slave trade, especially the Cuban and the Brazilian, had a serious effect on the working of the Hodge contract after 1851-2. The Queen's Yards at the British settlements were never as full after 1851 as before and some of the Company's ships remained under-employed. In fact before the renewal of the contract in 1851, the Company and the Emigration Commissioners had carefully examined this problem and speculated on the possibility of reopening the Kroo Coast emigration and expanding the scheme, if possible, up to the Niger Delta, as far as the Bonny River.[2] The only difficulty was the fact that the Niger Delta was already becoming a region of great labour demand, in consequence of the growing coastal trade in palm oil. It was observed that nearly all the hundred or more vessels owned by Liverpool merchants engaged in the palm oil trade 'between Sierra Leone and the Bonny river', needed a great deal of local labour. It was calculated that each of the vessels employed about 10 to 12 labourers; which meant that some 500 to 600 blacks were engaged as canoe boys, firemen, stewards, etc. by Liverpool coastal merchants. The *Petrel*, owned by Wilson and Dawson of Liverpool, had already started a regular coastal labour migration service between the Niger Delta and the Kroo Coast to import Kroo labour into the Bonny River. The vessel, during its last voyage to the Kroo Coast had returned about 63 Kroo labourers from the Niger Delta who had already served their term of engagement and were due for return passage to their country.[3] What chances of success then, under such new competition, had the Hodge Company if their service was now extended to the Kroo Coast and the Niger Delta?

---

1. C.O. 268/43, No. 410, February 11th, 1851, Grey to MacDonald. See also Law officers legal opinion on the *Atlantic* emigration at Sierra Leone, L.O. No. 1015 and 4718.
2. C.O. 386/57, June 8th, 1850, Commissioners to C.O.
3. C.O. 386/57, June 8th, 1850, Commissioners to C.O.; C.O. 318/185 and 186, June 8th, 1850, same to same.

While encouraging the Hodge Company or any other private ships to extend the emigration to the Kroo Coast or the Niger Delta if possible, the Commissioners could not advise the Government to finance 'such an uncertain service'. Soon afterwards British Guiana offered to sustain the Hodge contract and to finance the extension of the recruitment on the coast.[1] The Commissioners became merely the channel of communication in the conclusion of the final agreement between the Company and the Government of British Guiana. The new contract was to last for six years, the Company agreeing to import 15,000 labourers into British Guiana at a bounty of £7 per head.[2] By July 1853 the Colonial Office terminated the office of Government Emigration Agent at Sierra Leone and the Company took over the payment of Fisher's salary.[3]

The Company's vessels remained under such limited Government superintendence as would tend to prevent abuse; but responsibilities relating to financial arrangements and other matters reverted to the new contractors—the Hodge Company and British Guiana.

Meanwhile the Company requested the Commissioners' permission to send Fisher to the Kroo Coast to arrange with the local Chiefs of that place for emigrants. The request was approved.[4] By 1853 the Company was making further requests: unless some new emigration agency was employed, it argued, and effective canvassing for emigrants adopted, the emigration could only be continued by kidnapping, since not enough slave ships were being recaptured on the coast. While British Guiana raised the per capita bounty for the Company's ships to $43·20[5] the Company asked for permission to double Fisher's 'head-money', which the Emigration Commissioners also sanctioned.[6] A further request asked for government protection against competition from other emigration Companies allegedly forming in England for the African emigration traffic. The Government refused the request but on reading a prospectus published by one of the new Companies apprehended serious trouble if such Companies should come out to the West Coast:

---

1. C.O. 386/89, September 20th, 1852, Commissioners to C.O.
2. C.O. 386/89, April 16th, 1853; C.O. 386/90, December 22nd, 1853, same to same.
3. C.O. 386/90, September 7th, 1853, same to same.
4. C.O. 386/89, September 20th, 1852, same to same.
5. C.O. 318/196, January 12th, 1852, Commissioners to C.O.
6. C.O. 386/89, April 25th, 1853, same to same.

It is certainly impossible to view without apprehension the announce-
ment which that prospectus contains of a proposed emigration from
West Africa coupled with promise of a market for Rum in that locality.[1]

It appeared however that the Hodge Company, anxious for
protection against possible competition, had raised a false alarm
with the Government. No such Company was ever heard of again.
Curiously enough, the first cause for real alarm in 1853 was about
the action of the Hodge Company itself.

If the decline in the foreign slave trade diminished the volume
of their business, and the Government refused protection against
competition, the Company exerted itself to keep up its new contract
with British Guiana. At Sierra Leone where the payment of 'head-
money' had been doubled since 1852, the reports of the Governors
showed that the incidence of kidnapping reached a very high level
by 1853.[2] By August one of the Company's vessels, *Elphinstone*,
was reported on the Kroo Coast to have arrived without a Surgeon,
and this soon after the outbreak of smallpox on board. The Commissioners wrote to remind the Company about the clause in the
Passengers' Act which required that every vessel carrying up to 50
passengers must have a Surgeon on board.[3]

In the meantime the Government of Liberia was protesting
against the activities of the Hodge Company on the Kroo Coast, a
Proclamation having been made by the President of the Republic
against any further recruitment from that Coast. In Parliament
embarrassing questions were being asked about the emigration
contracts. The Colonial Office and the Commissioners were stirred

---

1. *Ibid.*, April 21st, 1853, same to same.
2. C.O. 268/45, No. 32, March 22nd, 1853, Newcastle to Kennedy about 'Traders
   within the Colony laying claim to respectability who are not only cognisant of
   this traffic, but likewise abet it by supplying the dealers in it with goods on
   credit.'; C.O. 268/45, No. 45, April 27th, 1853, same to same about persons
   already convicted of the crime; C.O. 268/45, No. 52, May 15th, 1853, same to
   same, about persons kidnapped and sold in the Colony but at last redeemed;
   C.O. 268/45, No. 58, June 2nd, 1853, same to same about 'the system of slave
   dealing lately brought to light in the Colony of Sierra Leone'; C.O. 268/45,
   No. 51, November 23rd, 1855, Labouchere to Hill about the Governor's Proclamation and other measures for the suppression of slave dealing in the
   Colony; C.O. 268/47, No. 68, December 29th, 1855, same to same about the
   case of 44 slaves recently smuggled into the Colony for sale; C.O. 268/47,
   No. 95, February 27th, 1856, same to same about three canoes arriving in the
   vicinity of the Colony with 119 slaves on board.
3. C.O. 38/90, August 20th, 1853.

into action. Consular Officers and members of the Admiralty on the West Coast were asked to investigate the proceedings on the Kroo Coast.[1] At home the Commissioners were instructed to furnish a report to the Secretary of State

> as may show that the Regulations in the West African Colonies are sufficient to prevent the possibility of fraud, violence or underhand means of compulsion being used.[2]

But investigations at the Kroo Coast confirmed that the Company's agents had exceeded the emigration boundaries; that the agency of local chiefs was utilized; that an advance payment of $10 per head on emigrants procured was offered to the local agents. The Proclamation by the President of Liberia, it was reported, had been occasioned by the smuggling of emigrants through the Liberian port of Monrovia.[3] By 1854 the Hodge Company was in serious hot water and offered to terminate the contract.[4] The Emigration Commission tried to establish its own innocence in the scandal.[5] But questions asked in Parliament still had to be answered anyway. Though by its later proceedings on the Kroo Coast the Hodge Company became in many respects only an English counterpart of the French Regis contract at the coasts of Dahomey, yet it was clear that under the Company's services liberated African Emigration had enjoyed a level of careful supervision and regularity which had been unknown to it prior to that contract. Perhaps this was why every effort was made by the Commissioners and the Secretary of State absolutely to absolve that 'respectable Firm' from any blame in the final report on the Kroo Coast emigration:

> Its endeavours to procure a free emigration [the British public was informed about the Hodge Company in 1854] have been carefully guarded from abuse on the part of those conducting it, and were promptly dis-

---

1. C.O. 386/90, July 29th, 1853.   2. C.O. 386/107, January 18th, 1854.
3. C.O. 386/90, July 29th, 1853, Commissioners to C.O.
4. C.O. 318/202, April 16th, 1853; C.O. 386/107, January 18th, 1854, Commissioners to C.O.; *General Report for 1853*, PP. 1854, Vol. XXVIII, 71.
5. C.O. 386/90, December 22nd, 1853, Commissioners to C.O. 'Throughout the arrangement', they pointed out, 'this Board was not the contracting party, but a channel of communication between Mr Rose of Hyde and Hodge and the British Guiana Government'; and although 'some additional regulations or details may have taken place between' the contracting parties, the Board could neither claim any responsibility for this, nor testify that any illegal plans had entered the contract agreements.

continued when it appeared impossible to obviate mischief arising from it through the misapprehension of the natives.

The Government itself was equally free from any improper proceedings in the emigration scheme:

> The Government has jealously and effectively provided against any use of violence, misrepresentation or undue influence in inducing Africans to emigrate; and, in regard to the Liberated Africans under its charge, has scrupulously abstained from the exercise of any compulsion.[1]

There was, of course, much specious reasoning and not a little falsification of facts in this special pleading. The facts were that between 1854 and 1865, after the Hodge Company had given up, private emigration vessels still transported some 2,000 or more Africans to the West Indies;[2] that between 1858–9, with the sudden revival of the foreign (Cuban) slave trade, the Hodge Company was back for another two years' contract, 946 emigrants having been landed in Sierra Leone in December 1858 and later despatched by the Company.[3] In 1860, 1,782 Africans were landed at St Helena in three slavers; in 1861, 845 of them were landed in one slaver.[4]

By 1861, the Hodge contract was finally dropped. Government had lost interest in the business as long ago as 1854. By 1860, in fact, official restrictions were being applied to check emigration.

The fact that the decline of the foreign slave trade was diminishing the number of captured slaves and therefore of emigrants does not, however, fully explain official indifference to emigration since 1854. The West India planters still clamoured for African labour after that year and, despite a thriving Asiatic emigration scheme, had continued until 1871 to demand the reopening of the 'cheaper' African emigration scheme. By this time Lord Kimberley in the Colonial Office had decided to treat the persistent demand of the planters for African labourers with utter silence and neglect: 'It will be more prudent to do nothing'.[5] It is necessary to trace the growth of

---

1. C.O. 386/107, January 18th, 1854, Commissioners to C.O.
2. C.O. 386/188, *Returns of African Emigrants, 1854 to 1865.*
3. C.O. 318/226, December 21st and 31st, 1858, Commissioners to C.O.; PP. 1859–ii, xx, 138–9, No. 396, February 25th, 1858; Labouchere to Acting Governor Walker, *Eighteenth General Report*, PP. 1857–8, Vol. xxiv (2395) 401.
4. C.O. 318/235, January 29th, 1862, Murdoch to Elliot.
5. C.O. 318/267, Walcott to Herbert, September 2nd, 1871; C.O. 318/262, Murdoch to Herbert, September 27th, 1871 and C.O. Minutes; C.O. 318/262,

official indifference to emigration in more detail, as this may enable a better understanding of the change in official policy.

In December 1859 some 500 captured Africans were reported waiting at Sierra Leone, but the Government prescribed near impossible conditions for the private vessels which engaged to remove them to the West Indies. Many were enlisted into the West India Regiment.[1] In 1861 some 200 liberated Africans were despatched to the Gambia on the request made by D'Arcy, Governor of the Colony, for defence purposes.[2] The Emigration Commissioners, uncertain on the thinking of the Ministers, became confused as to whether to continue engaging transport vessels or not. When Jamaica applied to receive its share of the captured Africans who remained in the Queen's Yard, the Commissioners merely regretted 'that Jamaica should lose the advantage of this large body of labourers'. Uncertain about the new Government policy towards liberated Africans, they stated that 'considerable as is the expense of maintaining those people it would not be advisable to take any further proceeding in this country for sending them to the West Indies'.[3] Significantly, by this time the Government was in fact sponsoring a delegation of black people from the new world to Lagos and the Niger hinterland, to establish a rehabilitation centre for liberated Africans to whom encouragement was being given to return to West Africa.[4] In April 1861 the Commissioners were instructed to cancel the engagement of the ship, *Athenais*, and to pay the owner compensation of £350 instead.[5]

By July another 500 Africans were reported captured at Sierra Leone, and the Commissioners could not take any action for their removal, but were obliged rather to inquire from the Secretary of State whether there was any plan 'to dispose of these Africans in any other way'.[6] Meanwhile the Secretary of State, Newcastle, decided that from April 1st, 1862, the colonies should finance African emigration entirely out of their own budgets. A definite intention to prohibit further recruitments from West Africa was clearly

---

same to same, October 19th, 1871 and Minute by Taylor; C.O. 318/262, Minute by Lord Kimberley, October 19th, 1871.
1. C.O. 386/108, December 21st, 1859 and January 18th, 1860.
2. C.O. 386/108, April 13th, 1861; C.O. 268/47, No. 188, June 11th, 1861, Newcastle to Hill.
3. C.O. 386/108, *ibid*.
4. F.O. 2/28, F.O. to Lodder, Lagos, June 11th, 1859.
5. C.O. 386/108, April 30th, 1861.   6. *Ibid*., July 12th, 1861.

implied and had produced its first desired effect when Trinidad immediately dropped out of the scheme. Other colonies still continued, with increasing difficulties deliberately put in their way.[1]

The West India interests became incensed at this sudden change of Government attitude. By the end of July the West India Committee met and delegated their Chairman, McGregor, to inquire from the Colonial Office about the new attitude towards the emigration scheme.[2] Still no change came after this appeal.

At last the West India interests forced a heated and revealing debate in Parliament. Stephen Cave attacked the Government:

> We fail to take a broad and comprehensive view of this great question. The Emperor of the French strains every nerve to pour labourers into his colonies. Spain risks a war with England to increase her population in Cuba. The people of England have determined to have as much sugar and cotton as they require without asking questions. It must be made by free labour. It cannot be made by free labour without immigration. Yet we persist in viewing immigration as a concession to the planters to be grudgingly and suspiciously bestowed. Seven hundred re-captured Africans are at this moment at Ascension, and it seems nobody's business to take them away. . . . Again we saddle the planter who employs the immigrant with two-thirds of the cost of his introduction, thereby confining immigration to a very narrow limit.[3]

Further official restrictions had since been applied at Sierra Leone where the Governor was instructed not to permit further recruitments to emigration vessels.[4]

Palmerston replied to Cave's motion on emigration. His statement not only caused that motion to be at last withdrawn but the information he gave plainly revealed the *volte-face* in policy. Palmerston explained that all the European Powers including Britain were beginning to acquire spheres of influence or possessions in Africa, that full development of the economic resources of these new acquisitions would require human labour, and that, like any other colonial power, Britain needed now to conserve the labour resources in her own Settlements:

> They want all the labour for cultivation and improvement that the

---

1. C.O. 318/233, Walcott to Rogers, August 31st, 1861 and C.O. 318/240, Murdoch to Rogers, February 11th, 1863.
2. *Ibid.*, July 31st, 1861.   3. *Hansard*, 1861, CLXI, 958.
4. C.O. 268/47, No. 80, March 17th; No. 99, June 22nd, 1860, Newcastle to Fitzjames.

population will afford, and every man sent away is a man withdrawn from the development of the natural resources of the country.[1]

In the meantime the new policy of economic development was already replacing the old one of destitution long pursued at Sierra Leone. A new firm called the British and West African Cotton Company had just been formed, and was receiving every official support in the purchase of some 10,000 acres of land at Sierra Leone where the project of cotton cultivation in West Africa was to be started. Both the Commissioners and the Secretary of State strongly advised the Governor of Sierra Leone to exert all his efforts in the interests if this Company, because 'at the present moment the cultivation of cotton is so important in a national point of view'.[2]

The problem of labour was to be one of the greatest difficulties to be faced both by merchants and by colonial Governments in the subsequent development of Britain's West African imperial estate during the century. Already by 1863 the American Civil War was having its impact on the great cotton industries of Britain. West Africa, especially most parts of the Niger hinterland, was seen as a potential source of supply of that vital raw material.

The British industrialists required cultivators who were not only adapted to the West African climate but who might also be very knowledgeable about cotton agriculture. There was no better answer to this problem than the black exiles in North America, Canada and the West Indies. But again, as in the previous demand for their exportation, a strong philanthropic note accompanied the clamour for their mass repatriation to Africa. By 1859, as pointed out before, the Government had sponsored a delegation to Lagos and the Yoruba country.[3] But by 1863 some of the British industrial societies were already growing impatient of delay and called upon the authorities to hasten the policy of mass repatriation, in order 'to rescue the Negroes from the unfavourable climate of Canada and Northern U.S.A. and from the growing prejudices of the white population'. Many of the exiles in the new world had treated this kindness as hypocritical, having been previously rescued by those same people to their new abode from the hostility of the African climate, and the tyranny of the African chiefs. Their scorn for the new rescue measure was clearly shown in the reply to the offer:

---

1. *Hansard*, 1861, CLXIV, 1658, July 26th, 1861.
2. C.O. 386/108, January 22nd, 1861.
3. Ajayi, *Christian Missions in Nigeria 1841–1891* (London, 1965) pp. 191–2.

The mortality among the coloured immigrants in Canada is no greater than among others; if Africa is the real home of the Negroes, so is Europe the real home of the American European. A colonisation man and a bitter pro-slavery man are almost controvertible terms.[1]

Meanwhile in the West Indies, as fresh importations of African labour became increasingly difficult because of the dramatic change in the Imperial Government's policy, the planters were given a free hand in the exploitation of those who had already been imported. The British Government sanctioned many new regulations which were introduced by the colonies with a view to obtaining more 'effective labour' from the immigrants. By the early 1850s the promise of a free return passage no longer applied, and many who were entitled to it were denied it:

When prospects of obtaining free emigrants dwindled, the West India colonies ceased to have much interest in sending back emigrants; rather the reverse.[2]

Gratuities of £1 began to be offered to Kroo labourers who agreed to renounce their right to a free return passage.[3] The reduction of wages by the planters was also sanctioned and took the form of a 25 per cent increase in the amount of task performed with wages remaining the same at an average of 33 cents per day.[4] When many of the planters took the extreme measure of making the labourers work without any wages at all, only the fears expressed by some of the Governors of a possible strike or labour upheaval in the West Indies forced the Emigration Commissioners to investigate the situation and report to the Government:

Some of the employers in defiance of their contracts had refused to pay the labourers the stipulated wages in money alleging that their labour was not worth the rations and food issued to them in addition to the expense of their support and medical attendance during sickness. The insufficiency of labour and all other irregularities now charged against them are clearly traceable to the hardship of giving them scarcely anything more than food and clothing for their services.[5]

---

1. *The African Times*, Organ of the African Aid Society, April 23rd, 1863, cited in Ajayi, *op. cit.*, p. 47, footnote 2.
2. Laurence, K. O., *op. cit.*, p. 158.
3. PP. 1850, Vol. XL, 350, November 16th, 1849, Commissioners to C.O.
4. PP. 1847–8, Vol. XLVI, 557–63, Stipendiary Magistrates' Returns, July 1848; PP. 1847–8, XLVI, 432, No. 324, April 10th, 1848, Grey to Light.
5. C.O. 386/87, October 21st, 1850, Commissioners to C.O.

The planters now valued the labour of the African immigrant at not more than 5d. per day, and claimed that this amount was more than offset by the higher expenses incurred in feeding and maintaining them. But the Emigration Commissioners saw the obvious contradiction in the planters' action:

> When we contrast these at best doubtful accounts with the eagerness which is shewn for immigrants of this class . . . it becomes questionable [how reliable the planters' complaints against their labourers are].[1]

These findings, however, still did not prevent the Government from sanctioning more serious acts of oppression against the labourers. When the colonies subsequently passed the so-called vagrancy laws, Lord Grey at the Colonial Office quickly sanctioned them in order to ensure that the labourers, now denied freedom of movement outside the estates, remained confined there to work for longer hours. By 1850 compulsory taxation was imposed 'which they would not be able to pay except by labouring for wages and which labour was to be enforced under the penalty of labour avowedly penal'.[2] The Colonial Office readily approved. By 1863 five-year indentures of immigrant labourers had replaced the 3-year labour contracts which had been the practice since 1852.[3]

The British Anti-Slavery Society, which had maintained a curious silence for so long over the emigration policy, was stirred into action in 1850 by the increasingly oppressive measures agreed upon between the colonies and the home Government. The Society had become appalled not by the principle of emigration but rather 'by the defective nature of those schemes' now introduced.[4] The Government roughly dismissed the Society's protest, declaring its intention to stick to its existing labour policy in the interest of the West India Colonies:

> In the West Indies the discontinuance of Sugar cultivation which has been and must again be the result of a want of labour would lead to the abandonment of the colonies by the European population and educated classes and would thus destroy the only apparent means of elevating

---

1. *Ibid.*, November 7th, 1849.
2. C.O. 386/57, October 31st, 1849, same to same.
3. Laurence, K. O., *op. cit.*, pp. 172–3; PP. 1850, XL, 661, July 28th, 1849; PP. 1852–3, LXVII, 484, *Report of Superintendent of Immigrants, to Trinidad*, March 31st, 1861.
4. C.O. 386/87, September 26th, 1850, Commissioners to C.O.

the emancipated classes and preventing their relapse into barbarism and idolatry.[1]

Despite the official determination to uphold it, emigration policy was abandoned soon afterwards. For suddenly in West Africa British interests and policies, as Palmerston's speech would show, were already changing by the 1860s and in a way that again profoundly affected the liberated Africans in Sierra Leone. Eventually, in fact, even those who had been refused their right to a free return passage and were held in the West Indies as hostages for those in West Africa who had failed to emigrate, were, thanks to the new interests of British policy, encouraged and enabled to return to West Africa.

Until late in the century, before many of the liberated Africans as exiles from the new world began to return in larger numbers, the liberated Africans in Sierra Leone became the corner-stone of the commercial developments and other British enterprises in the West African interior, especially the Niger hinterland. The authority whose opinion had carried the greatest weight with the British Government in the reversal of the emigration policy was Macgregor Laird. From 1854, after the historic success of the Niger expedition and after Barth's travels and glowing reports about commercial prospects in Central Africa, Laird's persuasive campaign for the return of the exiles from the West Indies and for the end of emigration policy was matched in force only by that of his memoranda and motion in 1842–43, for their compulsory emigration to the new world.

After 1854, the more his commercial expeditions or trading vessels were attacked by the hinterland natives of the Niger Delta, the more Laird campaigned seriously with the British Government for an end to emigration policy and for the utilisation of liberated African agency instead, to break the hostility of their heathen kith and kin who opposed British commercial penetration of the West African hinterland. Laird lost no time in finding a praise-name for the liberated Africans—'most efficient native agents', through whose agency British commerce 'may be introduced naturally, unobtrusively, and rapidly into the remotest regions of the interior'. They alone held the answer to the problem of native African hostility to the full development of British commercial enterprise in the West African interior:

The power of the Tribes of the Delta to impede the navigation of the

1. *Ibid.*

stream is owing to their command of arms and ammunition procured from the coast. This superiority will speedily cease with the opening of the trade above them, and the introduction of free Africans who in Sierra Leone and the West Indies have been in contact with a superior race and have acquired European habits and wants. Before the commercial value of central Africa can be largely developed this class of men must be introduced. They will form the retail dealers of British goods and collectors of produce. This class does not exist at the present and hence the failure commercially of the different attempts of trade in the interior.[1]

Lord Palmerston's speech in Parliament in 1861 had already removed the mystery about the official attitude to emigration policy. But in Macgregor Laird's commercial expeditions, and in the use which was made later of the labour and services both of liberated Africans and of Kroomen in the development of British enterprise in the Niger hinterland, the decline and death of liberated African emigration to the West Indies after 1860 fully and practically explains itself. This part of the story, an account of the vital role played by liberated African agency in the development of British commercial and political interests in West Africa, particularly the Niger hinterland after 1860, will form the theme of another work.

---

1. F.O. 2/23, February 8th, 1855, Laird to Clarendon; F.O. 2/23, Laird to Hammond, December 4th, 1856 and to Secretary to Admiralty, February 12th, 1856; F.O. 2/23, Laird to F.O., November 18th, 1856.

Conclusion

Some critics of Eric Williams' *Capitalism and Slavery* have seemed to argue, in spite of solid statistical evidence and of the implication for Government policy of trade facts, figures and statements about the West Indian economic situation in 1807 and 1833, that the economic facts or situations were only coincidental or secondary to the humanitarianism which they imply or see to be the dominant factor in the official minds which decided on abolition in 1807 and 1833. In other words, if the West Indian economic position in 1807 and 1833 was what *Capitalism and Slavery* stated it to be as regards the quantity of labour on the plantations and the production and the sale of sugar, that was no proof at all that those conditions actually decided Parliament and the Ministers to pass the abolition act:

> What is lacking is any hard evidence that the sort of economic con-
> siderations which are alleged to have dominated ministers and members
> of Parliament in fact did so. We have no indication at all of how these
> supposedly compulsive demands were translated into ministerial de-
> cisions and parliamentary votes.[1]

Dr Anstey has also strongly protested the steadfastness and con-
tinuity of official policy in regard to the abolition of the slave trade,
as well as the unflinching and selfless devotion of successive British
Governments and Ministers to that cause:

> What must strike any student of the Foreign Office records relating to
> Africa for the half-century after 1815 is that the notion that action
> against the slave trade on both humanitarian and commercial grounds
> was a good and proper concern of policy became the received conviction
> of the Office, something which did not require to be argued afresh as
> one generation of officials succeeded another, as one Foreign Secretary

---

1. Anstey, in *Seminar* (Edinburgh, 1965) p. 25.

gave place to his successor. To borrow the terminology of Robinson and Gallagher, the notion became an important part of the 'official mind'.[1]

In some sense this study is an attempt to reach that vital part, the secret part, of the official mind, which neither *Capitalism and Slavery* and its critics nor any other slave trade studies, with the documentary facts available to them, were in a position to reach. Since most of its performances are done in secret and outside public knowledge, the secret part of the official mind often leaves the real nature of, and the actual reasons behind its actions, naked and uncomplicated by the trappings and beguilements of logic, sophistry and rationale. The motives in this case are always clear, leaving no room for doubt or uncertainty.

In the secret records of the emigration policy the unsuspecting official mind has left its actions and motives quite clear enough, and this study therefore does not need to draw long conclusions for the reader who has gone through its pages.

But in view of the oft-told story that Christian Europe, in the hey-day of the Atlantic slave trade, had justified the traffic as the best means of bringing to Africans the joys and blessings of the Christian religion, much of the high rationale which surrounded liberated African emigration policy in parliamentary debates, as well as the sophistry with which officials tried to explain away in public the many abuses of the labourers, will all perhaps occasion very little surprise to students of the subject. But there will perhaps be little doubt that in the scheme for liberated African emigration, in the treatment given to the liberated Africans immediately on recapture and later in the plantation colonies, many of the old stories and problems and arguments—about British humanitarianism, economic self-interests, and about international non-cooperation in the nineteenth-century abolition movement—acquire important new perspectives for modern historians.

In their writings about the Atlantic slave trade and the international abolition movement, not a few historians have achieved fame by creating the image of one lone nation, Britain, unostentatiously fighting a virtuous, selfless cause against the intransigence and uncooperativeness of other, less virtuous nations. Indeed, the nineteenth-century philanthropic or anti-slavery movement is still proudly held by many imperial historians as a perfectly selfless act, the brightest feather in the cap of British paternalism or imperial

---

1. *Ibid.*, p. 29.

trusteeship. Of course the Granville Sharps, Thomas Clarksons, Fowell Buxtons, Wilberforces, the Denmans of the Naval Squadron and other illustrious names in that great movement must indeed remain as the 'Saints' for their unalloyed devotion to the anti-slavery cause. It may be said, however, that through the policy of its successive governments, Britain was as much involved in the unsavoury politics of abolition, and therefore as much entitled to a claim of singular honour or virtue in the abolition movement as any of the avowed slave trading nations in the mid-nineteenth century.

Appendix I

Substance of a Plan of a Settlement, to be made near Sierra Leone, on the Grain Coast of Africa, intended more particularly for the service and happy establishment of Blacks and People of colour to be shipped as freemen, under the direction of the Committee for relieving the Black poor, and under the protection of the British Government. By Henry Smeathman, Esq. who resided in that country near four years (London, 1786).

(1) Any person desirous of a permanent and comfortable establishment, in a most pleasant, fertile climate, near SIERRA LEONE where land is cheap, may do it on the following advantageous conditions.

(2) They will be carried out at five guineas each person, and supplied weekly during the voyage, with 5 lb. Bread, 1 ditto Beef, 3 ditto Pork, ¾ ditto Molasses, 1½ ditto Flour, 1 ditto Pot Barley, ½ ditto Suet, ½ ditto raisins, 1 pint Oatmeal, 1½ ditto Peas, 2 ditto Rum for grog; with Pimento, Ginger, &c.

(3) They will also have the same allowance, for 3 months after their arrival, and which will cost 31.15s. ster. for each person.

(4) Those who can afford to go as steerage, steward-room, or cabin passengers, will be accommodated accordingly.

(5) On their arrival in Africa, a convenient tract of land will be purchased for the community, to be their joint property. A township will then be marked out, and houses run up by the joint labour of the whole, for immediate shelter: this may easily be effected there, as materials are so near at hand, that 10 or 12 men may erect very comfortable habitations, in a few days.

(6) Each person will be allowed, by common consent, to possess as much land as he or she can cultivate, to which they may always add as much more as their necessity, or convenience may require.

(7) It is proposed to take out proper artificers, for erecting the necessary buildings, and dividing the lands.

(8) Beside the produce obtained from their own lands, individuals, by moderate labour, will have other easy means of procuring, not only the necessaries, but also the comforts of life. Fowls, hogs, goats, and sheep, are very cheap, being propagated with a rapidity

unknown in Europe; plenty of fish may be easily caught; and the forests abound with venison, wild-fowl, and other game.

(9) Such are the mildness and fertility of the climate and country, that a man possessed of a change of clothing, an axe, a hoe, and a pocket knife, may soon place himself in an easy situation. All the clothing wanted is what decency requires; and the earth turned up of 2 or 3 inches, with a light hoe, produces any kind of grain.

(10) These favourable circumstances, combine with the peaceable temper of the natives, promise the numerous advantages resulting from the quiet cultivation of the earth, and the exportation of its productions, which may be very advantageously exchanged for European manufactures.

(11) The climate is very healthy to those who live on the productions of the country. The cause why it has been fatal to many whites is, that they have led most intemperate lives; have subsisted chiefly on dried, salted, rancid and other unwholesome provisions; and have indulged beyond all bounds, in the use of spirits. They have been also cooped up in ships, small craft, or factories, stationed for the advantage of trade, in closed rivers or creeks, not choosing healthy spots, as is now proposed. Add to this, that the surgeons of ships trading thither, have hitherto been generally ignorant of the proper mode of treating diseases in that climate; or they have not been sufficiently supplied with medicines. Many persons have perished for want of good diet or nursing, and not a few from the total neglect of that mutual assistance, which the settlement proposed will furnish.

(12) The adventurers on this new establishment will be under the care of a physician, who has had 4 years practice on the coast of Africa, and as many in the Indies; and who being well provided, accompanied by skilful assistants, in surgery, midwifery, &c. and by several experienced women, they will enjoy every necessary assistance.

(13) It is also intended that the adventurers shall be accompanied by a clergyman, and a schoolmaster and mistress, at the expense of the whole community.

(14) Such will be the situation of those who cultivate their plantations for their own advantage: but many, instead of working wholly for themselves, may choose occasionally to serve the agent, or any other individual, for hire: some will employ their money in cultivation and trade: in that case the labourers will be supplied with provisions, and paid for their daily labour in the currency of the country.

(15) Only 8 hours of fair labour each day will be required, in summer or winter; and on Saturdays only 6 hours. The sabbath will be set apart as a day of rest, instruction, and devotion.

(16) The colonies being under the protection of the British Government, will consequently enjoy both civil and religious liberty, as in Great Britain.

(17) Disputes relative to property, or offences committed among themselves, will be settled according to the laws, by their own peers, in a town meeting.

(18) Offenders against the natives, in neighbouring districts, will be amenable to the laws of the country, unless the agent shall be able to compound for the penalty.

(19) In addition to those persons who are able to pay for their passage, it is intended to conduct this enterprise, on the most humane principles: it will be extended to others who have not money, on condition of agreements for their respective hire, to be calculated according to the ages and abilities of the parties; so that every one may be sure of having a comfortable provision made, after a short period, on the reasonable terms of moderate labour.

(20) And whereas many black persons, and people of colour, refugees from America, disbanded from His Majesty's service by sea or land, or otherwise distinguished objects of British humanity, are at this time in the greatest distress, they are invited to avail themselves of the advantage of the plan proposed.

(21) The committee, appointed for the relief of the Black Poor, having represented their unhappy situation to the Right Hon. the Lords Commissioners of the Treasury, Government has agreed to furnish them, not only with a passage and provision, but also with clothing, provisions for 3 months after their landing, together with all sorts of tools and implements of husbandry, necessary for the establishment of a new colony, according to the schedules annexed.

(22) Such persons will be also entitled to the necessary allotment of land, and other benefits, in as great a latitude as will render their lives easy.

(23) An opportunity so advantageous may perhaps never be offered to them again; for they and their posterity may enjoy perfect freedom. Settled in a country congenial to their constitutions, and having the means, by moderate labour, of the most comfortable livelihood, they will find a certain and secure retreat from their former sufferings.

HENRY SMEATHMAN.

SCHEDULES ABOVE REFERRED TO

(24) The Weekly Allowance of Provisions for the Voyage, and for 3 months after their Arrival:

Clothing at the rate of £21·15s. for each Man.

1 Blue Jacket
1 Striped Flannel ditto
1 Pair of Canvass Trowsers
1 Pair of Flannel ditto
2 Pair of Shoes
4 Shirts
2 Knives
1 Razor
1 Hat
Bedding
Cloths for the Women in proportion.

Tools and Utensils at the rate of 19s. 2d. value for each person.

1 Hoe
1 Wood Axe
1 Pewter Bason of 2 lb.
1 Wooden Cann and drinking Horn

For a Company of twelve persons.

1 Iron Pot of 5 Gallons
1 Ditto   2 Gallons
1 Ditto   1 Gallon
1 Iron Water Cistern of 20 Gallons
2 Pails
1 Iron Crow
1 Whip

Appendix II

Extracts from the Amended Memorandum for the Guidance of Officers who are to Effect the Removal of Liberated Africans from Foreign Stations to the West Indies. (Issued by the Colonial Office, 1844)

Liberated Africans placed at the disposal of the British Government at Foreign Stations are to be forwarded to the West Indies under the following Regulations.

Officers Responsible
The Officers by whom it is proposed that this Duty should be performed are the Superintendent of Liberated Africans at the Havannah; H. C. Ouseley Esq. who has hitherto attended to a similar service, at Rio; the British Consul at Boa Vista; and for the present the junior British member of the Mixed Commission at Loanda.

Receiving Colonies
The Liberated Africans placed at the disposal of Great Britain are to be sent by these Officers to the following Colonies, in the order in which they are here named, viz. Jamaica, British Guiana, and Trinidad.

Forwarding the Emigrants
The Africans are to be forwarded with the least possible delay, in order that they may not longer than necessary remain a burthen on the British Treasury, nor be detained from reaching places where they can earn their own subsistence and become members of a civilized community.

Shipping
As soon as a sufficient number of emigrants are ready, the officer will endeavour to procure a conveyance for them in a suitable *British* vessel, *but he will in no case forward them under the present Instructions in any foreign ship.*[1]

Scale of Victualling
The Officers should insert in their agreement a Scale of victualling, and they will also stipulate for a suitable medicine chest, properly

1 Underlined in the original.

filled, and will see that one is on board the vessel which is engaged before she sails. The Officers at the several Stations named in this Memorandum should adopt the same (the scale of rations) as far as circumstances admit.

The British Passengers' Act

Although this law does not extend to vessels sailing from Foreign Ports, the Officer should take care that the number embarked does not exceed either the limits fixed by this measure, viz. three persons including the Crew for every five tons, or one passenger for every twelve supercicial feet of the deck where the passengers live.

Surgeon

The Emigrants are never if possible to be embarked in ships which do not carry a Surgeon. But it may happen that at some of the less frequented stations named in this Memorandum, it may be impossible to meet with vessels which carry such an Officer, or to supply the deficiency on the spot. Rather than expose the people in such cases to the evil of an indefinite detention, under perhaps an equal risk, at the place where they are, the officer will be at liberty to agree for their passage, if they appear entirely fit for it.

Vaccination

Should the necessary means be procurable, all the emigrants should be vaccinated as soon as possible after embarkation, excepting only those who bear the marks of having had the natural small pox.

Clothing

Each emigrant ought to have a blanket or some other warm woollen covering, and if the clothing furnished by the public at the time of each African's liberation appear insufficient for this purpose or for the wants of the voyage, the officer will cause the defect to be supplied.

Officers' Reports

The Officer will report quarterly to the Secretary of State the number of vessels in which passages have been engaged by him, and the number of emigrants forwarded by each opportunity, with their destinations and the rates of Bounty to be paid, the number remaining at his station, and any other particulars relating to the service.

Remuneration

His remuneration will consist of a payment of 5/- for each emigrant forwarded by him, for which together with any amount he may have had to defray for extra clothing for the emigrants draw bills.

Source: Extracts from the Official Memorandum and Amendments thereto found in C.O. 318/162 and C.O. 386/49.

Appendix III

Articles of a Treaty concluded between King Siacca of Gallinas and Commander the Honourable Joseph Denman.

1. King Siacca engages totally to destroy the factories belonging to the white men without delay.

2. King Siacca engages to give up to Commander Denman all the slaves who were in the Barracoons of the white slave dealers when he entered the river, and have been carried off into the bush.

3. King Siacca engages to send these bad white men out of his country by the first opportunity, and within four months from this date.

4. King Siacca binds himself in the most solemn manner that no white man shall ever, for the future, settle in his country for the purpose of slave-dealing.

5. Captain Denman, on the part of Her Britannic Majesty, promises never to molest any traders engaged in legitimate commerce of the River Gallinas but that, on the contrary, Her Majesty's ships shall afford every assistance to King Siacca's subjects, and take every opportunity of promoting his commerce.

6. The Governor of Sierra Leone will use his influence to get the Sierra Leone people to open the trade with King Siacca's country.

7. No white man from Sierra Leone shall settle down in King Siacca's country without his full permission and consent.

8. All complaints that King Siacca may have to make hereafter against any of Her Majesty's ships, he is requested to forward at once to Sierra Leone; and a full investigation, and such redress as the occasion may require, is solemnly promised by Commander Denman on the part of Her Britannic Majesty.

> Done at Dumbacorro, in the River Gallinas, this 21st day of November, 1840.
>
> (*Signed*) PRINCE MANNA
> his X mark
> LUSINI ROGERS
> his X mark
> JOHN SELEPHA ROGERS
> his X mark
>
> (*Signed*) JOSEPH DENMAN
> Commander and Senior Officer on the Sierra Leone Station.

Convention for the Total Supression of the slave trade, agreed upon by Mr William Tucker, Captain of Her Britannic Majesty's ship *Iris*, and senior officer in command of Her Britannic Majesty's ships and vessels on the West Coast of Africa, and King Pepple and the Chiefs of the Bonny dominions.

It is agreed, and the two Contracting Parties hereby covenant and agree.—

1. That the slave trade shall be totally and for ever abolished in the dominions subject to the jurisdiction of King Pepple and the chiefs of Bonny; and that no slaves shall be passed through or exported from those dominions from the date of the ratification of this agreement.

2. That in consideration of the total abolition of the slave trade for ever, and that no slaves shall ever be permited to pass through or be exported from the said dominions, Great Britain engages to pay King Pepple, on the ratifications of this agreement, goods to the amount of 10,000 dollars per annum for five years.

3. That on each future time of making the annual payment, the man-of-war bringing the annual gift shall furnish Great Britain with a document stating whether slave trade has, to their knowledge, existed there, and that no slaves have been passed through the dominions subject to the jurisdiction of King Pepple and the Chiefs of Bonny during the preceding year.

4. That if, at any time whatever, either from want of that document, or from any other circumstance, it shall appear that the slave trade has been carried on in, from, or through the dominions subject to the jurisdiction of King Pepple and the Chiefs of Bonny, the gifts mentioned in the preceding Article will be discontinued, the slave trade put down by force, and King Pepple and the Chiefs of Bonny will subject themselves to severe acts of displeasure on the part of Great Britain.

5. That King Pepple shall make a proclamation and a law, prohibiting all his subjects, or persons depending on him, from selling any slaves to be transported from the dominions subject to his jurisdiction, or to abet or assist in any such, under penalty of severe punishment.

6. That at the particular request of King Pepple, the said gift shall be paid to him in dollars—viz., 10,000 dollars per annum year by year, for five years, upon the document required being received as proof of his having fulfilled the above Articles.

7. That should Great Britain at any future time permit the slave

trade to be carried on again, the King and Chiefs of Bonny shall be at liberty to carry on the slave trade also.

Done at the Parliament House, Bonny Town, this 20th day of August, 1841.

WILLIAM TUCKER.
KING PEPPLE.

Appendix IV

Instructions to the Commander of The Emigration Vessel H.M.S. Growler.

(Source C.O. 386/53)

1. The Commander will see that the Embarkation and Disembarkation of the passengers is effected in the manner best adopted for their safety and convenience.

2. No passenger is to be received on board unless with the knowledge and approval of the commander; nor is he to allow any passenger to be received except such as are duly reported to him for the purpose by the Emigration Agents. The surgeon should inspect the emigrants as early as possible to ascertain that they are in good bodily health and fit for the voyage.

3. Upon the embarkation of the people, the Commander will cause immediate measures to be taken for berthing them properly and dividing them into messes of convenient size.

4. During the voyage he will take proper measures for insuring the regular issue of all the articles of Food specified in the victualling scale subject to any recommendation from the Surgeon to the contrary. As the emigrants would not be able to complain for themselves care should be taken that there is no neglect to cook their Food properly.

5. He will establish written Regulations for the maintenance of good order, cleanliness and decency on board. Copies of two different sets of Regulations used on board two Transports formerly employed in carrying African Emigrant are annexed,which may be of service in framing the intended Rules. The Commander will at the earliest opportunity after completing his first voyage, transmit to the Colonial Land and Emigration Commisioners a copy of the Regulations he shall establish, accompanied by any remarks he may wish to make on the manner in which they have worked.

6. The Commander will pay the utmost attention to the ventilation of the ship and to the preservation of cleanliness, giving due regard to any representations which may be made to him on these points by the surgeon, as necessary for the health of the people.

7. He should take great care to preserve dryness between Decks. For this purpose the swing stores should be used when necessary,

and unless for very special reasons, only stones and dry rubbing should be employed in cleaning the deck.

8. He will require that the bottom boards of the berths be frequently removed during the voyage, and after disembarkation of the passengers he is to require that those boards are lifted and washed, and that the parts underneath are thoroughly cleansed and whitewashed, with wash of a proper consistency, made of unslaked lime.

9. In case there should have been any infectious sickness on board, the vessel is, under the advice of the Surgeon, to be well and frequently fumigated, more especially when under refit, and chloride of lime may be used when necessary, as well as airing stoves in the Hold, when fires can be made there with safety.

10. Upon arriving at the Colony to which he has been directed to proceed, the Commander will acquaint the Governor with the instructions under which he is acting, and if he have any passengers on board furnish a properly authenticated List of all whom he may have brought in the vessel. He will then receive the Governor's directions relative to their disembarkation.

11. The Commander will keep a journal of his proceedings in respect to the conveyance of Emigrants, and report in it all circumstances worthy of note which may come within his observation. This journal he will transmit as soon after the expiration of each voyage to the West Indies as the opportunity for sending it may offer, to H.M. Col: Land and Emigration Commissioners in London. He will address to the same Board all other correspondence connected with the Emigration Service in which he is engaged.

12. For his services to the Colonies, he will be allowed 7/- per diem, commencing from the date of sailing from England, for which allowance he will draw Bills half yearly on H.M's Commissioners of Colonial Land and Emigration in the form annexed.

FORM OF BILL

Place & date.............   ....184......

£   S   D   Three days after sight pay to............or order the sum of........Pounds.........Shillings being one half year's allowance due to me on the —— of —— 184– as Officer in command of H.M.S. *Growler* engaged in conveying emigrants from Africa to the West Indies.

To H.M. Colonial Land & Emign Comrs   *Signature*...............
    9, Park Street, Westminster

Instructions to the Surgeon of
The Growler

1. Upon joining the ship the Surgeon will see that the medicines, the surgical instruments, and the medical comforts are on board.

2. It will be the duty of the Surgeon, previously to the embarkation of the passengers on the coast of Africa, personally to inspect and examine all persons designated to him as intended passengers by the proper Officer of the Colonial Government and to ascertain whether they be in good bodily health and not incapacitated from labor by any lasting infirmity; and he will then furnish to the same Officer a Certificate stating the result of his examination.

3. All Passengers who have not had the small-pox, or previously undergone vacination, must be vacinated before being admitted on board. A fresh supply of vacine matter is herewith transmitted to the Surgeon for this purpose, and he will endeavor to renew his supply at all proper opportunities.

4. During the voyage it will be his duty to take medical charge of the passengers, and to do his utmost to enforce all the Regulations which may be sanctioned by the Commander of the Vessel, for the maintenance of cleanliness, decency, and good order.

5. The Surgeon is expected to render every aid which may be required of him in superintending the embarkation and disembarkation of the emigrants, and their berthing and division into messes, and to promote the observance of the Regulations which may be established on board for the maintenance of good order, and for the promotion of cleanliness and ventilation offering any advice on any of these points which he may consider necessary, with a view to the preservation of the health of the Passenger.

6. Should experience prove that any of the articles in the Dietary are unsuited to the constitution of the passengers, the Surgeon will report the circumstance to the Commander with a view of effecting such alterations in the scale as may be deemed necessary.

7. The Surgeon will use his discretion in respect to any requisitions to be made by him for the victualling of the sick.

8. The Surgeon will keep a full and distinct medical journal showing on what day each passenger was entered for treatment, and on what day discharged, and whether cured, remaining sick at the end of the voyage, or dead, and giving in detail daily an account of the symptoms, and medicines prescribed; and if there be any causes connected with the voyage which appear likely to have occasioned

the disease he is to assign them and point out whether there seems to him any practicable method of obviating them for the future, more especially if the complaint be of an infectious nature. He will also carefully note any alterations which he might think it desirable should be made in the Dietary, the medicines, and the medical comforts. He will further append to his journal copies of all written reports which he has found it necessary to make to the Commander with any decisions upon them which have been communicated to him by that officer. At the expiration of each voyage, he will deliver two copies of his journal, when thus Completed, to the Commander for transmission, one to the Commissioner for Land & Emigration, and the other to the Director General of Naval Hospitals and Fleets.

9. With regard to the medical treatment of the Officers and Crew, the Surgeon and Assistant Surgeon are to be guided by the instructions issued to them for the service afloat generally.

10. The Surgeon will, for the present, receive 2/– for each African conveyed to the West Indies, and landed alive, and the Assistant Surgeon 1/–. This allowance will not be applicable to coming back from the West Indies. The Surgeon and Assistant Surgeon will apply to the Colonial Secretary at Guiana and Trinidad, respectively, for directions on the manner in which they are to obtain this allowance, which it is intended should be paid to them in the Colony at the end of each voyage.

Instructions to the Chief Emigration Agent for the West India Colonies

1. One of Her Majesty's Steamers will repair almost immediately to the Coast of Africa for the purpose of taking Emigrants from Sierra Leone and the Kroo Coast to the Colonies of British Guiana and Trinidad.

2. The Chief Agent for Emigration will select forthwith and despatch to the places which he judges best on the Kroo Coast a few Subordinate Agents to endeavour to collect emigrants for Her Majesty's Steamer.

3. The Subordinate Agents may explain that the Steamer is one of Her Majesty's vessels of war.

4. The Chief Agent will also be at liberty to furnish the subordinate Agents for their use with any printed papers which may from time to time be officially communicated to him for the purpose

containing information relative to the respective West India Colonies. The intelligence thus conveyed will consist of any general statements which it may be practicable to supply from authentic sources, of the average rates of money wages for different kinds of labour. The other advantages afforded by employers and the sort of labour which is most in demand.

5. The different Agents will inform all emigrants from the Coast of Africa, whether from Sierra Leone or elsewhere, that they will be entitled to demand a free passage back after 5 years from their arrival.

6. The Chief Agent will assign to the Subordinate Agents, with the approval of the Governor, moderate salaries in addition to an allowance of half a dollar a head to each of them for all emigrants despatched from his station. The Chief Agent's report of such salaries with any remarks which they may require in explanation, being transmitted by the Governor at the earliest opportunity to the Secretary of State for confirmation.

7. The Subordinate Agents are to be placed nowhere except within the proper limits of the Kroo Coast nor on any pretence to go or be sent to any place where slave trading has prevailed, a rule which is enjoined on penalty of the immediate dismissal of any officer convicted of its violation.

8. In case it should be necessary to establish any Depot on the Kroo Coast for the reception of emigrants waiting for the steamers, the Chief Agent will make the requisite arrangements and report thus through the Governor of Sierra Leone for approval; but he will avoid every unnecessary measure of this description.

9. On the first and if possible each succeeding voyage of the steamer, it would be desirable that the Chief Agent should proceed in her to visit the other Agents and attend to the embarkation of the people on the Kroo Coast. With regard to the mode of returning to Sierra Leone he should make an early report on the means of communication coastwise, and in the meanwhile may incur with the Governor's approval, expenditure indispensable for that purpose and may hire a coaster expressly for it if no better arrangement can be made.

10. While these arrangements are made on the Kroo Coast, the steamer is also to be available for the conveyance of any emigrant who may be procurable at Sierra Leone.

11. The Chief Agent should spare no endeavour to secure, if possible, the presence of an interpreter in the steamer for each voyage.

12. He will inspect personally every emigrant to ascertain that he goes with his free consent and has not been deceived but really understands the nature of the countries to which he is going.

13. He will see that each emigrant has such clothing or blankets as may be requisite for decency and for health during the voyage.

14. He will render all the assistance in his power to facilitate the embarkation of the emigrants, and will furnish the officer in command with a nominal list (in form A) of all the passengers embarked. He will sign this list himself, and see that there be appended to it a certificate from the Surgeon on Board that he has examined all the emigrants previous to embarkation, and found them to be in good bodily health, and with no deformity or mutilation incapacitating them from labour.

15. He will transmit through the Governor for the information of Her Majesty's Government a quarterly return of Emigration according to the form B and he will make a general report at the close of every year upon the mode in which the plan may have worked, and upon the alterations if any, which may have occurred to him as desirable for its improvement.

16. The Chief Agent will continue to receive a salary of £300 per annum but divided in future between British Guiana and Trinidad, and will also receive the allowance of a Dollar a head for each emigrant despatched respectively to those two colonies.

17. For his salary and head-money he will draw Bills Quarterly upon the Colonial Land and Emigration Commissioners being careful duly to advise their Secretary of each Bill, and also to transmit a certificate from the Governor of Sierra Leone that he has been in the performance of his duties for the period referred to as well as a statement signed by the Officer in command of the steamer showing the number of emigrants despatched by him during the quarter to British Guiana and Trinidad respectively.

18. For the pay and head-money of the Sub-Agents, and for all miscellaneous and petty disbursements the Chief Agent will also draw Bills duly advised on the same Board, carefully forwarding at the same time any accounts which may be necessary, together with proper receipts for all sums paid by him. As regards the amount of head-money paid by him to the Sub-Agents he should transmit a certificate signed by himself of the accuracy of the numbers in respect of whom payment is thus made—All Bills to be drawn at 60 days sight.

For Naval Officers accompanying Private Emigration Transports

Heads of Instructions for the Naval Officer on board the African Emigrant Transport ———

I. When on service the Naval Officer will wear the Uniform established for his rank agreeably to the practice of Her Majesty's Navy.

II. The duties of the Officer will be chiefly to see that the vessel on board of which he shall be placed does not proceed for emigrants to any other part of the Coast of Africa than Sierra Leone (or, if wished by the master, the British possessions in the Gambia or on the Gold Coast) and the Kroo Coast, and to satisfy the officers of any cruisers who may be met with on the voyage, that he is proceeding with the sanction and authority of Her Majesty's Government.

III. Within the limits of the British possessions in Africa the Officer will not be held in any way responsible for the selection of the emigrants to be put on board, as this duty will pertain solely to the Master of the vessel and the Government Emigration Agent, or his representatives on the spot—On the Kroo Coast, however, being beyond the limits of British jurisdiction it will be the duty of the Officer, in case the Government Emigration Agent be not in attendance there, to make himself sufficiently acquainted with the proceedings to be able to certify that none of the emigrants embark otherwise than entirely with their own free will, and that nothing occurs which in any way bears a character of slave-trading.

IV. Should the vessel for any reason touch at any other place in Africa than those above named, the Officer will immediately on his arrival in Jamaica report the circumstances to the Governor of that Colony, stating at the same time the object of the visit, the nature of his proceedings and the length of stay.

V. It is not intended that the vessel should remain at Sierra Leone or the Kroo Coast more than twenty one days in all, unless it be otherwise specially agreed between Mr. Hook, the Emigration Agent and the Master of the vessel.

VI. The terms under which the vessel is to be licensed for the service are contained in the accompanying paper which is forwarded for the information of the Officer on board.

VII. He is in no way to interfere in the management or navigation of the ship.

VIII. He will be furnished with a proper Admiralty Pass, to satisfy any of the officers of Her Majesty's Cruisers by whom the vessel may be visited. He is to offer no obstacle to any lawful visit by the Officers of British or Foreign vessels of War engaged in the prevention of the slave trade.

IX. On the disembarkation of the emigrants in Jamaica the duty of the Officer will cease, and he will be allowed a passage back to England, at the expense of Government, in the first mail steamer.

X. His remuneration will consist of a Gratuity of £150 to be paid to him in addition to his half pay.

XI. The Officer will keep a journal in duplicate of any circumstances worthy of note, which may fall within his observation. One copy he will deliver to the Governor of Jamaica, and the other he will deposit on his return to England, in the office of Her Majesty's Colonial Land and Emigration Commissioners.

Appendix V

MEMORANDUM of Agreement made this Twenty-first day of September, 1849, between Stephen Walcott, Esquire, Secretary to and on behalf of the Colonial Land and Emigration Commissioners of the one part, and John Hodge, one of the Partners and on behalf of the Firm of Messrs. Hyde, Hodge & Co., of the City of London, Merchants, of the other part.

WITNESSETH, That it is mutually agreed as follows:—

ARTICLE I. That from the 15th of December next to the 31st December 1850 inclusive, Messrs. Hyde, Hodge & Co. shall furnish a supply of suitable Vessels on the terms and in the manner hereinafter-mentioned for the conveyance of Liberated Africans from the Government Yards at Sierra Leone and St. Helena to the British West Indies, and that while the Contract is duly performed, no Liberated African shall be conveyed to the British West Indies at the expense of the British or Colonial Governments except in Vessels so furnished.

ART. II. That subject to the conditions hereinafter-mentioned Messrs. Hyde, Hodge & Co. shall choose the time of despatching their Vessels, giving, however, to the said Commissioners at least Three Weeks previous notice of the departure of each Ship, together with such particulars thereof as shall be necessary for obtaining the necessary Pass and License; but that the said Commissioners shall determine to what Port or Ports in the West Indies each Ship shall proceed.

ART. III. That the Emigrants shall be selected by the Emigration Agent or other person acting in that capacity at Sierra Leone or St. Helena hereinafter described as Emigration Agent, with the assistance of the Ship's Surgeon shall consider any person selected by the Emigration Agent as unfitted for the Voyage by the state of his health, the difference shall be decided by the Colonial Surgeon or in his absence by any other Officer to be appointed by the Governor.

ART. IV. That no Ship shall be employed in this Service which shall be rated lower than the Red Diphthong in Lloyd's List, nor unless she shall have been approved as fit for the conveyance of Emigrants both by the said Commissioners and by some Officer to be appointed for that purpose by the Governor of the Colony from which she shall be intended to convey Passengers; and the Officer appointed by the said Commissioners and by the said Governor shall be entitled at the expense of the Messrs. Hyde, Hodge & Co. to make all surveys and examinations both of the Ship and of the fittings thereof which they shall deem necessary for the purpose of ascertaining such fitness.

ART. V. That the Passengers shall be victualled according to the scale in the Schedule hereto annexed, marked A, and that the Vessel shall be provided with medical comforts and other stores for their use, enumerated in the Schedule marked B, also annexed, and with such supply of Medicines as the said Commissioners shall deem sufficient.

By a Supplementary Agreement the responsibilities of Messrs. Hyde, Hodge & Co. are to commence on the 15th of November instead of the 15th of December next.

ART. VI. That such provisions, stores, and medicines, shall be laid in if required by the said Commissioners before the Ships leave England and shall be of a quality to be approved by the Emigration Officer at the Port from which the Ship shall proceed. The said Commissioners shall determine the length of Voyage for which such provisions, &c. shall be laid in, not exceeding in any case Eight Weeks.

ART. VIII. That every Ship shall, if required by the Colonial Authorities, remain Six Days at Sierra Leone or St. Helena for the purpose of embarking her Passengers, and Eight Days at the Port of Disembarkation for the purpose of disembarking them.

ART. IX. That a Surgeon, to be appointed by the Commissioners, shall receive from the Messrs. Hyde, Hodge & Co. £25. and a free cabin passage out and home again, and shall be dieted at the Captain's table, at the expense of Messrs. Hyde, Hodge & Co. on condition of his taking the medical charge of the Officers and Crew of the Ship, as well as of any passengers that may be embarked. But the Captain of the Vessel shall be at liberty, if he thinks fit, as soon as he shall have landed all his passengers, to pay the Surgeon, or the Surgeon, after Thirty Days' stay in the Colony, shall be entitled to demand, the sum of Forty Pounds in satisfaction of his claim for maintenance in the Colony, and for his free passage home.

ART. X. That the rate of passage-money on every Liberated

African embarked from the Liberated African Yard, and landed alive in the West Indies shall be as follows:

For every Liberated African embarked at Sierra Leone if above 10 years of age	£6: 1: 10
If between 1 and 10 years of age	3: 0: 11
For every Liberated African embarked at St. Helena, if above 10 years of age	6: 16: 10
If between 1 and 10 years of age	3: 7: 5

Subject nevertheless to the following Conditions and Deductions:

1. That the passage-money payable on each Emigrant, shall be subject to a deduction for every day subsequent to the said 15th day of December next, during which such Emigrant shall have remained under Government superintendence after adjudication, at the rate of 3d. per diem in respect of Emigrants embarked at Sierra Leone, and of 6d. per diem in respect of those embarked at St. Helena, and also to a further deduction of £1. on every Emigrant who shall be sent to the Hospital or receptacle for sick persons, on his arrival in the West Indies.

2. That any Interpreters placed on board by or with the concurrence of the Emigration Agent at the Port of Embarkation, shall receive a steerage passage to the West Indies at the rate of £6 a head.

3. That no passage money shall be payable till twenty-one days after an account setting forth the full particulars of the claim, together with the following documents, shall have been left with the said Commissioners viz:—

FIRST—A List of the Passengers embarked at Sierra Leone or St. Helena, certified by the Governor and Emigration Agent of the Colony, distinguishing between Interpreters and Liberated Africans and stating with regard to Liberated Africans, whether they were adjudicated on before the said 15th day of December, 1849, or belong to the class on whom the fixed rate of £5 10s. per adult is to be payable under Article XII and if not, for how many days after adjudication they have been respectively under Government superintendence, and also stating which of them are above Ten years of age.

SECONDLY—A statement signed by the Immigration Agent at the Port of Disembarkation, or Officer acting in that capacity, and specifying which of such persons were landed alive, and how many were sent to the Hospital or other receptacle for sick persons, and further stating, that in all material respects the service appeared to him to have been performed in conformity with the conditions of this Agreement.

4. That the above-mentioned List of Passengers shall be conclusive evidence as to the number of days during which each African shall have remained under Government superintendence.

ART. XI. That if, at the termination of the Contract, any Africans shall still be remaining under Government superintendence, the Contractor shall pay, for every day during which any such African shall have so remained after adjudication, a forfeit of 3d. per diem, if such African shall have been kept at Sierra Leone, and 6d. per diem if at St. Helena. Provided, however, that no forfeit shall be payable on any such African who, within the three preceding weeks, has had an opportunity of emigrating and has refused, or has been unable to avail himself of it.

ART. XII. That if after adjudication Messrs. Hyde, Hodge & Co., shall have twice offered to any African an opportunity of embarking in their Ships for the West Indies, such offers being made at an interval of not less than 28 days, to be computed from the clearance of one Ship to the clearance of the other Ship, and if such African from sickness or from any other cause shall have refused to receive, or shall not have been selected by the Emigration Agent for receiving such passage and if by such refusal or non-selection the said Ship shall have been obliged to leave the Port of Embarkation with less than her legal complement of Emigrants, Messrs. Hyde, Hodge & Co. shall thereupon be discharged from all forfeit whatever in respect of such African. Provided nevertheless, that the Governor may at any time afterwards place such Africans on board any ship furnished by Messrs. Hyde, Hodge & Co., for this service, to be conveyed to the West Indies at the rate of £5 10s. per Adult.

ART. XIII. That the Master of any such Ship may refuse to receive on board any Emigrant whom he may consider unfitted by the state of his health for immediate conveyance to the West Indies, but in that case the Messrs. Hyde, Hodge & Co., shall remain subject to all deductions and forfeitures provided for by this Agreement in respect of the Africans so refused, and in computing the numbers of Emigrants placed on board for the purposes of Art. 12, the Africans so refused shall be considered to have been placed on board.

ART. XIV. That if at any time the Governor of Sierra Leone or St. Helena shall report to the Secretary of State, either that during the preceding three months no suitable Ship has been tendered by Messrs. Hyde, Hodge & Co. for the conveyance of Liberated Africans from the Colony, or that no such Ship has been so tendered during the then preceding two months, and that there are at the date of his report not less than 200 Liberated Africans under Government superintendence, it shall be competent to the said Commissioners to enforce the performance of this Contract, or in case the delay should not be explained to the satisfaction of the said Commissioners, to treat the Contract as at an end in respect of the Colony from which such report shall arrive, and in the latter case Messrs. Hyde, Hodge & Co. shall thereupon forfeit to the said Commissioners as liquidated damages the sum of £1,500 in case the Contract shall be terminated in respect of St. Helena, and half that sum in case it shall have been terminated in respect of Sierra Leone.

ART. XV. That the present Agreement is made by the Commissioners in their official capacity only, and that no liability whatever arising out of it is to attach to any of the said Commissioners, nor to the said Stephen Walcott, nor to the private estate and effect of any of them.

In Witness whereof, the said parties have hereunto set their hands the day and year above written.

Signed by the said Stephen Walcott as
such Secretary as aforesaid, and by   (*Signed*) S. WALCOTT
the said John Hodge, on behalf of the
Firm of Hyde, Hodge & Co. in the   (*Signed*) JOHN HODGE
presence of

(*Signed*) GEORGE M. BUTLER

SCHEDULE A

VICTUALLING SCALE FOR AFRICAN SHIPS

Women to receive the same ration as Men, and Children between the Ages of 1 and 10, to receive half a ration.

Biscuit............................½ lb.
Rice................................½ lb.   Vinegar ....½ pint
Beef, Pork, or Salt Fish......½ lb.   Palm Oil ....1½ Gill
   To be issued—the Salt Fish   Salt ....2 oz.
three times a week, the Pork and
Beef twice a week.   African Pepper ....2 oz.
Lime Juice....................½ oz.
Sugar ....2 oz.
Water ....1 Gallon

N.B. Yams or Cassada may be substituted for Rice to a limited extent, in proportions to be fixed by the Emigration Agent at Sierra Leone.

SCHEDULE B

ARTICLES TO BE SUPPLIED BY THE MESSRS. HYDE, HODGE & CO. FOR THE USE OF THE AFRICANS ON THE VOYAGE TO THE WEST INDIES.

For each Mess of Six Persons.

1 Kit ....
1 Wooden Platter..............
1 Mess Bread Basket............
1 Hawso Bucket.................

1 New Mat to serve as a Bed for each Person, with sufficient Knives, Spoons, Tin Drinking Mugs, &c. for the numbers embarked, and such a number of Blankets as shall be further deemed necessary by the Emigration Agent at the Port of Embarkation.

MEDICAL COMFORTS FOR EVERY 100 PASSENGERS

50 lbs. of Arrowroot	18 bottles of Wine
28 lbs. of Sago	10 gallons of Rum
10 lbs. of preserved boiled Mutton, in 1 lb. Tins	3 gallons of Vinegar
10 lbs. of preserved boiled Beef, in 1 lb. Tins	½ cwt. of Marine Soap
100 pints of Lemon Juice	6 quarts of Sir W. Burnett's Chloride of Zinc
100 lbs. of Sugar	25 lbs. of Chloride of Lime

Second Contract Agreement
(Source C.O. 386/88)

ARTICLES OF AGREEMENT FOR THE CONVEYANCE OF LIBERATED AFRICANS BETWEEN THE COLONIAL LAND AND EMIGRATION COMMISSIONERS AND MESSRS. HYDE, HODGE AND CO.

ART. I. That from the date of these presents to the 30th of June, 1852, the Contractors shall furnish a supply of suitable vessels on the terms and in the manner hereinafter mentioned for the conveyance of Liberated Africans from the Government Yards, or vessels at Sierra Leone, St. Helena, and Rio de Janeiro (hereinafter called the Ports of Embarkation) to the British West Indies, and that while the Contract is duly performed, no Liberated African shall be conveyed to the British West Indies at the expense of the British or Colonial Governments, except in vessels so furnished.

ART. II. That, subject to the conditions hereinafter mentioned, the Contractors shall choose the time of despatching their vessels, giving, however, to the said Commissioners at least three weeks' previous notice of the departure of any ship from England, together with such particulars thereof as shall be necessary for obtaining the necessary pass and licence, but that the said Commissioners shall determine to what port or ports in the West Indies each ship shall proceed.

ART. III. That, for the purpose of this Contract, the term Emigration Officer shall mean the Emigration Agent or other person acting in that capacity at Sierra Leone or St. Helena, and the British Consul or other person having authority to act for him at Rio de Janeiro.

ART. IV. That the Emigrants shall be selected by the Emigration Officer, with the assistance of the ship's Surgeon, and at Sierra Leone or St. Helena subject to the approval of the Governor; and that if the ship's Surgeon shall consider any person selected by the Emigration Officer as unfitted for the voyage by the state of his health, the difference shall be decided at Rio Janeiro by some medical man, to be appointed by the said Consul, and at Sierra Leone or St. Helena by the Colonial Surgeon, or in his absence by any other Officer to be appointed by the Governor.

ART. V. That no ship shall be employed in this service which shall be rated lower than the red diphthong in Lloyd's List, nor unless she shall have been approved as fit for the conveyance of Emigrants both by the said Commissioners and by some Officer to be appointed for that purpose by the Governor of Sierra Leone or St. Helena, or by the Consul at Rio de Janeiro, as the case may be; and the Officers appointed by the said Commissioners, and by the said Governor or Consul, shall be entitled, at the expense of the Contractors, to make all surveys and examinations both of the ship and of the fittings thereof, which they shall deem necessary for the purpose of ascertaining such fitness.

ART. VI. That the passengers shall be victualled according to the scale in the Schedule hereto annexed, marked A, and that the vessel shall be provided with medical comforts and other stores for their use, enumerated in the Schedule marked B, also annexed, and with such supply of medicines as the said Commissioners shall deem sufficient.

ART. VII. That such provisions, stores, and medicines shall be laid in, if required by the said Commissioners, before the ships leave England, and shall be of a quality to be approved by the Emigration Officer at the port from which the ship shall proceed. The said Commissioners shall determine the length of voyage for which such provisions, stores, and medicines, shall be laid in, not exceeding in any case eight weeks.

ART. VIII. That provisions shall be made for ventilation to the satisfaction of the Emigration Officer at the port from which the ship shall proceed.

ART. IX. That a Surgeon, to be appointed by the Commissioners, shall receive from the Contractors £25, if engaged for a single voyage, or payment at the rate of £100 per annum, if engaged for a succession of voyages; and in either case a free cabin passage out and home again, and shall be dieted at the Captain's table, at the expense of the Contractors, on condition of his taking the medical charge of the Officers and Crew of the ship, as well as of any passengers that may be embarked. But at the expiration of the engagement the Captain of the vessel shall be at liberty, if he thinks fit, as soon as he shall have landed all his passengers, to pay the Surgeon; or the Surgeon, after thirty days' stay in the Colony, shall be entitled to demand the sum of £40 in satisfaction of his claim for maintenance in the Colony, and for his free passage home.

ART. X. That the rate of passage-money on every Liberated African landed alive in the West Indies, shall be:—
If embarked at Sierra Leone.....................£6 1 10} per Adult
If embarked at St. Helena or Rio de Janeiro...£6 14 10} per Adult
Provided, nevertheless—

1. That every person above ten years of age shall be counted as an adult, and every person between one and ten as half an adult, and that no charge shall be made for infants under one year of age.

2. That the passage-money payable on each Emigrant shall be subject to a deduction, hereafter called 'maintenance-money', at the rate of 3d. per diem in respect of Emigrants embarked at Sierra Leone, and of 6d. per diem in respect of those embarked at St. Helena or Rio de Janeiro, for every day during which such Emigrant shall have remained under Government superintendence at Sierra Leone or St. Helena after adjudication, or at Rio de Janeiro after the day on which, in the opinion of the Consul, he shall have been fit to undertake a voyage to the West Indies; and also to a further deduction of £1 on every Emigrant who shall be sent to hospital

or other receptacle for sick persons, on his arrival in the West Indies.

3. That any interpreters placed on board by or with the concurrence of the Emigration Officer at the port of embarkation, shall receive a steerage passage to the West Indies at the rate of £6 a head, but shall be taken back to Africa, if necessary, at the expence of the Contractors.

4. That no passage-money shall be payable till 21 days after an account, setting forth the full particulars of the claim, shall have been left with the said Commissioners, together with the following documents, viz:—

First. A list of the passengers embarked, certified in respect of Sierra Leone or St. Helena by the Governor and Emigration Agent of the Colony, and in respect of Rio de Janeiro by the Consul, distinguishing between Interpreters and Liberated Africans, and stating with regard to Liberated Africans which of them are above ten years of age, whether they belong to the class on whom the fixed rate of £5 10s. per adult is to be payable under Article XII., and if not, the number of days in respect of which maintenance-money is chargeable against the Contractors.

Secondly. A statement, signed by the Immigration Agent at the port of disembarkation or Officer acting in that capacity, and specifying which of such persons were landed alive, and how many were sent to the hospital or other receptacle for sick persons, and further stating, that in all material respects the service appeared to him to have been performed in conformity with the conditions of this Agreement.

5. That the above-mentioned list of passengers shall be conclusive evidence as to the number of days for which the Contractors are to be charged with maintenance-money.

ART. XI. That if, at the termination of the Contract, any Africans shall still be remaining under Government superintendence, who within the three preceding weeks shall not have had an opportunity of emigrating, the Contractors shall pay the Commissioners the amount of maintenance-money which would have been payable on every such African, if such African had been embarked in the Contractor's vessels on the 30th of June, 1852.

ART. XII. Provided always, that if, during the period for which maintenance-money is payable, the Contractors shall have twice offered to any African an opportunity of embarking in their ships for the West Indies, such offers being made at an interval of not less than 28 days, to be computed from the clearance of one ship to the clearance of the other ship; and if such African from sickness or from any other cause shall have refused to receive, or shall not have been selected by the Emigration Officer for receiving such passage, and if the said ship, after staying six days in the port of embarkation, shall by such refusal or non-selection have been obliged to leave the said port with less than her legal complement of Emigrants, the Contractors shall thereupon be discharged from all forfeit or maintenance-money in respect of such African. Provided, nevertheless, that the Emigration Officer may at any time afterwards place such Africans on board any ship furnished by the Contractors for this service, to be conveyed to the West Indies at the rate of £5 10s. per adult.

ART. XIII. That the Master of any such ship may refuse to receive on board any Emigrant whom he may consider unfitted by the state of his health for immediate conveyance to the West Indies; but in that case the Contractors shall remain subject to all deductions and forfeitures provided for by this Agreement in respect of the Africans so refused; and in computing the numbers of Emigrants placed on board for the purposes of Art. XII., the Africans so refused shall be considered to have been placed on board.

ART. XIV. That if at any time the Governor of Sierra Leone or St. Helena, or the Consul at Rio de Janeiro shall report to the Secretary of State, either that during the preceding two months no suitable ship has been tendered by the Contractors for the conveyance of Liberated Africans, and that there are at the date of his report not less than 200 Liberated Africans under Government superintendence, or that no such ship has been so tendered during the then preceding three months, it shall be competent to the said Commissioners to enforce the performance of this Contract, or in case the delay should not be explained to the satisfaction of the said Commissioners, to treat the Contract as at an end in respect of the place from which such report shall arrive, and in the latter case the Contractors shall thereupon forfeit to the said Commissioners as liquidated damages the sum of £1,500 in case the Contract shall be terminated in respect of St. Helena or Rio de Janeiro, and half that sum in case it shall have been terminated in respect of Sierra Leone.

ART. XV. That the Contractors shall convey to Sierra Leone any Africans who shall be placed on board of any of their ships, bound to that port, by authority of the Governors of British Guiana or Trinidad at the rate of £4 10s. per adult.

ART. XVI. That the Contractors shall convey to British Guiana, Trinidad, or St. Lucia, any free Africans who shall be placed on board of any of their ships, bound to any of these Colonies, by authority of the Governors of Sierra Leone or St. Helena at the rate of £5 per adult.

ART. XVII. That all persons embarked by virtue of the two preceding articles shall be treated and victualled as hereinbefore provided, with regard to Liberated Africans, and that the passage-money payable on such persons shall be paid from Colonial funds; and if paid through the said Commissioners, after production to the said Commissioners of an account setting forth the particulars of the claim, together with certificates that such persons were placed on board by authority of the Governor of the Colony from which they were embarked, and after being properly treated on the voyage, were landed alive at the port of their destination, such certificate to be signed by the Emigration or Immigration Officer at such respective ports.

ART. XVIII. That the Contractors shall deliver to the Emigration Agent at the port of embarkation a receipt for all Government Stores, whether clothing or otherwise, which shall be placed on board for the use of the Emigrants, and shall pay to the said Commissioners the value of all such Stores as shall not be certified by a Government Officer at the port of debarkation to have been either accounted for to his satisfaction, or delivered up at the end of the voyage.

ART. XIX. That the Contractors shall not be entitled to claim compensation for any detention of their ships which may take place at Sierra Leone, St. Helena, or Rio de Janeiro, in order to secure the health, safety, or well being of the Africans on board; but if any detention in the West Indies shall take place by authority of the Government, not having been rendered necessary by any act or default of the Contractors or of any person employed by them, then for every day of such detention not exceeding eight days (which shall in all cases be allowed, if necessary, for the disembarkation of the Emigrants) the said Commissioners shall pay demurrage at the rate of 4½d. per ton register per diem, and victualling-money at the rate of 6d. per head per diem for every African victualled on board.

Appendix VI

The place of Origin of Liberated Slaves and other Africans introduced into the West Indies between 1841—1867 (as far as known)

Year	British Guiana				Jamaica				Trinidad			Other Colonies	
	Sierra Leone and Kroo Coast	St Helena	Rio and Havana	Elsewhere	Sierra Leone and Kroo Coast	St Helena	Rio and Havana	Elsewhere	Sierra Leone and Kroo Coast	St Helena	Rio and Havana	Sierra Leone and Kroo Coast	St Helena
1841–44	1,180	1,776	708	740*	1,524	601	—	408†	1,406	751	504	—	—
1845–49	3,089	1,816	—	—	1,418	1,979	539	—	1,281	1,621	375	1,490	—
1850–54	1,294	734	185	—	494	452	148	230	597	614	—	1,022	137
1855–59	—	346	—	—	—	—	—	362‡	—	315	—	—	891
1860–64	—	2,059	—	—	390	1,447	—	—	226	695	—	223	—
1865–67	—	42	—	—	—	11	—	—	—	—	—	—	—
Total	5,563	6,773	893	740	3,826	4,490	687	1,000	3,510	3,996	879	2,735	1,028
Grand Total	13,069				10,003				8,385			3,763	

* In 1841, origin unknown (740); † In 1841 and 1842 respectively from Bahamas (94) and (314) = 408; ‡ In 1850 and 1875 landed directly from captured slavers (230) and (362).

Year	Summary of Origin of Emigrants				
	Sierra Leone and Kroo Coast	St Helena	Rio and Havana	Else-where	Total No. of Emigrants
1841–44	4,110	3,128	1,212	1,148	9,598
1845–49	7,278	5,416	914	—	13,608
1850–54	3,407	1,937	333	230	5,907
1855–59	—	661	—	362	1,023
1860–64	839	5,092	—	—	5,931
1865–67	—	53	—	—	53
Total	15,634	16,287	2,459	1,740	36,120*
Grand Total		36,120			

* Excluding some 3,200 liberated Africans of unknown origin introduced in the West Indies between 1834–40. There is also no proper account given of emigrants landed in Mauritius and the Cape of Good Hope direct from captured foreign slavers.

Sources:

1834–49 inclusive:	PP. 1847, Vol. XXXIX, 496, 15
	PP. 1850, Vol. XXXIX, 228, 283
1849–51:	PP. 1851, Vol. XL, 625, 409
Since July 1st 1851:	PP. 1851, Vol. XXXI, 231, 869
1852–3:	PP. 1852–3, Vol. LXV, 287
1854:	PP. 1854, Vol. XLVI, 425
1854–5:	PP. 1854–5, Vol. XXXVI, 575
1856:	PP. 1856, Vol. XLIV, 269
1857:	PP. 1857, Vol. X (Sess. 1), 955
1857–8:	PP. 1857–8, Vol. XL, 561
1859:	PP. 1859, Vol. XVI (Sess. 1), 535
1860:	PP. 1860, Vol. XLV, 337
1861:	PP. 1861, Vol. XL, 521;
	PP. 1862, Vol. XXXVI, 415.

C.O. 386/54

Appendix VII

The African Squadron and the Suppression of the West African Atlantic Slave Trade

Record of captures and emancipation at Sierra Leone from 1808 to 1861 (as far as known) compiled from the Liberated African Register (L.A.R.) and the Official Returns (R) in the Archives at Fourah Bay College, Freetown, Sierra Leone.

Note: Records badly kept. Actual figures very probably far exceed the entries in the records. In cases where no entry appears, the information is lacking.

Key: M.C. = Mixed Commission Court; V.A.C. = Vice-Admiralty Court; V.E. = Variously employed (apprenticeship, public works, enlistment in the Military, etc.); R.A.C. = Royal African Corps; W.I.R. = West Indian Regiment.

Documentary Source	Slave Vessel	Nationality of vessel	Number of Slaves Emancipated or their Registration No.	Year	Date Emancipated	Emancipating Court	Method of Disposal	Warship	Commander	Remarks
LAR 1	Maria Paul	French	1 to 60	1808	10.11	V.A.C.	Public Works	Derwent	F. Parker	—
LAR 2 and 3	San Joaquim and San Domingo	—	61 to 74	1808	24.11	—	—	Derwent	F. Parker	—
LAR 4	Two Cousins	English	75 to 78	1808	25.11		—	Derwent	F. Parker	—
LAR 5	African	Dutch	79 to 81	1809	30.5	V.A.C.	—	Derwent	F. Parker	—
LAR 6	Pennel	English	82 to 99	1809	12.8		—	Minerva	A. Macauley	—
LAR 7	—	—	100 to 248	1809	6.11		—	—	—	—
LAR 8	Cuba or Marianna	American	249 to 358	1809	28.2		—	—	—	Illegal on Spanish papers
LAR 9	La Lucia	American	359 to 487	1810	9.4		37 Enlisted R.A.C.	—	—	On Spanish Papers
LAR 10	Doris	—	488 to 545	1810	17.7		—	Crocodile	—	Slaver carrying Spanish papers
LAR 11	Marianna	—	546 to 731	1810	2.5		—	Crocodile	—	Slaver carrying Spanish papers
LAR 12	Esperana	—	732 to 822	1810	14.5		—	Crocodile	—	Slaver carrying Portuguese papers
LAR 13	—	—	823 to 940	—	—		—	—	—	—
LAR 14	—	—	941 to 970	—	—		—	—	—	—
LAR 15	—	—	971 to 1017	—	—		—	—	—	—
LAR 16	—	—	1018 to 1074	—	—		—	—	—	—
LAR 17	—	—	1075 to 1151	—	—		—	—	—	—
LAR 18	—	—	1152 to 1233	—	—		—	—	—	Some numbers are empty

Appendix VII (cont.) For key and headings to columns see p. 191

LAR	Numbers	Notes
LAR 19	1234 to 1317	
LAR 20	1318 to 1418	
LAR 21	1419 to 1446	
LAR 22	1447 to 1456	
LAR 23	1457 to 1464	
LAR 24	1465 to 1551	
LAR 25	1552 to 1636	
LAR 26	1637 to 1747	
LAR 27	1748 to 1762	
LAR 28	1763 to 1860	
LAR 29	1861 to 1898	
LAR 30	1899 to 1957	
LAR 31	1858 to 1970	
LAR 32	1971 to 1991	
LAR 33	1992 to 1995	
LAR 34	1996 to 2051	
LAR 35	2052 to 2124	
LAR 36	2125 to 2169	
LAR 37	2170 to 2184	
LAR 38	2185 to 2190	
LAR 39	2191 to 2213	
LAR 40	2214 to 2352	
LAR 41	2353 to 2362	
LAR 42	2363 to 2504	
LAR 43	2505 to 2792	2778–2792 empty numbers, Probably the females
LAR 44	2793 to 2907	
LAR 45	2908 to 2938	
LAR 46	2939 to 3142	
LAR 47	3143 to 3153	
LAR 48	3154 to 3206	
LAR 49	3207	1 man named William Richmond
LAR 50	3208 to 3340	
LAR 51	3341 to 3407	
LAR 52	3408 to 3485	
LAR 53	3486 to 3653	

LAR	Name	Numbers	Date				Name		Notes
LAR 54	—	3654 to 3859	—	—	—	—	—	—	3772 marks end of 1st book dated quoted by last figures 3859
LAR 55	—	3860 to 4143	—	—	—	—	—	—	Some with Portuguese names, other brandmarked
LAR 56	—	4144 to 4224	—	—	—	—	—	—	Many with Portuguese names
LAR 57	—	4225 to 4337	—	—	—	—	—	—	
LAR 58	—	4338 to 4570	—	—	—	—	—	—	
LAR 59	—	4571 to 4618	—	—	—	—	—	—	
LAR 60	—	4619 to 4665	—	—	—	—	—	—	
LAR 61	Phoenix	4666	—	—	—	—	—	—	
LAR 62	—	4667 to 4669	—	—	—	—	Favorite	—	
LAR 63	—	4670	—	—	—	—	Princess Charlotte	—	
LAR 64	—	4671 to 4675	—	—	—	—	Creole and Astrea	—	
LAR 65	—	4676 to 4681	—	—	—	—	—	—	
LAR 66	—	4682 to 4683	—	—	—	—	—	—	
LAR 67	—	4684 to 4924	1814 30.3	V.A.C.	—	—	Macmillan	—	Seized at Rio Pongas many had names
LAR 68	—	4925 to 4986	1814 19.4	—	—	—	—	—	Condemned for being property of English convict
LAR 69	Nossa Senhora Da Victoria	4988 to 5420	1814 28.5	V.A.C.	—	—	Macmillan	—	Brand marks e.g. R, MF, A.
LAR 70	Plantain	5421 to 5433	1814 24.5	V.A.C.	—	—	—	—	Taken from the Soosoo country for being property
LAR 71	—	5434 to 5445	1814 22.6	V.A.C.	—	—	—	—	of an enemy
LAR 72	Gertrudis Da Graciosa	5446 to 5925	1814 8.7	V.A.C.	—	—	—	—	
LAR 73	Maria Joseffa	5926 to 5987	1814 21.7	V.A.C.	—	—	—	—	
LAR 74	Bom Successo	5988 to 6238	1814 30.8	—	—	—	—	—	
LAR 75	Delores or El Volador	6239 to 6273	1814 11.10	—	—	—	—	—	
LAR 76	—	6274	1814 11.10	—	—	—	—	—	
LAR 77	—	6275 to 6329	1814 14.11	—	—	—	—	Major Appleton	Seized by the collector of customs
LAR 78	Resurrexion	6330	1814 2.12	—	—	—	—	—	

Appendix VII (*cont.*) For key and headings to columns see p. 191

For key and headings to columns see p. 191

	Ship		Number							Notes
LAR 79	Princess Charlotte	—	6331 to 6388	—	2.12	—	—	—	—	—
LAR 80	Golondrina	—	6389 to 6532	1814	8.12	—	—	—	Major Appleton	—
LAR 81	—	—	6533 to 6552	1815	18.1	—	—	—		—
LAR 82	Vanganze	—	6553 to 6595	1815	21.6	—	—	—		—
LAR 83	S. Joge	—	6596 to 6660	1815	17.6	—	—	—		Seized at Goree and Senegal
LAR 84	—	—	6661 to 6666	1815	17.6	—	—	—		—
LAR 85	Resurrection	—	—	1815	17.6	—	Princess Charlotte	—		—
LAR 86	General Silveira	—	6726 to 6963	1815	21.6	—	—	—		—
LAR 87	Deligente	—	6964 to 6985	1815	24.6	—	—	—		—
LAR 88	Concessio	—	6986	1815	21.6	—	—	—		All men with Portuguese names
LAR 89	Triumpho Africana	—	6987 to 7004	1815	21.6	—	—	—		Two slaves without number sent to Joliff town
LAR 90	Dido	—	7005 to 7331	1815	25.8	—	—	—		—
LAR 91	Entrepida	—	(a) 7332 to 7576	1815	8.8	—	Pilgrim	—		—
LAR 92	Carmin	—	7577 to 7696	1815	8.8	—	—	—		—
LAR 93		—	7697 to 7701	1815	8.8	—	—	—		Seized at Goree and Senegal
LAR 94	Bon Sorte	—	—	—	1.8	—	—	—		—
LAR 95	Estrilla	—	7702 to 7758	1815	19.8	—	—	—		—
LAR 96	Dos Amegos	—	7759 to 7800	1815	19.8	—	—	—		—
LAR 97	Santa Anna	—	No. 7801 (1)	1815	19.8	—	—	—		—
LAR 98	San Joaquim	—	7802 to 7804	1815	21.8	—	—	—		—
LAR 99	—	—	7805 to 7843	1815	17.9	—	—	—		Seized at the Bananas and the settlement of Goree and Senegal.
LAR 100	—	—	7844 to 7860	1815	9.11	—	—	—		—
LAR 101	—	—	7861 to 7871	1815	5.12	—	—	—		—
LAR 102	Rosa	—	7872 to 8105	1816	3.2	—	—	—		—
LAR 103	Eugenia	—	8106 to 8148	1816	12.3	—	—	—		—
LAR 104	Juan	—	8149 to 8197	1816	12.3	—	—	—		—
LAR 105	Eugenia	—	8198 to 8230	1816	12.3	—	—	—		—
LAR 106	Los Dos Hermanoes	—	8231 to 8314	1816	8.5	V.A.C.	—	—		Ship with Spanish papers
LAR 107	Saint Antonio Milagroso	French	8704 to 9207	1816	13.5	—	—	—		Slaves with English or Portuguese names

LAR No.	Name	Nationality	Registration Nos	Date	Value	Vessel	Remarks
LAR 108	Delores	—	9208 to 9456	1816	13.5	—	Vessel described as 'H.M. colonial brig; 18 natives of Africa in an illegal state of slavery'
LAR 109	Princess Charlotte	—	9457 9475	1816	13.5	—	—
LAR 110	Temarario	—	9476 to 9492	1816	22.5	—	Many with English names
LAR 111	La Nueva Pez (Paz)	—	9493 9532	1816	19.6	—	—
LAR 112	Caveira	—	9533 to 9543	1816	19.6	—	—
LAR 113	Dos Amegos	—	9544 9692	1816	6.8	—	No. 9693 not used
LAR 114	H.M. Col. Brig. Prince Regent	—	9694 9758	—	—	—	—
LAR 115	Triumphante	—	9759 to 10,158	1816	25.11	—	Part of Dos Amegos's cargo. Vide Lar 113
LAR 116	Carmin	—	10,159 to 10,255	1817	4.1	—	—
LAR 117	Teresa	—	10,256 to 10,415	1817	4.1	—	—
LAR 118	Rodeur	—	10,416 to 10,447	1817	5.1 or 25.1	—	Several with Portuguese names
LAR 119	Caroline	—	10,448 to 10,465	1817	15.3	—	—
LAR 120	San Joanna	—	10,466 to 10,530	1817	15.3	—	—
LAR 121	Ceresa	—	10,531 to 10,582	1817	15.3	—	Several with Portuguese names
LAR 122	Esperanza	—	10,583 to 10,990	1817	9.5	—	Cargo of the Triumvirate
LAR 123	Labirinto	—	10,991 to 11,018	1817	31.5	—	—
LAR 124	San Juan	—	11,019 to 11,287	1818	12.2	—	—
LAR 125	Nepomecena Linda Africano	—	11,288 to 11,292	1818	12.2	—	—
LAR 126	—	—	11,293 to 11,310	1818	2.10	—	Taken by Mr. Kaerney
LAR 127	Hannah	—	—	1818	10.10	—	—
LAR 128	Descubridor and Concha	—	11,311 to 11,743	—	—	—	8 slaves lost Slave Registration Nos given
LAR 129	Sylph	—	11,744 to 12,107	1819	13.2	Tartar Pheasant	—
LAR 130	—	Portg	12,108	1819	6.5	—	—
LAR 131	Novo Felicidad	—	12,109 to 12,178	—	—	—	Not condemned
LAR 132	Neustra Senora de Ragla	Spanish	12,179	1819	13.9	Kelly	—
LAR 133	Fabianna	Spanish	12,180 to 12,192	1819	7.10	—	—
LAR 134	Centra	Portg	12,193 to 12,217	1820	3.6	—	—

Appendix VII (*cont.*) For key and headings to columns see p. 191

	Name	Nation	Numbers	Year		M.C.	Destination	Ship		
LAR 135	Esperanza	—	12,218 to 12,256	1819	27.12	M.C.	—	—	—	—
LAR 136	Francisca	Spanish	12,257 to 12,325	1820	8.2	—	—	—	—	—
LAR 137	Julietta	Spanish	12,326 to 12,334	1819	12.11	—	To Kissy Village	—	—	—
LAR 138	Virginia	Dutch	12,335 to 12,365	1819	15.11	—	To Charlotte Village	—	—	—
LAR 139	Eliza	—	12,366	1819	25.11	M.C.	To Bathurst Village	—	—	—
LAR 140	Nuestra Senora-de La Nieos (Nievs) Maria	Spanish	12,367 to 12,487	1820	3.1	—	To Gloucester and Leopole Village	—	—	—
LAR 141		Dutch	12,488 to 12,489	1820	10.2 or 15.2	—	—	—	—	—
LAR 142	Gazetta	Spanish	12,490 to 12,570	1820	18.3	—	—	—	—	—
LAR 143	Invincible the 2nd	—	12,571 to 12,597	1820	—	—	—	—	—	Privateer Schooner
LAT 144	La Marie	French	12,598 to 12,687	1820	19.2	—	All sent to Waterloo	—	—	—
LAR 145	—	—	12,688 to 12,696	1820	5.1	—	All sent to Gloucester	Myrmidon	—	—
LAR 146	Two Sisters	English	12,607 to 12,711	1820	20.9	—	To Gloucester	—	—	—
LAR 147	La Monserrat	—	12,712 to 12,795	1820	2.11	M.C.	Most sent to Charlotte	Pheasant	Kelly	—
LAR 148	—	—	12,796 to 12,840	1820	5.11	—	To Bananas and Bathurst	—	—	—
LAR 149	Anna Maria	Spanish	12,841 to 13,165	1821	16.5	—	—	—	—	—
LAR 150	Dona Eugenia	Portg	13,166 to 13,243	1821	19.5	M.C.	To Village	—	—	—
LAR 151	Constantia	Portg	13,244 to 13,334	1821	5.6	MC..	To Charlotte Village and to Waterloo	Thistle	—	—
LAR 152	Constantia	Portg	13,335 to 13,390	1821	5.6	—	—	—	—	—
LAR 153	Ana Maria	Spanish	13,391 to 13,418	1821	11.5	M.C.	To Villages	Tartar	—	—
LAR 154	Gavioa or Gavion	Spanish	13,419 to 13,467	1821	16.5	—	All sent to Kissy	Tartan	—	—
LAR 155	Adelaide	Portg	13,468 to 13,675	1821	17.9	M.C.	To various Villages and to Public Works	Pheasant	—	—

LAR	Name	Nationality	Numbers	Year	Date	M.C.	Disposition	Ship			Notes
LAR 156	La Caridad	Spanish	13,676 to 13,811	1821	7.11	M.C.	To various Villages	Myrmidon	—	—	
LAR 157	El Nueva Vergen	Spanish	13,812 to 13,917	1821	7.11	M.C.	—	Myrmidon	—	—	
LAR 158	Rosalia	Spanish	13,918 to 13,975	1822	31.1	—	To Villages	—	—	—	
LAR 159	El Conde De Villa Flor	Portg	13,977 to 14,141	1822	13.3	—	Some Apprenticeship and some to Villages	Iphigenia	—	—	
LAR 160	Dichosa Estrella	Spanish	14,142 to 14,170	1822	18.6	—	Apprenticed, some sent to Villages	Morgiana	—	—	
LAR 161	L'ursule	French	14,171 to 14,371	1822	24.5	—	To Villages	Iphigenia	—	—	
LAR 162	Le Vigilent	French	14,372 to 14,671	1822	24.5	—	To Villages	Iphigenia	—	—	
LAR 163	Le Petit	French	14,672 to 14,868	1822	27.7	—	Some to hospital, some to Waterloo	Iphigenia	—	—	
LAR 164	Betszy Dies De Feverio	Portg	14,869 to 14,878	1822	22.6	—	All to Charlotte Village	Iphigenia	—	—	
LAR 165	L'Esperanza	Portg	14,879 to 15,025	1822	8.6	M.C.	Some to hospital, some apprenticed, some to villages	Morgiana	—	—	Many Brandmarked (A)
LAR 166	Conceicao	Portg	15,026 to 15,079	1821	26.9	—	—	—	—	—	
LAR 167	Veova or (Vegua)	Spanish	15,080 to 15,297	1822	25.6	—	Some sent to Leopold	Myrmidon and Iphigenia	—	—	
LAR 168	Yoanaue and Iecanen	Spanish	15,298 to 15,309 (12) Persons	1822	25.6	—	Employed in Govt.	H.M.S. Iphegenia	—	—	
LAR 169	Esperanza Felis	Portg	15,310 to 15,344	1822	4.7	—	To Bathurst	—	—	—	
LAR 170	Defeucon Da Patria	Portg	15,395 to 15,474	1822	4.7	—	To Leopold	—	—	—	
LAR 171	Estrella	Portg	15,475 to 15,766 (292) Persons	1822	6.8	—	To Villages	H.M.S. Thistle	—	—	
LAR 172	Nymfadelmar	Portg	15,767 to 15,768	1822	28.8	—	To Hastings	H.M.S. Thistle	—	—	
LAR 173	San Joze Sallacan	Portg	15,679 to 15,785 (17) Persons	1822	28.8	—		H.M.S. Thistle	—	—	
LAR 174	Josefa	Spanish	15,786 to 15,557 (182) Persons	1822	5.10	—	To Regent and Fourah Bay	H.M.S. Driver	—	—	
LAR 175	Aurora	Netherland	15,968 to 16,145	1822	29.11	M.C.	To Villages	H.M.S.	—	—	

Appendix VII (cont.) For key and headings to columns see p. 191

For key and headings to columns see p. 191

	Name	Flag	Persons	Reg. Nos.	Year	No.	Court	Disposal	Vessel	Commander	Notes
LAR 176	Commerciante	Portg	(157) Persons	16,146 to 16,312	1822	15.11	M.C.	To Villages	Cyrene H.M.S.	—	—
LAR 177	S. Raphael	Spanish	(167) Persons	16,313 to 16,629	1822	16.11	M.C.	To Kissy and Hospital	H.M.S. Driver	—	—
LAR 178	St. Antonio Delisboa	Portg	(191) Persons	16,630 to 16,728	1822	3.12	M.C.	To Villages	H.M.S. Bann	—	—
LAR 179	Juliana da Praca	Portg	(99) Persons	16,729 to 16,926	1822	30.12	M.C.	To Leopold	H.M.S. Bann	—	—
LAR 180	Conceicao	Portg	(191) Persons	16,927 to 17,011	1822	18.1	—	To Villages	H.M.S. Bann	—	—
LAR 181	Caroline	French	(85) Persons	17,012 to 17,044	1822	24.12	—	To Vilages	—	—	—
LAR 182	Magdalena Da Fraca	Portg	(122)	17,045 to 17,165	1822	23.1	—	—	H.M.S. Cyrene	—	—
LAR 183	Nova-Sorte	Portg	(114) Persons	17,169 to 17,286	1822	6.2	M.C.	To Villages	—	—	—
LAR 184	Sincerridade	Portg	(118) Persons	17,287 to 17,298	1823	17.3	M.C.	To Villages	H.M.S. Snapper	—	—
LAR 185	Fabiana	Spanish	(12) Persons	17,299 to 17,307	1823	21.10	V.A.C.	To Villages	H.M.S. Gwen Glendower	—	—
LAR 186	—	Spanish	(9) Persons	17,308 to 17,634	1823	11.11	—	Settled at York To Villages	—	M. James Johnston	—
LAR 187	—	—	(327)	—	1823	17.12	M.C.	Variously Employed	H.M.S. Owen Glendowen	—	—
LAR 188	Bomcominho	Portg	14 Persons	17,635 to 17,646	1824	15.5	M.C.	To Villages and V.E.	H.M.S. Bann	—	—
LAR 189	Alex Grant	British	—	17,647 to 17,652	1824	30.5	V.A.C.	To York	—	—	Ashuntee prisoners brought by the slaver 'Alex Grant'
LAR 190	Fl Vencedor	Braz	(6) Persons	—	1824	5.6	V.A.C.	To Villages	H.M.S. Victor	—	—
LAR 191	—	—	—	—	1824	24.1	—	Employed in Freetown as stone labourers	H.M.S. Bann	—	—
LAR 192	—	—	—	17,304	—	—	—	2 to hospital and John Liverpool	H.M.S. Owen Glendowen	—	One man only; there were many others not given Slave Registration Nos, No Expl. Seized in the Gambia
LAR 193	—	—	—	17,776 to 17,779	1824	18.9	V.A.C.	—	—	Capt. Findley	—

LAR	Nat.	Ship	Numbers	Year	Date	Code	Disposition	H.M.S.	Officer	Notes
LAR 194	—	—	17,780 to 17,782	1824	Aug	—	To Leopold	—	Capt. Findley	Seized at St. Mary's Capt. seized in the Gambia
LAR 195	Braz	Diana	17,783 to 17,898 (116) Persons	1824	15.11	M.C.	V.E. and To Charlotte	H.M.S. Victor	—	—
LAR 196	Braz	Los Dos Amigos	17,899 to 18,153 (255) Persons	1824	4.11	M.C.	To Villages	H.M.S. Victor	—	—
LAR 197	Portg	Aviso Aviso	18,154 to 18,577	1824	12.11	—	To Villages	H.M.S. Stone	—	—
LAR 198	Portg	Bella Eliza	18,578 to 18,946 (369) Persons	1825	31.1	M.C.	—	H.M.S. Bann	—	—
LAR 199	—	—	18,947 to 19,078	1825	29.1	V.A.C.	To Villages	—	Alfred William Percival	—
LAR 200	Spanish	Espanola	19,079 to 19,348	1825	19.3	—	—	Athol	—	From Espanola
LAR 201	Portg	Bom Fim	19,349 to 19,494	1825	19.3	—	—	H.M.S. Swinger	—	—
LAR 202	French	S. Eleonore	19,495 to 19,622	1825	—	V.A.C.	To Villages	Roxburg castle	General Turner	In Sierra Leone Harbour Judge Rendale
LAR 203	Braz	Bom Jesus Dos Navigantes Brigant Sunmaca Bom. J. D. N.	19,623 to 19,888	1825	10.4	M.C.	To Gambia	H.M.S. Esk	—	—
LAR 204	—	—	19,889 to 19,988	1825	8.10	V.A.C.	To Villages	—	General Turner	At York Island Sherbro
LAR 205	Spanish	Segunda	19,989 to 20,011	1825	—	—	To Villages	H.M.S. Maid Stone	—	—
LAR 206	Spanish	Gakega	20,012 to 20,285	1825	23.11	M.C.	To Villages	H.M.S. Brazen	—	—
LAR 207	Spanish	Clarita	20,286 to 20,321 (274) Persons	1825	18.11	M.C.	—	—	—	—
LAR 208	Portg	Uniad Ninfa	20,322 to 20,570	1825	4.11	M.C.	To Wilberforce V.E. and To Villages	H.M.S. Athol	—	—
LAR 209	Spanish	Habana	20,571 to 20,798	1826	3.1	M.C.	—	H.M.S. Brazen	—	—
LAR 210	Spanish	Ana	20,799 to 20,928	1826	3.1	—	—	H.M.S. Red Wing	—	—
LAR 211	Spanish	Teresa	20,929 to 20,934	—	—	—	—	H.M.S. Sloop Red Wing	—	—
LAR 212	Portg	Parguito	20,935 to 21,319	1826	10.1	M.C.	To Public Works Barracks	H.M.S. Swinger	—	—
LAR 213	Netherlands	L'Amable Claudine	21,320 to 21,353	1826	6.2	—	—	H.M.S. Athol	—	—

Appendix VII (*cont.*) For key and headings to columns see p. 191

LAR	Ship	Flag	Numbers	Date	Value	Class	Destination	Vessel	Notes
LAR 214	Charles	Netherlands	21,354 to 21,596	1826	15.3	—	—	Brig Conflict	—
LAR 215	Iberia Sanjbao Segunda Rosalia	—	21,597 to 22,013	1826	21.3	M.C.	—	Brazen	—
LAR 216		Braz	22,014 to 22,199	1826	21.3	—	—	Esk	—
LAR 217	—	—	22,200 to 22,247	1826	10.3	—	—	Major General Turner	—
LAR 218	Edward	—	22,248 to 22,282 (35) Persons	1826	15.3	—	—	Major General Turner	Landed at Cape Coast
LAR 219	—	—	22,283 to 22,286	—	—	—	To Villages	H.M.S. Esk	—
LAR 220	Esperanca	—	22,287 to 22,290 (4) Persons	1826	9.6	M.C.	To York and D. Hamilton	Athol	—
LAR 221	Activo	Braz	(163) Persons	1826	1.5	—	Taken charge of by dept.	—	—
LAR 222	Netuno	Braz	22,291 to 22,374 (84)	1826	8.6	M.C.	To Villages	Esk	—
LAR 223	Necarno	Spanish	22,375 to 22,597	1826	1.7	—	—	—	—
LAR 224	La Fortuna	Netherlands	22,548 to 22,682	1826	17.7	—	—	Brazen	—
LAR 225	Principe de Guinea	—	22,683 to 23,261 (579)	1826	26.9	M.C.	—	Maidstone	—
LAR 226	Intripeda	Portg	23,262 to 23,486	1826	26.9	—	—	—	—
LAR 227	Perpetuo Defensor	Braz	23,487 to 23,724	1826	—	—	—	H.M.S. Maidstone	Branded
	Perpetuo Defensor	Braz	23,725 to 23,814	1826	6.7	—	—	—	—
LAR 228	Snelheid	Netherlands	23,815 to 23,837	1826	16,11	M.C.	—	H.M.S. Brazen	—
LAR 229	—	—	23,838 to 23,856 (19)	1826	4,12	V.A.C.	—	—	—
LAR 230	—	—	23,857 to 23,856 (26)	1826	7,12	V.A.C.	To Villages	—	—
LAR 231	—	—	23,883 to 23,888	—	7.1	—	To Wellington	H.M.S. Steam	Sir Neil Cambell
LAR 232	Paulata	Spanish	23,889 to 24,077 (189)	1827	16.3	—	To Villages	H.M.S. Maidstone	—

LAR	Name	Nationality	Numbers	Year			Disposal	Ship	
LAR 233	Lynx	Dutch	24,078 to 24,328 (251)	1827	21.2	M.C.	—	H.M.S. Esk	—
LAR 234	Invencible Invinciyal	Braz	24,329 to 24,678 (250)	1827	10.3	M.C.	—	H.M.S. Esk	—
LAR 235	Emelia Aemelia	Spanish	24,579 to 24,753 (175)	1827	10.3	M.C.	—	H.M.S. North Star	—
LAR 236	Fame Fama	Spanish	24,754 to 24,848 (95)	1827	10.3	M.C.	—	H.M.S. North Star	—
LAR 237	Venus	Braz	24,849 to 25,036 (188)	1827	9.4	M.C.	—	H.M.S. Esk	—
LAR 238	Dos Amegos	Braz	25,037 to 25,344 (308)	1827	9.4	—	—	H.M.S. Esk	—
LAR 239	Conceiao De Maria	—	25,345 to 25,542 (198)	1827	15.5	M.C.	—	H.M.S. North Star	—
LAR 240	—	—	25,543 to 25,551 (8)	1827	1.5	V.A.C.	—	—	Logan Hook
LAR 241	Amegostaes Amegos	Braz	25,552 to 25,554	1827	16.5	—	—	H.M.S. North Star	—
LAR 242	Creola Creole	Braz	25,555 to 25,843 (289)	1827	1.6	M.C.	Enlisted in Army	H.M.S. Maidstone	—
LAR 243	Silverenah Silevrinha	Braz	25,854 to 26,052 (209)	1827	19.6	M.C.	—	—	—
LAR 244	Tonenha	Portg	26,053 to 26,110 (58)	1827	21.7	M.C.	To Hospital and Kissy	H.M.S. Northstar	—
LAR 246	Ioninha Diana	Braz	26,657 to 26,740 (84)	1827	8.12	—	—	H.M.S. Sybille	—
LAR 247	Gertrudis Gertrudes	Spanish	26,741 to 26,895	1828	2.8	M.C.	To Villages	H.M.S. Sybille	—
LAR 248	Fanny	Netherlands	26,896 to 27,148	1827	25.5	M.C.	To Villages	H.M.S. Sybille and Plumber	—
LAR 249	Vaodora	—	27,149 to 27,193 (15)	1828	16.6	—	—	H.M.S. Eden	—
LAR 250	Victoria	Spanish	27,194 to 27,210 (17)	—	17.6	—	—	H.M.S. Eden	—
LAR 251	Vingador or Vinzidor	Braz	27,211 to 27,834 (624)	1828	16.6	M.C.	To Villages	H.M.S. Sybille	—
LAR 252	Feliz Victoria	Spanish	27,835 to 27,836	1828	23.6	M.C.	Employed as Seamen	—	—
LAR 253	Emprendedor	Spanish	27,837 to 27,839	1828	14.7	—	To their country	—	—

Appendix VII (*cont.*) For key and headings to columns see p. 191

For key and headings to columns see p. 191

	Name	Flag	Numbers			M.C.	Destination	Ship	Captor	Remarks
LAR 254	Josephine	Portg	27,840 to 27,916 (77)	1828	17.8	—	To Villages	—	—	—
LAR 255	Nova-Virgem	Braz	27,917 to 28,241	—	—	—	To Why-Not-Estate	—	—	—
LAR 256	Clementina	Braz	28,242 to 28,398 (158) Persons	1828	18.9	—		H.M.S. Clinker	—	—
LAR 257	Henrietta	Netherlands	28,399 to 28,704 (306) Persons	1828	3.10	M.C.	Ran Away	H.M.S. Aden	—	—
LAR 258	Santa Effigenia	Braz	28,705 to 28,921 (217) Persons	1828	26.11	—	—	—	—	—
LAR 259	Zepherina	Braz	28,922 to 29,075 (158) Persons	1828	9.12	M.C.	To Wellington	—	—	—
LAR 260	Compeadore	Spanish	29,079 to 29,290 (212) Persons	1828	19.12	—	To Villages	—	—	—
LAR 261	Arcenia	Braz	29,291 to 29,559 (269) Persons	1828	19.12	M.C.	—	—	—	—
LAR 262	Minerya de Conceicao	Braz	29,560 to 29,641 (82) Persons	1828	—	M.C.	—	—	—	—
LAR 263	Penhade Franca	Braz	29,642 to 29,810 (169) Persons	1828	19.12	M.C.	To York	—	—	—
LAR 264	Eljuan	Spanish	29,811 to 30,188 Persons	1828	19.12	M.C.	—	—	—	Rec. 10.12.1828 Distrib. 21.12.1829 Slaver was condemned 17.1.1829
LAR 265	Triumpho	Braz	30,189 to 30,310	1828	30.12	M.C.	—	—	—	Slaver was condemned 26.1.1829
LAR 266	La Coquette	Dutch	30,311 to 30,493	1829	27.1	—	—	—	—	—
LAR 267	Bella Eliza	Braz	30,494 to 30,708	1829	21.2	—	Sent to Bathurst	—	—	Slaver Cond. 27.2.1829 Several of the slaves had Brandmarks (P)
LAR 268	Vingador	Portg	30,709 to 30,928	1829	24.1	—	Variously employed (V.E.) Freetown	Primrose	5 Griffen Hofe	Cond. 3.3.1829
LAR 269	Aurelia	Braz	30,929 to 30,957	1829	4.3	—	—	—	—	—
LAR 270	Jules	Netherlands	30,958 to 31,633	1829	3.3	—	—	Eden (Owen)	Owen	—
LAR 271	Jeune Eugenia	Netherland	31,164 to 31,209	1829	10.3	—	—	Eden (Owen)	Owen	Cond. 24.6.1829
LAR 272	Uniac	Braz	31,210 to 31,575	1829	4.3	—	—	Sybille	F. Collier	Many of them branded Slaver Cond. 13.2.1829
LAR 273	El Almirante	Spanish	31,576 to 31,991	1829	21.3	—	Employed at Bananas—Bathurst	Black Joke	J. A. Collier	—
LAR 274	Donna Barbara	Braz	31,992 to 32,342	1829	14.4	—		Paul Fry	Collier	Many Branded

LAR No.	Name	Nationality	Numbers	Year	Date		Disposal	Ship	Officer	Remarks
LAR 275	Corolina	Braz	32,342 to 32,738	1829	6.4	—	V.E.	Sybille	Collier	—
LAR 276	Jules	—	32,739 to	1829	19.5	—	—	Eden	W. J. W.	—
LAR 277	Mensageria	Braz	32,740 to 32,850	1829	19.5 30.5	—	—	Eden	Owen	Branded (S) on right breast
LAR 278	Hirondello	Netherland	32,857 to 32,905	1829	13.5	—	—	Eden	Owen	Cond. 24.6.1829
LAR 279	La Ranchita	Spanish	32,912 to 33,170	1829	18.5	—	V.E.	—	—	Cond. 24.6.1829
LAR 280	Hossio	Portg	33,171 to 33,336	1829	9.5	—	—	Sybille	Collier	Cond. 24.6.1829
LAR 281	Ceres	Braz	33,337 to 33,464	1829	13.9	—	V.E.	Plumper	J. M. Greer	Cond. 22.9.1829
LAR 282	Clarita	Spanish	33,465 to 33,665	1829	14.9	—	—	Medina	E. Webb	Cond. 19.9.1829
LAR 283	Emelia	Braz	33,666 to 34,100	1829	13.9	—	—	Sybille	F. A. Collier	Branded Cond. 22.9.1829
LAR 284	Santa Jago	Braz	34,101 to 34,248	1829	24.9	—	Sent to Bathurst	Medina	E. Webb	Cond. 30.9.1829
LAR 285	Laure	French	34,249 to 34,494	1829	19.11	—	—	Clinker	G. W. Matson	—
LAR 286	Octavio	Spanish	34,495 to 34,829	1829	19.11	—	Sent to Bathurst	Black Joke	Collier	—
LAR 287	Christina	Spanish	34,830 to 35,045	1829	27.11	—	—	Dallas	G. W. Matson	Cond. 14.1.1830
LAR 288	Tentadora	Braz	35,046 to 35,365	1829	16.12	M.C.	—	Dallas	—	—
LAR 289	Emelia	Braz	35,366 to 35,513	1830	14.1	—	Employed at Waterloo	Clinker	C. W. Matson	(Letter 7.8.1830)
LAR 290	Emelia	Braz	35,514 to 35,641 / 118 (Persons)	1830	1.5	—	—	Clinker	A. Gordon	Cond. 1.5.1830
LAR 291	Noalendia	Braz	35,642 to 35,800	1830	—	—	—	Atholl	E. Webb	Cond. 17.5.1830
LAR 292	Menzanares	Spanish	35,801 to 36,148	1830	—	—	—	Medina	Collier	—
LAR 293	Maria De La Conception	Spanish	36,149	1830	—	—	Sent to Bathurst (14.7.1830)	Black Joke	—	—
LAR 294	Maria De La Conception	Spanish	36,150 to 36,227	1830	—	—	Sent to Native country at own request	—	—	—
LAR 295	Altimara	Spanish	36,228 to 36,426	1830	26.4	—	Sent to Wellington	—	—	—
LAR 296	Nova Resolutio	Braz	36,427 to 36,467	1830	13.4	—	Sent to Wellington	Medina	E. Webb	Cond. 13.5.1830
LAR 297	Premeira Rosalia	Braz	36,469 to 36,710	1830	15.3	—	Employed at Aberdeen Regent, Bathurst	Sybille	Collier	(Branded) Cond. 13.5.1830
LAR 298	Umbelino	Braz	36,711 to 36,873	1830	16.3	—	—	Sybille	Collier	Cond. 13.5.1830
LAR 299	Nossa Senhora Datina	Braz	36,874 to 37,111	1830	21.2	—	—	Dallas	Collier	Cond. 13.5.1830
LAR 300	Loreta al Corunerea	Spanish	37,112 to 37,295	1830	21.3	—	—	Plumper	J. Adams	Cond. 27.5.1830
LAR 301	Santiago Alias Polasque	Spanish	37,296 to 37,429	1830	25.8	M.C.	—	Athol	A. Gordon	—

Appendix VII (*cont.*) For key and headings to columns see p. 191

	Name	Nationality	Numbers	Year	Date	M.C./V.A.C.	Destination	Vessel	Officer	Notes
LAR 301	Santiago	Spanish	37,430 to 37,448	1830	27.5	—	—	1. Alex (Athol)	Gordon	Cond. 31.8.1830
LAR 302	Velos Passagera	Spanish	37,449 to 37,978	1830	9.10	—	Sent to Gambia	Primrose	E. Broughtton	Cond. 16.10.1830
LAR 303	Nouva Isabelita	Spanish	37,979 to 38,117	1830	22.10	—	Sent to Lumley	Atholl	E. Gordon	Cond. 29.10.1830
LAR 304	Pasirito	Spanish	38,118 to 38,347	1830	37.10	—	Sent to Kissy and Wilberforce	Puss	E. Webb	Brigantine Restored to owner
LAR 305	Maria	Portg	38,348 to 38,382	1830	20.11	—	Sent to Wellington	—	—	—
LAR 306	Nympha	Portg	38,383 to 38,549	1830	1.12	—	Sent to York	Conflict	G. Smithers	Liberated Africans kidnapped in colony and sold into slavery
LAR 307	La Caroline	French	38,550 to 38,553 4 Persons	1830	18.12 19.12	—	Sent to Goree	Conflict		
LAR 308	La Laure	French	38,554 to 38,653	1829	Oct	M.C.	Sent to Aberdeen	Athole	A. Gordon	M.C. refused to deal with this document
LAR 309	Maria	Spanish	38,654 to 39,150	1831	6.1	—	—	Plumper	J. Adams	Cond. 19.1.1831
LAR 310	Primaira	Spanish	39,151 to 39,460	1831	4.1	—	—	Black Joke	J. Hayes	Cond. 14.3.1831
LAR 311	La Virginie	French	39,461 to 39,551	1831	22.3	V.A.C.	—	—	—	Cond. 13.4.1831
LAR 312	Marinerito	Spanish	39,552 to 39,927	1831	24.5	—	—	Black Joke	J. Hayes	Cond. 3.6.1831
LAR 313	Potosi	Spanish	39,928 to 40,110	1831	22.8	V.A.C.	—	—	—	
LAR 314	—	—	40,111 to 40,164	1831	24.9	V.A.C.	Sent to York	—	—	Seized in 8 canoes by W. B. Prate of Liberated African Dep.
LAR 315	—	—	40,165 to 40,174	—	20.9	V.A.C.	Sent to Bananas	—	—	Seized off Isles de Los by Gov. A. Findlay
LAR 316	Regulo	Spanish	40,175 to 40,337	1831	13.10	—	Sent to Wilberforce	Black Joke	—	Children App to pers in Kissy
LAR 317	Rapido	Spanish	40,338 to 40,339	1831	14.11	—	Sent to Wilberforce	—	—	Cond. 7.11.1831
LAR 318	—	—	40,340 to 40,355	1831	24.9	V.A.C.	—	—	—	Seized by W. B. Pratt under Gov. A. Findlay
LAR 319	—	—	40,356 to 40,378	1831	1.12	V.A.C.	Sent to Bananas	—	—	Seized by W. B. Pratt under Gov. A. Findlay, Place of seizure Larjah
LAR 320	Fasquito	Spanish	40,371 to 40,598	1832	March	—	—	Black Joke	Hayes	Cond. 20.3.1832
LAR 321	Segunda Teresa	Spanish	40,599 to 41,043	1832	14.4	—	Apprenticed 244.1832. Latter sent to H.M.S. Forester 14.7.1834	Peluens	R. Medislo	Cond. 21.4.1832

LAR No.	Name	Nationality	Register Nos.	Year	Tonnage	V.A.C.	Employment	Brisk	E. Harris	Branded
LAR 322	Preuve	Spanish	41,044 to 41,317	1832	5,6	—	—	—	—	Branded
LAR 323	—	—	41,318 to 41,332	1832	24,5	V.A.C.	—	—	—	Seized by J. Campbell
LAR 324	John and David	—	41,333 to	1832	24,5	V.A.C.	—	—	—	Seized by N. M. Donnell =
LAR 325	—	—	41,334	1832	24,5	—	—	—	—	Seized by N. M. Donnell
LAR 326	Carolina	Spanish	41,335 to 41,703	1832	11,9	—	Apprenticed to H.W.H. Graham	Favorito	J. H. Harrison	—
LAR 327	Dasan Guna	Spanish	41,704 to 41,912	1832	11,4	—	Apprenticed to Mary A. Damay	Charybdis	R. B. Cranford	Branded
LAR 328	Veloz Mariana	Spanish	41,913 to 42,177	1833	31,5	—	—	—	Curlen Henry D. Trotter	—
LAR 329	Indie	Spanish	42,178 to 42,285	1833	22,6	—	—	Favorite	Joseph Harrison	—
LAR 330	Josefa Segunda	Spanish	42,286 to 42,478	1833	22,6	—	—	Pluto	Ross Sulivan	The Majority brand-marked with B. on Right or left arm
LAR 331	Socorro	Spanish	42,479 to 42,785	1833	17,7	—	—	Iuncula	Josiah Thompson	—
LAR 332	Caridad	Spanish	42,786 to 42,892	1883	19,10	—	—	Trinculo	Rich Warren	—
LAR 333	Virtude	Portg	42,893 to 43,205	1833	21,11	—	Variously employed	Brisk	Josiah Thompson	—
LAR 334	El Primo	Spanish	43,204 to 43,538	1833	10,12	—	—	Isis	James Polking-Horne	The Majority brandmarked with a P. on right arm
LAR 350	Minerva	Spanish	47,433 to 47,890	1835	28,2	—	V.E.	Pelorus	Rich Heredith	The Majority marked M on left shoulder blade
LAR 351	Maria	Portg	47,895 to 47,898	1835	28,2	—	—	Fair Rosamond	Lieut. George Rose	One marked XX on the lower back
LAR 352	Iberia	Spanish	47,889 to 48,203	1835	11,3	—	V.E.	Buzzard	Lieut. Antony will Mihard	—
LAR 353	Manuel	Spanish	48,204 to 48,578	1835	24,3	—	V.E.	Forester	Lieut. George Gover Miall	—
LAR 354	Bienvenida	Spanish	48,579 to 48,945	1833	23,4	—	V.E.	Buzzard	Lieut. Anthony Will Mihward	—
LAR 355	Ligitimo Africano	Portg	48,946 to 49,131	1835	9,5	—	V.E.	Forester	George Gover Miatt	—
LAR 356	Numero Dos	Spanish	49,132 to 49,272	1835	20,7	—	V.E.	Forester	Lieut. George Gover Miall	—
LAR 357	Volador	Spanish	49,273 to 49,700	1835	26,8	—	—	Fair Rosamond	Lieut. George Rose	—
LAR 358	Simeramis	Spanish	49,701 to 50,126	1835	14,10	—	V.E.	Buzzard	Lieut. Thomas Hobert	—
LAR 359	Argos	Spanish	50,127 to 50,492	1835	24,11	—	Many men and Boys sent to River St. Mary's Gambia	Charybdis	Lieut. Samuel Meren	Many brandmarked with an M on right shoulder

Appendix VII (*cont.*) For key and headings to columns see p. 191

										Notes
LAR 360	Conde De Los Andes	Spanish	50,493 to 50,761	1835	30.11	—	—	Britomart	Lieut. William Henry Quin	—
LAR 361	Theresa	Portg	59,762 to 50,963	1836	1.1	—	—	Britomart	Lieut. Will Henry Quin	—
LAR 362	Morma	Spanish	50,964 to 51,181	1836	6.1	—	—	Buzzard	Lieut. Thomas Lorey Roberts	—
LAR 363	Yebria	Spanish	51,182 to 51,419	1836	3.2	—	—	Fair Rosamond	Lieut. George Rose	—
LAR 364	Isabella 2nd and 4th Estrella	Spanish	51,420 to 51,751	1836	3.2	—	—	Princut	Lieut. Henry Joseph Peyet	—
LAR 365	Gazetta	Spanish	51,752 to 51,974	1836	3.2	V.E.	—	Pylades	Lieut. Will. Langford	—
LAR 366	Ligera	Spanish	51,975 to 52,166	1836	3.2	—	—	Buzzard	Lieut. Thomas Lorey Roberts	—
LAR 367	Vandolero	Spanish	52,167 to 52,509	1834	9.3	V.E.	—	Lynx	Lieut. Henry Vere Hantley	—
LAR 368	Seis Hermanos	Spanish	52,510 to 52,680	1836	13.3	—	—	Thalia	Robert Wauchope	—
LAR 369	Mandillo	Portg	52,681 to 52,937	1836	15.6	—	—	Buzzard	Lieut. Patrick Campbell	The Majority brandmarked with an O on right arm
LAR 370	Felicia	Spanish	52,938 to 53,292	1836	2.8	—	—	Buzzard	Patrick Campbell	Many brandmarked with an P on left shoulder blade
LAR 371	Joven Carolina	Portg	53,293 to 53,675	1836	13.8	—	—	Buzzard	Lieut. Patrick Campbell	Many especially the children, brandmarked with an P. on left breast
LAR 372	Felix	Portg	53,676 to 54,156	1836	22.10	—	—	Thalia	Robert Wauchope	—
LAR 373	Esperanza 1.	—	54,157 to 54,573	1836	22.10	V.E.	—	Pylades	Will Langford	—
LAR 374	Atalaya	—	54,574 to 54,661	—	—	—	—	—	—	—
LAR 375	Esperanza 2nd	—	54,562 to 55,057	—	—	V.E.	—	—	—	—
LAR 376	Victoria	—	55,057 to 55,373	—	—	V.E.	—	—	—	—
LAR 377	Quatro De Abrill	Portg	5,5374 to 55,831	—	—	V.E.	—	—	—	—
LAR 378	Olympia	—	55,832 to 56,083	—	—	—	—	—	—	—
LAR 379	Velox	—	56,084 to 56,542	—	—	—	—	—	—	—
LAR 380	Saria	—	56,543 to 56,563	—	—	—	—	—	—	—

Marked in various ways

LAR	Name	Nat.	Number range	Year	Value	Notes
LAR 381	Lachugino	Spanish	56,564 to 56,612	—	—	
LAR 382	Gala	Spanish	56,613 to 56,713	—	—	
LAR 383	Incompre Hencidal	—	56,714 to 57,299	—	—	
LAR 384	Cabo Verde	Portg	57,300 to 57,751	—	—	V.E.
LAR 385	Aurelia	Portg	14,785 to 14,790	—	—	Enlisted W.I.
LAR 386	Temerario	Portg	57,752 to 57,987	—	—	V.E.
LAR 387	Esperanca	Portg	57,988 to 58,076	—	—	
LAR 388	Josephine	Portg	58,077 to 58,442	—	—	
LAR 389	Latonia	Portg	58,423 to 58,742	—	—	
LAR 390	Dolores	Spanish	58,743 to 59,021	—	—	
LAR 391	La Fayette	Portg	59,022 to 59,432	—	—	
LAR 392	Cabro De Africa	Portg	59,433 to 59,533	1837	22.6	
LAR 393	Providen	Portg	59,534 to 59,725	1837	10.7	
LAR 394	Amelia	—	59,726 to 60,092	—	—	
LAR 395	Primaroza	Portg	60,093 to 60,228	1837	28.10	
LAR 396	Vibora De Cabo Verde	Spanish	60,229 to 60,443	—	—	
LAR 397	Felicidade	Port	60,444 to 60,724	—	—	
LAR 399	Ligeria	Portg	60,725 to 61,004	1837	20.12	
LAR 399	Princenca Africano	Portg	61,005 to 61,226	1838	10.1	
LAR 400	Deixa Falar	Portg	61,227 to 61,412	1838	10.1	
LAR 401	Gratidas	Portg	61,413 to 61,782	1838	19.1	
LAR 402	Felicidades	Portg	61,793 to 62,196	1838	17.4	
LAR 403	Dous Irmaos	Portg	62,201 to 62,411	1838	19.5	
LAR 404	—	—	62,442 to 62,472	—	—	
LAR 405	Prova	Portg	62,473 to 62,666	—	—	Fair
LAR 406	Pasqvita Felix	Portg	62,667 to 62,853	—	—	Rosamond
LAR 407	Prova 2nd	—	62,854 to 63,148	—	—	V.E.
LAR 408	Dulcinea	Portg	63,149 to 63,397	—	—	
LAR 409	Liberal	—	63,398 to 63,986	—	—	
	(Presumably)					
LAR 410	Imprudes	Portg	63,987 to 64,305	—	—	
LAR 411	Gertrudes	Portg	64,407 to 64,533	1839	10.1	
LAR 412	Violente	Portg	64,534 to 64,720	1839	10.1	
LAR 413	Magdalene	Portg	64,721 to 65,022	1839	17.1	
LAR 414	Ontario	Spanish	65,023 to 65,221	1839	17.1	
LAR 415	Labradora	Portg	65,222 to 65,469	1839	13.4	

Appendix VII (*cont.*) For key and headings to columns see p. 191

LAR	Ship	Flag	Registration Nos.	Year	Date	Court	Disposition	Remarks
LAR 416	—	—	65,470 to 65,486	1839	24.4		Sent to Waterloo	—
LAR 417	Liberal	Portg	65,487 to 65,526	1839	11.5		V.E.	Brisk —
LAR 418	Passos	Portg	65,527 to 65,607	1839	11.5	M.C.		—
LAR 419	Felucca	Spanish	323	1837	22.8			—
LAR 420	SI	Spanish	65,608 to 65,965	1839	June			—
LAR 421	Meroed	Spanish	65,966	1839	8.7			One Brandmarked with OO on left shoulder
LAR 422	Cazolidade	Spanish	65,967 to 66,054	1839	16.7			—
LAR 423	Jacay	Portg	66,055 to 66,250	1839	19.7			—
LAR 424	Sedoan Trade	Spanish	66,251 to 66,271	1839	25.7			—
LAR 425	Pomba De Africa	Portg	66,272 to 66,391	1839	25.7			—
LAR 426	Constitucao Sete De Abril	Portg	66,392 to 66,729	1839	15.8			Many Branded
LAR 427		Spanish	66,730 to 67,143	1839	30.10			—
LAR 428	Vinc Edora Edora	Portg	67,144 to 67,193	1839	24.12			—
LAR 429	Andoriner	Portg	67,194 to 67,200 (50)	1839	24.12		All Sent to Waterloo	—
LAR 430	Brig-Destimeda	—	29 Persons	1839	3.12	V.A.C.		These slaves were given no registration numbers
LAR 431	Novo Abismo	Portg	67,201	1840	8.4	V.A.C.	Was located or Settled in the Freetown on 11.4.1840	One slave only and with registration No. 67201
LAR 432	Eliza Davidson	Spanish	67,202 to 67,203	1840	18.4	M.C.	Both put aboard H.M.S. Wanderer 30.5.40	Two slaves only
LAR 433	St. Antonio Victorso	Portg	67,204	1840	21.5	M.C.		One slave only
LAR 434	Olympia Raimondo	Port	67,205 to 67,573	—	—			—
LAR 435	Primiers	—	67,574 to 67,592	—	—			—
LAR 436	Brig Claudine	—	67,593 to 67,635	1840	18.9			—

LAR 437–469 Vacancy in covering Sept 1840 to May 1845

From 18th September 1840 to 28th May 1845 there are practically no more information about proceedings regarding captures of slave vessels and emancipations by the courts at Sierra Leone. Hence the L.A.R. Nos. 437–469 give no account of slaves Nos. 67,636–75,374. About these latter, however, the Liberated African Dept's Letter Book (L.A.D.L.B. the only source of information about proceedings at Sierra Leone during this period) gives some scanty information—and mainly about emigration and the embarkation of Liberated Africans from the Queen's Yard.

Reference	Ship	Nationality	No. of Persons	Date		V.A.C./M.C.	Emigration	H.M.S. Vessel	Remarks
L.A.D.L.B.	Belvica	Portg	8 Persons	1842 Feb	—	—	—	H.M.S. Pluto	—
L.A.D.L.B.	(Brig)	—	174 Persons	1842 July	—	—	—	—	—
L.A.D.L.B.	St. Christopher	British	56 Persons	1843 March	—	V.A.C.	—	—	—
L.A.D.L.B.	St. Christopher	British	63 Persons	—	—	—	Emigrated	—	—
L.A.D.L.B.	Madagascar	—	No. Not Stated	1843	—	—	—	—	'been in the Yard this morning ... no one was willing to go on board the Madagascar in consequence of the small-pox being on board' Terry to Governor 17.4.1843
L.A.D.L.B.	Furio	Portg	429 Persons	1843	—	M.C.	—	—	—
L.A.D.L.B.	—	—	529 Persons	1843	—	—	—	—	220 men, 130 women with the rest children—All Yuroba
L.A.D.L.B.	Cyprus	Portg	1 Man	1844	11.9	—	—	—	—
L.A.D.L.B.	Santa-Anna	—	1 Boy	—	—	—	—	—	—
L.A.D.L.B.	Veterano	—	1 Girl	—	—	—	—	—	—
LAR 470	—	—	75,375 to 75,999	1845	18.5	V.A.C.	Many Emigrated to Trinidad, Many Children sent to School in the Villages	—	—
LAR 471	Africawo	—	76,000 to 76,523	1845	8.9	V.A.C.	Many Emigrated to Demerara/to Berbice	—	—
LAR 472	Isabel	Brazilian	76,524 to 76,871	1845	5.12	V.A.C.	—	Styx and Albatrose	—
LAR 473	—	—	76,872 to 76,874	1846	5.1	—	Emigrated	H.M.S. Heate	—
LAR 474	—	—	76,875 to 76,882	—	—	—	—	—	—
Col. Secr's Letter Book 1845–46	Espiga, Sierra-Leone Packet and Recuperador	Brazilian	Not stated	1846	—	V.A.C.	—	—	These slaves were brought from *Sherbro* by *Mandingoes* and seized by a Mr. Palmer at Kent

Appendix VII (*cont.*) For key and headings to columns see p. 191

Col. Secr's Letter Book 1845-6 Letter of 3.4.1846	Beigs Princeza Venganzio	Branzilian	—	1846 April	—	—	—	—	—
LAR 475	Paqueta de Rio	Branzilian	76,883 to 77,429	16.11	1846	V.A.C.	Many Enlisted	H.M.S. Cygnet	—	Two of the lot died. So total emancipated, 547
LAR 476	Reyaao-quitoa	Branzilian	77,430 to 77,929	19th May	1847	V.A.C.	Many sent to Wilberforce and Willington	H.M.S. Devastation	—	Of the 500 persons, 8 died
LAR 477	Not Known	—	77,930 to 78,219	25.5	1847	V.A.C.	—	H.M.S. Brig of War King Fisher	—	290 persons 11 died 279
LAR 478	—	—	78,220 to 78,430	11.6	1847	V.A.C.	—	H.M.S. Brig of War King Fisher	—	Total of 208 persons emancipated
LAR 479	Beaulah (alias Brig Name Unknown)	—	78,431 to 78,905	13.7	1847	V.A.C.	—	Waterwitch	—	17 Died, and 458 persons were emancipated
LAR 480	Emprende-dora	—	78,906 to 79,400	21.8	1847	V.A.C.	—	H.M.S. Albatrose and Graper	—	12 Died and 483 emancipated
LAR 481	18th Oct	Branzilian	79,401 to 79,453	21.8	1847	V.A.C.	—	H.M.S. Wanderer	—	—
LAR 482	Graca	Braz	79,454 to 79,896	26.8	1847	V.A.C.	—	Acteon	—	—
LAR 483	Lebro	Braz	79,897 to 80,085	30.8	1847	V.A.C.	—	Sealark	—	—
LAR 484	Esperanca	Braz	80,086 to 80,304	30.8	1847	V.A.C.	—	Contest	—	Example of Male Names Mecongoo, Voongo, Peudar, Pinzar / All Men
LAR 485	Theodozia	Braz	80,305 to 80,324	15.9	1847	V.A.C.	—	Mariner	—	
LAR 486	Faceirinha	Braz	80,325 to 80,573	14.10	1847	V.A.C.	—	Ferrett	—	20 Died and 230 were emancipated
LAR 487	Tibesin Iesebam (alias)	Braz	80,575 to 80,884 / 304 Slaves	14.10 / 29.9	1847 / 1847	V.A.C. / —	—	Bittern	—	304 emancipated
Letter Book Entry of 5.10.1847									
LAR 488	Maria	Braz	80,885 to 81,099	8.11	1847	V.A.C.	—	Dart	—	207 of whom 107 were boys.
LAR 489	—	—	81,100 to 81,106	—	—	—	—	Dart	—	Slaves taken off shore of Rio Pongas

							Delivered to the Department		
LAR 490	Not Stated	—	2 Men	—	—	—	—	—	—
LAR 491	—	—	81,107 to 81,219	1848	10.1	V.A.C.	—	—	Captured by *Mr, Palmer* off York in Mandingo Canoes. 1 girl given up to her father as freeborn
LAR 492	Agua	Braz	81,220 to 81,945	1848	10.1	V.A.C.	Several emigrated to Jamaica or Demerara — Grapler	—	—
LAR 493	Malaga	Braz	81,946 to 82,668	1848	11.1	V.A.C.	H.M.S. Ferrett	—	754 slaves, 360 of them boys
LAR 494	—	—	82,689 to 82,693	1848	11.4	V.A.C.	—	—	These slaves fled into the Colony for protection
LAR 495	Dosamigos	Braz	82,694 to 83,078	1848	28.4	V.A.C.	H.M.S. Steamer Bonetta Firefly Grappler Grecian	—	—
LAR 496	Guhyba	Braz	83,079 to 83,300	1848	12.5	V.A.C.	—	—	—
LAR 497	Anderina	Braz	83,301 to 83,790	1848	13.5	V.A.C.	—	—	—
LAR 498	Bella Miquilina	—	83,791 to 84,307	1848	19.6	V.A.C.	—	—	517 Emancipated
LAR 499	Pensarmento	—	84,304 to 84,420	1848	13.7	—	—	—	500 Emancipated
Return 1 in (LADLB)	Curiosa	—	299 Persons	1848	4.8	—	—	—	With the 299 persons Total no. emancipated in the colony up to now = 84,719
Return 2	Canoe Libinty	—	42 Persons	1848	20.9	—	—	—	Total now = 84,761
Return 3	San Antonio	—	286 Persons	1848	23.11	—	—	—	Total = 85,047
Return 4	Brazelencia	—	666 Persons	1848	23.11	—	—	—	Total = 85,713
Return 5	Quarto Andorinha	—	361	1848	12.12	—	—	—	Total = 86,074
Return 6	—	—	100	1849	1.1	—	Liberated into Lib. Afr. Department — H.M.S. Alert	—	Total = 86,174
Return 7	Jeciuto	Mexican	289	1849	12.2	—	—	—	Total = 86,463
Return 8	—	—	11	—	—	—	Penelope	—	Total = 86,474
Return 9	Catnerina De Bomfin	Braz	589	1849	8.5	—	—	—	Total = 87,063
Return 10	—	—	215	1849	—	—	Alert	—	Were not adjudicated landed from H.M.S. Alert (Total 87,278)

Appendix VII (*cont.*) For key and headings to columns see p. 191

For key and headings to columns see p. 191

Return	Nat.	Ship	191	1849	20.11	Vessel	Total
Return 11						Alert	Landed 20.11.1849 (Total = 87,469)
Return 12	Braz	Conquesador	316	1849	24.11		(Total = 87,785)
Return 13	Braz	Proserpine	227	1849	6.12		Total now = 88,012
Return 14	Braz	California	264	1849	22.12		Total = 88,276
Return 15		California	33				Back from quarantine Total now = 88,309
Return 16			112	1850	9.1	H.M.S. Alert	Total now 88,421
Return 17			15	1850	4.3	H.M.S. Heroine	Total = 88,436
Return 18			30	1850	8.4	H.M.S. Heroine	Total = 88,466
Return 19			23	1850	30.4	H.M.S. Heroine	Total = 88,489
Return 20	Braz	Rosina	151	1850	10.5		Total = 88,640
Return 21	Braz	Nova	115	1850	29.6		Total = 88,755
Return 22	Braz	Espienlacao Fleurde Maris	266	1850	9.7		Total = 89,021
Return 23	Braz	Caramaru	330	1850	17.7	H.M.S. Rawger	Total = 89,351
Return 24			23	1850	4.9		Total = 89,374
Return 25	Braz		242	1850	7.10		Total = 89,616
Return 26	Braz	Felix	235	1850	23.11		Total = 89,851
Return 27	Braz	Brazil	275	1850	10.12		Total = 90,126
Return 28			9	1850	1.2	H.M.S. Hound	Total = 90,135
Return 29			5	1851	15.1	H.M.S. Centaur	Total = 90,140
Return 30			33	1851	25.2	H.M.S. Cygnet	Total = 90,173
Return 31			24	1851	29.4	H.M.S. Volcano	Total = 90,197
Return 32	Braz	Gualdade	55	1851	18.1		Total = 90,252
Return 33			259	1851	17.2		Total = 90,511
Return 34			106	1851	10.4		Total = 90,617
Return 35		Pepito	63	1851	8.11	H.M.S. Alecto	Total = 90,680
Return 36			2	1851	30.8		Total = 90,682

Return	Source	No.	Year	Date	Ship	Note / Total
Return 37	Canoe	22	1851	2.10	—	Mainly boys Total = 90,704
Return 38	—	56	1851	2.11	H.M.S. Spy	Mainly boys Total = 90,760
Return 39	—	62	1852	—	H.M.S. Electo	Mainly boys Total = 90,822
Return 40	—	20	—	—	H.M.S. Sealark	Total = 90,842
Return 41	—	2	—	—	—	Escaped from Slavery in Sherbro Total = 90,844
Return 42	—	31	1852	16.10	H.M.S. Polyphemos	Total = 90,875
Return 43	—	10	1852	28.12	—	Total = 90,885
Return 44	—	10	1853	—	H.M.S. Firefly	Total = 90,895
Return 45	—	57	1853	—	—	All boys and girls rescued from Slavery. Total = 90,952
Return 46	—	30	1853	13.12	—	All boys and girls Total = 90,982
Return 47	—	9	—	—	H.M.S. Tartan	Total = 90,991
Return 48	—	49	1854	—	—	Mainly Children Total = 91,040
Return 49	—	139	1854	—	—	Nearly all of them children Total = 91,179
Return 50	—	44	—	—	—	Rescued from Slavery Total = 91,223
Return 51	—	19	1855	—	—	Total = 91,242
Return 52	—	1 only no. (91.243)	1855	—	—	Total = 91,243
Return 53	—	3	1855	—	—	Total = 91.246
Return 54	—	44	1855	—	—	Total = 91,290
Return 55	—	2	1855	—	—	Total = 91,292
Return 56	—	44	1855	—	—	Total = 91,336
Return 57	—	86	1856	—	—	Total = 91,422
Return 58	Canoes within Colony	119 Persons	1856	—	—	Nearly all children Total = 91,541
Return 59	Canoes within Colony	36	1856	—	—	Total = 91,577
Return 60	A Schooner	70	1857	—	H.M.S. Antilope	Total = 91,647
Return 61	Abbot Deverung	213	—	—	H.M.S. Jenser	With many boys and girls Total = 91,860

Appendix VII (*cont.*) For key and headings to columns see p. 191

Return 62	A Canoe	—	4I	1857	—	—	H.M.S. Antilope	—	Total = 91,901
Return 63	I.H. Record	—	187	1857	—	—		—	Total = 92,088
Return 64	Cunard	—	219	1857	—	—	H.M.S. Sappho	—	Total = 92,307
Return 65	—	—	94	1857	—	—	H.M.S. Steamship Vesuvius	—	Total = 92,401
Return 66	Canoe	—	1	1859	—	—	—	—	Total = 92,402
Return 67	Two Canoes	—	50	1859	—	—	—	—	Total = 92,452
Return 68	Two Canoes	—	75	1859	—	—	—	—	Total = 92,537
Return 69	A Canoe	—	25 Persons	1859	—	—	—	—	Total = 92,552
Return 70	—	—	11 Persons	1859	—	—	—	—	Total = 92,563
Return 71	Two Canoes	—	97 Persons	1859	6.10	/	—	—	Mainly children Total = 92,660
Return 72	1 Canoe	—	58 Persons	1859	6.10	—	—	—	Total = 92,718
Return 73	A Borgantine No name	—	460 Persons	1859	9.11	—	H.M.S. Spiture	—	Captured off Whydah Total = 93,178
Return 74	A Canoe	—	21 Persons	1859	8.12	—	—	—	Total = 93,199
Return 75	A Canoe	—	34 Persons	1860	—	—	—	—	Total = 93,233
Return 76	Bark clara Windsor	—	590 Persons	1861	—	—	H.M.S. Espon	—	Nearly all children Total = 93,823
Return 77	A Canoe	—	11	1861	—	—	—	—	Total = 93,834
Return 78	Flight	—	495	1861	—	—	H.M.S. Falcon	—	Nearly all boys and girls Total now = 94,339

Bibliography

Primary Sources (divided into i, ii, iii, iv and v)

i. Government Manuscript Records

The Colonial Office and the Foreign Office documents in the Public Record Office, London, form the most important sources for this research.

Most important for the study of the emigration scheme are:

C.O. 386 (Emigration)—a document untouched so far by any other study. Also important are—

C.O. 267 and 248—Sierra Leone

C.O. 318, West Indies, Miscellaneous.

C.O. 147—Lagos

F.O. 84, Slave Trade series

F.O. 2, Fernando Po.

ii. Printed Sources—Parliamentary Papers and Official Reports

Annual Reports of the Colonial Land and Emigration Commissioners on Liberated African emigration. These Reports are referred to as General Reports.

1843	Third General Report: PP. 1843, Vol. xxxxx, 621, 15
1844	Fourth General Report: PP. 1844, Vol. xxxi, 178, 11
1845	Fifth General Report: PP. 1845, Vol. xxvii, 617, 83
1846	Sixth General Report: PP. 1846, Vol. xxiv, 706, 1
1847	Seventh General Report: PP. 1847, Vol. xxxiii, 809, 131
1847–48	Eighth General Report: PP. 1847–48, Vol. xxvi, 961, 41
1849	Ninth General Report: PP. 1849, Vol. xxii, 1082, 1
1850	Tenth General Report: PP. 1850, Vol. xxiii, 1204, 55
1851	Eleventh General Report: PP. 1851, Vol. xxii, 1383, 333
1852	Twelfth General Report: PP. 1852, Vol. xviii, 1499, 161
1853	Thirteenth General Report: PP. 1852–53, Vol. xl, 1647, 65, and Appendix 159
1854	Fourteenth General Report: PP. 1854, Vol. xxviii, 1833 and Appendix 77
1855	Fifteenth General Report: PP. 1854–55, Vol. xvii, 1853
1856	Sixteenth General Report: PP. 1856, Vol. xxiv, 2089, 325 and Appendix 20

1857   Seventeenth General Report: PP. 1857 (Sess. 2), Vol. XVI,
        2249, 33
1858   Eighteenth General Report: PP. 1857–58, Vol. XXIV, 2395,
        401
1859   Nineteenth General Report: PP. 1859 (Sess. 2), Vol. XIV,
        2555
1860   Twentieth General Report: PP. 1860, Vol. XXIX, 2696
1861   Twenty-first General Report: PP. 1861, Vol. XXII, 2843, 20

iii. Papers Relating to Slave Captures and Liberation at Sierra Leone

Number of slaves captured and liberated at Sierra Leone from 1808
to 1846:

> PP. 1829, Vol. XXV, 275, 25
> PP. 1842, Vol. XLIV, 561, 531
> PP. 1845, Vol. XLIX, 212, 567
> PP. 1847–48, Vol. LXIV, 116, 1

Number of slaves captured and liberated after 1846 up to 1865:

1847–1852   PP. 1850, Vol. LV, 1166, 89
            PP. 1850, Vol. LV, 151, 75
            PP. 1852, Vol. LV, 201, 337
1855–1859   PP. 1861, Vol. LXIV, 35
1860–1864   PP. 1865, Vol. LVI, 527

Expense of the anti-slavery Naval Squadron on the West Coast:

> PP. 1814–15, Vol. VII, 368, 409
> PP. 1817, Vol. XVII, 491, 492, 217, 221
> PP. 1822, Vol. XXII, 177, 641
> PP. 1842, Vol. XLIV, 561, 531
> PP. 1847–48, Vol. LXIV, 26, 49
> PP. 1847–48, Vol. XXIII (Part III), 361, 415

General Expenses on the maintenance of liberated Africans in Sierra
Leone:

> PP. 1845, Vol. XLIX, 471, 635

iv. Papers and Correspondence relating to Liberated African Emigration:

Resolutions and Memorials of West Indian planters to the Colonial Office:

> PP. 1839, Vol. XXXV, 304, 129
> PP. 1839, Vol. XXXV, 290, 95
> PP. 1839, Vol. XXXV, 289, 133

Order-in-Council of 1838 repealing West Indian Ordinances respecting apprenticeship and emigration:

> PP. 1840, Vol. XXXIV, 224, 365

Reports of Select Committees on West Africa:

> PP. 1842, Vol. XI, XII, 551, XIII

Papers relating to emigration:

> PP. 1843, Vol. XXXIV, 438, 603

Additional instructions to Governor of Sierra Leone for removal of restrictions on liberated African emigration:

> PP. 1844, Vol. XXXV, 284, 275

Further correspondence:

> PP. 1844, Vol. XXXV, 530, 297

Memorials by Jamaica House of Assembly on emigration:

> PP. 1844, Vol. XXXIV, 266, 251
> PP. 1845, Vol. XXXI, 66, 207

Proclamation by Governor of Sierra Leone to promote emigration:

> PP. 1845, Vol. XXXI, 158, 319

Reports by Guppy and Butts on emigration:

PP. 1847–48, Vol. XLIV, 732, 23

Suggestions by the West India Committee and planters on emigration:

PP. 1847–48, Vol. XXII, 536, 467
PP. 1847, Vol. XXXIX, 325, 115
PP. 1847–48, Vol. XLIV, 32, 519
PP. 1847–48, Vol. XLVI, 749, 323
PP. 1847, Vol. XXXIV, 191, 1
PP. 1847–48, Vol. XXIII, 245, Pt. III, I

Regulation of labour between masters and labourers:

PP. 1847–48, Vol. XLV, 63, 7

Cultivation of sugar and supply of labour:

PP. 1847–48, Vol. XXIII, Pt. I, 395

Loans and other measures for promoting emigration:

PP. 1847–48, Vol. XLV, 399, 75
PP. 1850, Vol. XL, 643, 271
PP. 1846, Vol. XXX, 322, 453
PP. 1847–48, Vol. XLIV, 927, 499

v. Papers and Correspondence relating to the Niger and to liberated Africans in the Niger Hinterland:

Rights of liberated Africans as British subjects:

PP. 1852–53, Vol. IV, 319
Vol. LXV, 291

Correspondence relating to the conveyance of H.M. Mails to West Africa:

PP. 1852, Vol. XLIX, 284

Papers relating to the reduction of Lagos:

> PP. 1852, Vol. LIV, 221

Papers relating to the cultivation of cotton in West Africa:

> PP. 1857, Vol. XXXVIII, 255

Slave trade correspondence, Africa (Consular):

> PP. 1861, Vol. LXIV, 1
> PP. 1862, Vol. LXI, 1

Papers relating to the occupation of Lagos:

> PP. 1862, Vol. LXI, 339, 365

Report of Select Committee on West Africa:

> PP. 1865, Vol. V, 1

Papers relating to outrages committed by black British subjects on the Niger: The Onitsha Murder Trial:

> PP. 1882, Vol. XLVI, 3430, 571

Secondary Sources

(a) *Private Papers, Newspapers and Documents of Societies*

G. W. Johnson Papers (In the University of Ibadan Library, Nigeria)

Herbert Macaulay Papers (In the University of Ibadan Library, Nigeria)

Nigerian Newspapers (In the University of Ibadan Library Nigeria)

Publications of the Anti-Slavery Society (Denison House, Vauxhall Bridge Street, London, S.W.1)

Publications of the Aborigines Protection Society (Rhodes House, Oxford)

Church Missionary Society Documents (Archives at Salisbury Square, London E.C.4)

Other Relevant Publications: Nigeria and West Africa Pamphlets (at the C.O.L., London)

(b) *Ph.D. Theses in various University Libraries*
Ajayi, J. F. A., *Christian Missions and the Making of Nigeria, 1841–1891,* Ph.D. London, 1958
Herskovits, J., *Liberated Africans and History of Lagos Colony to 1886,* D.Phil. Oxford, 1960
Jones, M. A., *The Role of the United Kingdom in the Transatlantic Emigration Trade 1815–1875,* D.Phil. Oxford, 1955
Laurence, K. O., *Immigration into Trinidad and British Guiana 1834–1870,* Ph.D. Cambridge, 1958
Pilgrim, E. I., *Anti-Slavery Sentiment in Great Britain its Nature and its Decline, 1841–1854,* Ph.D. Cambridge, 1952

(c) *Select Bibliography*
Adderley, C. B., *Review of the Colonial Policy of Lord Russell's Administration,* London 1869
Allen, Capt. W., *A Plan for the Immediate Extinction of the Slave Trade* London, 1849
Allison, A., *Universal Free Trade,* London 1852
Anon., *Sugar, Slavery and Emancipation, 1854* (Reprint from the Anti-Slavery Reporter)
Anon., *Our Free Trade Policy Examined,* London 1846
Anon., *Slave Trade Tracts,* Cambridge University Library
Baikie, W. B., *Narrative of an Exploring Voyage,* London 1856
Bandinel, J., *Some Account of the Slave Trade in Slaves from Africa,* London 1842
Barnes, Rev. C. W., *Adventures on the West Coast of Africa,* London 1864
Bartlett, C. J., *Great Britain and Sea Power,* London 1962
Beaton, Rev. P., *Six Months in Reunion,* 2 Vols., London 1860
Bell and Morrell, *Select Documents on British Colonial Policy 1830–1860,* Oxford 1928
Bell, T. M., *Outrage by Missionaries at Onitsha,* Liverpool 1883
Bevan, W., *The Operation of the Apprentice System in the British Colonies,* 1838
Blyden, E., *The West African University,* 1873; *The Return of the Exiles,* 1891; *Address on West Africa,* London 1901
Bridge, H., *Journal of an African Cruiser* edited by N. Hawthorn, London 1845
Brodie, W., *Modern Slavery and the Slave Trade,* 1850
Brougham, H., *An Inquiry into the Colonial Policy of the European Powers,* 2 Vols., Edinburgh 1803

Burn, W. L., *Emancipation and Apprenticeship in the British West Indies*, London 1937

Burton, R. F., *Wanderings in Western African*, London 1863

Butt-Thompson, F. W., *Sierra Leone in History and Tradition*, London 1926

Buxton, C., *Slavery and Freedom in the British West Indies*, London 1860

Buxton, T. F., *The African Slave Trade and its Remedy*, 1839

Campbell, P. C., *Chinese Coolie Emigration*, London 1922

Campbell, R., *Pilgrimage to my Motherland*, Philadelphia 1861

Cave, S., *Papers relating to Free Labour and the Slave Trade*, London 1861

Clarkson, T., *A History of the Abolition of the Slave Trade*, 2nd edition, London 1829; *Not a Labourer wanted in Jamaica*, London 1842

Cole, W., *Life in the Niger, or Journal of an African Trader*, London 1862

Coupland, R., *The British Anti-Slavery Movement*, London 1933

Crooks, J. J., *History of the Colony of Sierra Leone*, Dublin 1903

Cumpston, I. M., *Indians Overseas*, London 1953

Davy, J., *The West Indies Before and After Emancipation*, London 1854

Delany, M. R., *Report of the Niger Valley Exploring Party*, New York 1861

Denman, Lord, *Letters to Lord Brougham on the Final Extinction of the Slave Trade*, 1848

Denman, J., *West India Interests, African Emigrants and the Slave Trade*, London 1848; *The Slave Trade, the African Squadron and Mr. Hutt's Committee*, London 1849

Du Bois, W. E. B., *The Suppression of the African Slave Trade*, New York 1896

Duval, M. Jules, *Histoire de l'Emigration européenne, asiatique et africaine au XIXe siecle: see causes, ses caracterers, ses effets*, Paris 1862

Evans, D., *The Commercial Crisis*, 1848

Freyre, G., *The Masters and the Slaves*, translated by S. Putham, 1946

Gaston-Martin, *Esclavages dans les Colonies Francaises*, Paris 1948

Hastings, A. C. G., *The Voyage of the Dayspring*, London 1926

Hitchins, F. H., *The Colonial Land and Emigration Commissioners*, Philadelphia 1931

Hoare, P., *Memoirs of Granville Sharp*, London 1820

Horton, J. A. B., *West African Countries and Peoples*, 1868

Hutchinson, T. J., *Impressions of Western Africa*, London 1858; *Ten Years Wandering Among the Ethiopians*, London 1861

Ingham, E. G., *Sierra Leone after a Hundred Years*, London 1894

Johnson, J. F., *Proceedings of the General Anti-Slavery Convention*, London 1843

Johnston, H. H., *British West Africa and the Trade of the Interior*, London 1889

Kingsley, Mary, *West African Studies*, London 1901

Klingsberg, F. J., *The Anti-Slavery Movement in England*, New Haven 1926

Kuczynski, R. R., *Demographic Survey of the British Colonial Empire*, Vol. i., Oxford 1948

Laird, M., 'Remedies for the Slave Trade', *Wesminster Review*, 1840

Laryle, Capt., *Abolition de l'Esclavage dans les Colonies Anglaises*, 1840

Lawrence, W. B., *Visitation and Search*, Boston 1858

Legcyt, A., *L'Emigration européenne, son importance, ses causes, ses effets, avec un appendice sur l'Emigration Africaine, Hindoue et Chinoise*, Paris 1861

Lloyd, C., *The Navy and the Slave Trade*, London 1949

Mannix and Cowley, *Black Cargoes, 1518–1865*, London 1963

Mansfield, J., *Remarks on the African Squadron*, 1848

Mathieson, W. L., *Great Britain and the Slave Trade 1839–1865*, London 1929; *British Slave Emancipation 1838–1849*, London 1932

Mellor, G. R., *British Imperial Trusteeship 1783–1850*, London 1951

Merivale, H., *Lectures on Colonisation 1839–1861*, Oxford 1928

Morrell, W. P., *The Colonial Policy of Peel and Russell*, Oxford 1930

Olivier, Lord, *White Capital and Coloured Labour*, London 1929

Ollivier, J., *Free Trade in Negroes*, London 1849

Premium, B., *Eight Years in British Guiana*, London 1848

(Reports) *Reports by Directors of the Sierra Leone Company*, London 1792; *Reports of the African Institution*, London 1815

Richard, H., *Memoirs of Joseph Sturge*, 1864

Ritchie, J., *Thoughts on Slavery and Cheap Sugar*, 1844

Robinson, R. and Gallagher, J., *Africa and the Victorians*, London 1961

Sewell, W. G., *Ordeal of Free Labour in the West Indies*, New York 1861

Soulsby, H. G., *The Slave Trade and the Right of Search in Anglo-American Relations 1814–1862*, Baltimore 1933
Stephen, G., *Anti-Slavery Recollections*, London 1854
Stephen, J., *England Enslaved by her own Slave Colonies*, London 1826
Stokes, R., *A Regulated Slave Trade*, 1850
Wadstrom, C. B., *An Essay on Colonisation*, 2 Vols., London 1794
Wakefield, E. G., *A View of the Art of Colonisation*, London 1849
Wilson, J. L. and Trotter, H. D., *The British Squadron on the Coast of Africa*, London 1851
Williams, E. C., *Capitalism and Slavery*, Carolina 1944
Wyndham, H. A., *The Atlantic and Slavery*, London 1935

Later Works
Ajayi, J. F. A., *Christian Missions in Nigeria 1841–1891*, Longmans 1965
Biobaku, S., *The Egba and their Neighbours*, Oxford 1957
Boahen, A. A., *Britain, the Sahara and the Western Sudan, 1788–1861*, Oxford 1964
Coleman, J. S., *Nigeria: Background to Nationalism*, California 1958
Dike, K. O., *Trade and Politics in the Niger Delta 1830–1885*, Oxford 1956
Flint, J. E., *Sir George Goldie and the Making of Nigeria*, Oxford 1960
Fyfe, C. H., *History of Sierra Leone*, Oxford 1962; *Sierra Leone Inheritance*, London 1964
(Seminar Edin. Univ. 1965), *The Transatlantic Slave Trade from West Africa*
Herskovits, J., *A Preface to Modern Nigeria 'The Sierra Leoneans in Yoruba'*, Wisconsin 1966
Newbury, C. W., *The Western Slave Coast and its Rulers*, Oxford 1961

(d) *Journal Articles*
Buxton, T. F. V., 'The Creole in West Africa', *Journal of the African Society*, Vol. XII, 1913
Fyfe, C. H., 'Four Sierra Leone Recaptives', *Journal of African History*, Vol. 2, No, 1. 1961; 'The Life and Times of John Ezzidio', *Sierra Leone Studies N.S. No. 4*, June, 1955; 'Old Calabar and Freetown', *Journal of the Historical Society of Nigeria*, Vol. 2, No. 1, 1960

Gallagher, J., 'Fowell Buxton and the New African Policy 1838–1842', *Cambridge Historical Journal*, Vol. x, No. 1, 1950

Gertzel, C., 'Relations Between African and European Traders in the Niger Delta 1880–1896', *Journal of African History*, Vol. 3, No. 2, 1962

Leslie Bethel, 'The Mixed Commissions for the Suppression of the Transatlantic Slave Trade in the 19th Century', *Journal of African History*, Vol. vii, No. 1, 1966

Loatan, A. B., 'Brazilian Influence on Lagos', *Nigeria*, No. 69, August, 1961

Roberts, G. W., 'Immigration into the British Caribbean', *Population Studies*, Vol. 7, 1953–54.

Rodriques, J. H., 'The Influence of Brazil on Africa and of Africa on Brazil', *Journal of African History*, Vol. 3, No. 1, 1962

Shepperson, G., 'Negro American Influences on the Emergence of African Nationalism', *Journal of African History*, Vol. 1, No. 2, 1960

Turner, L. D., 'Some Contacts of Brazilian Ex-slaves with Nigeria', *Journal of Negro History*, Vol. 1, 27, No. 1, 1942

Verger, P., 'Nigeria, Brazil and Cuba', *Nigeria 1960*.

Index